Julia Laite is a reader in moder... versity of London. Her first boo... *Ordinary Citizens* (2011), exami... commercial sex in twentieth-cent... one has written for the *Guardian*, *Open Democracy* and *History & Policy*, and appeared on BBC Radio 4's *Woman's Hour* and *Making History*, as well as the television programme *Find My Past*. She discovered Lydia Harvey during research for her first book and has been searching for her story in archives around the world ever since. She lives in Cambridge with her partner and their two children.

Praise for *The Disappearance of Lydia Harvey*

'A gripping, unputdownable masterpiece of scholarly historical research and true crime writing. Julia Laite explores the sordid world of crime, sex and international policing in 1910 by focusing on the individuals caught up in an elaborate web of exploitation. Readers who loved *The Five* will find this story and its skilful telling equally as enthralling'
Hallie Rubenhold, author of *The Five*

'Demonstrates how, with determination, sensitivity and a careful dose of imagination, extraordinary recoveries are possible ... Laite has taken her slim archival trace and immeasurably enriched it; she has reclaimed a woman's life and restored a more complex reality to the record'
Sarah Watling, *Guardian*

'With an inventive mix of sources, Laite brilliantly summons up one girl's life, dreams and suffering. It's ingenious history writing'
Mail on Sunday

THE DISAPPEARANCE OF LYDIA HARVEY

A TRUE STORY OF SEX, CRIME AND
THE MEANING OF JUSTICE

JULIA LAITE

PROFILE BOOKS

This paperback edition first published in 2022

First published in Great Britain in 2021 by
Profile Books Ltd
29 Cloth Fair
London
EC1A 7JQ
www.profilebooks.com

1 3 5 7 9 10 8 6 4 2

Typeset in Garamond by MacGuru Ltd
Printed and bound in Great Britain by
CPI Group (UK) Ltd, Croydon, CR0 4YY

A CIP catalogue record for this book is available from the British Library.

ISBN 978 1 78816 443 6
eISBN 978 1 78283 654 4
Audio ISBN 978 1 78283 843 2

To Will

Contents

RESEARCH NOTE

The lives in this book were found in fragments, and they have been reconstructed using a large number of very small details. These include birth, marriage, death and migration records from digitised genealogical web sites; character-searched information from digitised newspapers; and police, court and institutional records from archives around the world. These scraps, glimpses and clues, often little more than a tiny detail in a margin, have been carefully contextualised using both broad and local histories, which have helped me place these historical actors in their time and place.

I have stitched these details together with threads of imagination, but this imagining has followed careful rules. There is no detail offered here for which I do not have historical evidence. The weather columns of local newspapers have told me if it was sunny, cold or raining. Historical photographs, novels and travel stories have helped me re-create scenes. Three major archival case files and dozens of other related ones from four different countries have been carefully interlaced to form a picture of almost-forgotten lives.

There are thousands of missing pieces to this puzzle – evidence that has been lost, destroyed or never written down in the first place. Perhaps there are bit and pieces still lying in an archive somewhere: uncatalogued, un-indexed, as yet unfound. In the places where I cannot know or even glimpse what happened or why, I have carefully deployed the historian's tool of 'maybe', 'perhaps' and 'must have'. There are places where the accounts conflict, and where it is difficult to say which clue is more convincing. I have left these moments unreconciled.

This is a true story. But it is also a story that insists we think carefully about who gets to do the telling.

HISTORICAL ACTORS

Ernest Anderson: A detective inspector with the Criminal Investigation Department, Scotland Yard

Emily Louisa Badeley: A piano teacher from Oamaru, New Zealand; Lydia Harvey's mother

Marie Balandras: A French landlady in North Soho who had a habit of renting rooms to criminals.

Alex/Alexander Berard: A pseudonym of Alessandro di Nicotera

Marguerite Bescançon: A young French woman who was brought from Paris to London by traffickers

Victoria Bricot: A young French woman who was brought from Paris to London by traffickers

Frederick Bullock: Metropolitan assistant police commissioner and central authority on the 'white slave' traffic

Walter Burmby: A Metropolitan Police sergeant, C Division, Soho

Marguerite Carl: A young woman who boarded a steamship in London bound for New Zealand in May 1910; may be the same person as 'Florrie'

Antonio Carvelli: An Italian man alternatively known as Aldo Cellis, Anton Courrier, Anthony Coty, etc.;

a musician, indent agent, translator, Latin teacher, bookmaker, thief and trafficker

Luigi Carvelli: A maestro and classical composer from Calabria who played first horn in the Brighton Municipal Orchestra; Antonio Carvelli's father; 'Serenata Napoleatana' is his most well-known surviving work

Aldo Cellis: A pseudonym of Antonio Carvelli, and the name by which Lydia Harvey knew him

William Coote: A well-known anti-trafficking campaigner; general secretary of the National Vigilance Association and the International Bureau for the Suppression of the 'White Slave Traffic'

Anthony Coty: A pseudonym of Antonio Carvelli

Anton Courrier: A pseudonym of Antonio Carvelli

Alec Denis: A pseudonym of Alessandro di Nicotera

Florrie: A young woman who was trafficked from New Zealand to Buenos Aires, and possibly on to London; may be synonymous with Marguerite Carl

William Hall-Jones: The New Zealand high commissioner in London

Harry George Cannon Harvey: A solicitor in Dunedin, Oamaru and Christchurch, New Zealand; Lydia Harvey's father

Lydia Rhoda Harvey: A young woman who was trafficked from New Zealand to Buenos Aires and London in 1910; sometimes used the pseudonym Doris Williams

Mireille Lapara: A young French woman who was brought from Paris to London by traffickers

Marguerite Leroy: A young French woman who was

brought from Paris to London by traffickers and was
  later deported

Eilidh MacDougall: A social worker in London and 'lady
  assistant' to the Metropolitan Police

William Mead: A Metropolitan Police constable at C
  Division, Soho with an eye for illicit opportunities

George Nicholls: A Metropolitan Police detective sergeant
  working for the head of the Criminal Investigation
  Department; fastidious, discreet, with a talent for
  speaking French

Alessandro di Nicotera: An Italian man alternatively known
  as Alex/Alexander Berard and Alec Denis; a mechanic,
  army deserter, waiter, bookmaker and trafficker

Herbert Ockenden: A merchant mariner, based in Australia

Charles Peneau: A French teenager with respectable
  parents, who was charged with pimping in April 1910

Camelia Rae: A French woman working at a 'one-woman
  brothel' in Wellington, New Zealand, also known as
  'Tit'; a close friend and/or business associate of Antonio
  Carvelli and Veronique White

Annie Sawyer: A woman known as the wife of Alexander
  Berard, aka Alessandro di Nicotera

Guy Hardy Scholefield: The New Zealand Press Association
  correspondent in London

Tit: A pseudonym of Camelia Rae

Marie Vernon: A pseudonym of Veronique White

Joseph Ward: The prime minister of New Zealand in 1910

Veronique Sarah White: A well-travelled Australian woman,
  who made her living in the sex industry; also known as
  Vanda Williams, Marie Vernon and Kathleen Williams

Doris Williams: A pseudonym of Lydia Harvey

Kathleen/Vanda Williams: Pseudonyms of Veronique
   White

Vera Wilson: An English woman much maligned by the
   parents of her pimp, Charles Peneau; a police informant

*The problem is one of infinite complexity. In a word
– those who constitute it are human beings.*

Maude Royden, 'The Problem of the Undesirables', 1916

PROLOGUE

In January 1910, just a few months shy of her seventeenth birthday, Lydia Harvey disappeared. She bade farewell to the motley crew at Mrs Logan's boarding house in downtown Wellington, New Zealand, where young men and women, new arrivals to the city, took their meals together in a threadbare dining room after long days of work. She wrote to her mother, who had her hands full of children back home in the small provincial town of Oamaru, telling her that she had taken a job as a nursemaid to a rich couple, who were bringing her with them to London. She gave notice to Mr Harlow at the photography studio where she had recently got a job, where families in nice clothes and lines of orderly children came to buy Kodak cameras and develop pictures of their travels. Then she boarded a brand-new steamship, with 500 third-class berths and a triple-expansion steam engine, which could cut through the waves of the Pacific and land her in Buenos Aires in less than a month's time. Then, she seemed to disappear.

A working-class, provincial girl like Lydia was meant to be a respectable servant in the home of a wealthier woman: scrubbing, cooking and caring for children for well over seventy hours each week. This was, in fact, why she had first come to the big city, joining a small army of young women who left rural and provincial towns the world over, travelling sometimes ten and sometimes 10,000 miles, on trains, roads and steamships, to answer the hungry call of the urban middle classes for live-in domestic servants. For more than a century this had been the natural order of things: working-class young women were essential fixtures in middle- and upper-class households, without whom the wealthy would have to scrub, cook and care for themselves.[1]

But as the twentieth century dawned, this system was in crisis, and the demand for servants far outstripped the supply. More and more young women were expressing their opinions on domestic service with their feet. Like many others, Lydia was desperate to pull herself out of this low-paid, low-status job and, seizing one of the growing opportunities for young women in shop work, she had landed a post at a photographer's studio. It was a move up, but she still wore plain cotton and unfashionable hats, and her purse was empty by the end of the month.

A new world of travel, luxury and consumer goods lay just beyond her grasp. She had seen the nice dresses and the fine shoes in the windows of shops and in the thin pages of catalogues; she had held the cameras and the travel photographs. Each morning as her commuter train snaked its way to Mr Harlow's photography studio, she saw the steamships at anchor in Wellington's wide blue harbour, waiting to carry people to Sydney, London and New York. As she returned home, she walked among the young women who smoked cigarettes and danced the night away, who kissed young men in corners, who had begun to claim the dangerous, exciting spaces of the city as their own. So when she met a beautiful woman and a handsome man who said they would give her nice dresses and help her to travel, she made the wager of a lifetime.

Three weeks later, a once-unaffordable steamship ticket was in her hands. But when the handsome man and beautiful woman met her beneath the Buenos Aires sun, their masks began to slip. Six harrowing months later, Lydia was finally found in London by Metropolitan Police detectives, shivering in a hand-me-down dress and trying to catch the eye of passing men under the electric lights of Piccadilly Circus. They brought her back to Great Marlborough Street Police Station, and here she told her story, or at least the parts the police wanted to hear and the parts she elected to reveal.

Lydia's story, however it was told, unfolded in an era that was obsessed with the idea of the exploited prostitution of young, white women. The public was hungry to read such melodramatic, sexualised stories of innocence and ruin, and books with titles like *From Dancehall to White Slavery* and *The Girl who Disappeared* became early twentieth-century bestsellers. To the authors of cheap novels and newspaper exposés, Lydia Harvey was another bit of fodder for a salacious plot or an eye-catching headline. To those who campaigned for better laws and policies to 'rescue' and 'reform' trafficking victims, Lydia Harvey was a morality tale. In the eyes of moralisers and sensationalisers alike, Lydia Harvey was a *girl* – that is, an unmarried, working-class young woman who was dangerously unformed. Girls like Lydia were in need of protection and control, in order to prevent their being lost to the twilight world of vice and prostitution.

Early feminists saw girls like Lydia a little differently. To women's suffrage campaigners, whose movement was gaining

1: As the panic over 'white slavery' and 'the traffic in women' swept the world in the early twentieth century, many feminists and women's suffrage campaigners argued that this particular kind of exploitation was a direct product of women's underpaid and unpaid labour in other sectors. This image, created by M. Hughes of the Suffrage Atelier in Britain, was used as a postcard around 1910.

strength at the same time as she crossed the Pacific, the Lydia Harveys of the world were at the sharpest end of gender inequality. They were the ultimate victims in a society where women were given no political say and where iniquitous economic systems forced girls to choose between the hardships of exploited labour and the miseries of prostitution.

To the London police, meanwhile, Lydia Harvey was seen as a tool to be used to prosecute her traffickers, who were 'beasts in human clothing' and 'fiends in the shape of a man': the most despised of all criminals.[2] But she was also considered by them to be part of a legion of 'inveterate liars': one of the women who walked slowly down the West End pavements night after night.[3] To those who sought to rescue girls from these lives of prostitution, meanwhile, Lydia was a project, a creature to save and reform. And to the traffickers who followed her as she walked the London streets, she was a willing if naïve ally in their bid to get rich in one of the world's most lucrative underworld industries.

Inside the stories other people told about her, the real Lydia Harvey disappeared again and again. She was no one. Who she was, what she wanted, what happened afterwards: none of this mattered. She joined a legion of missing girls, whose brief appearances in newspapers and books remained uncomplicated by their past experiences of poverty, abuse or their exploitation in other kinds of work. No one took any notice of their dreams, ambitions and desires. In the hands of newspaper reporters and moral reformers, stories like Lydia's served as cautionary tales for any young working-class woman who longed for adventure and travel, for better pay or better working conditions and, if they dared to imagine it, for a life of luxury and romance. The end of the story was always an imagined punishment for girls who had, in the parlance of the time, been 'ruined': 'Her slavery lasts some five or six years as a rule,' noted one dramatic writer, 'and then she is flung out upon the streets, her character gone, her hope dead, her body diseased, to die before long either in a workhouse or a Lock Hospital.'[4] The missing girls in these ubiquitous stories were condemned to a short life of misery, disease and degradation; they 'vanished forever beneath the slime of the underworld' and remained 'literally nameless and unknown'.[5]

But Lydia Harvey is not nameless, or unknown. She refused this story. In a Soho police station in July 1910 she gave a witness statement that would form the key piece of testimony that saw her traffickers brought to some semblance of justice. This witness statement, and the archive file into which it was tucked, opened up a small window onto the full and extraordinary life of a young woman who crossed two oceans, walked the streets of world cities, denounced her abusers and reinvented herself. This book tells the story of her incredible journey and the people whose lives entwined with hers along the way. It reconstructs the events that led up to one forgotten yet dramatic trial, and follows the threads of its remarkable afterlife.

Lydia Harvey has almost disappeared from the historical record. After the trial was over, she was sent home. Her New Zealand-bound steamship travelled down the Thames and out of sight, and she slipped off the archive page. The police officers signed off on their final reports; the newspapers reported the trial's outcome; her traffickers, once they had served their time, melted back into the underworld; and

Lydia's grateful letters to her social worker dried up. For the historian, that would usually be where her story would end: a useful illustration, an anecdote, a glimpse of a life we could not know beyond the archive file in which we found her, its pages crumbling at the edge.

Lydia Harvey, and millions of young women like her, left very few traces in the archives. If we are lucky, we can find birth, marriage and death certificates: enough to include them on a branch of a family tree. There may survive a handful of school records or health reports or, if they lived in a country that kept census returns, we might be fortunate enough to have a brief snapshot of their household on census night. Of course some young women kept diaries, and many wrote letters, but precious few of these remain. Can we blame their authors for burning them in the grate or tossing them in the bin – for thinking that their words didn't matter?

Lydia and similar young women are usually missing from the great histories that have been written about this tumultuous era. Their stories of adventure and risk, of work and abuse, were rarely recorded, and even more rarely remembered. At first no one looked for them; and now, fifty years after historians first began writing about women in the past, we have yet to incorporate them into popular historical understanding. They are still, at best, footnotes to histories of supposedly more important things.

This is especially true of poor, vulnerable and marginalised girls and young women who were often, in the words of Saidiya Hartman, 'only visible in the moment of their disappearance'.[6] Hartman writes about young black women who were killed in the Atlantic slave trade, about whom nothing remains but a line in a ledger, briefly describing their death. White Western girls like Lydia were given the opportunity to make a deeper mark on the historical record, but it remains true that the moment that rendered Lydia visible was one of extreme duress. It is only because of her pain and suffering, and her vulnerability to coercion, control and judgement by both criminals and state authorities, that we can see her at all.

This glimpse I had caught of Lydia Harvey could have been left that way: a small story woven into a broader history of trafficking, migration, work and crime in the early twentieth century. But the more I put her into this wider historical context, the more she herself faded from view. And so I tugged at the threads of the archive in which she briefly appeared, and began to unravel the stories inside. This book starts with the presumption that her life, as well as the lives of those who trafficked her, those who investigated the case, those who helped her and those who told her story, deserve histories of their own. It insists that these small histories can tell us just as much, if not more, about the early twentieth-century world as those sweeping histories that dominate our bookshelves, in which girls like Lydia become nobodies. And it shows how breathtakingly human such stories can be.

So how can we find a nobody of a girl – a girl who was supposed to disappear – from more than a hundred years' distance? A decade ago, such things would not really have been possible. We can only find more glimpses now of Lydia in her world because of the immense changes that our own has witnessed. We do not have more information. The gone is still gone, and parts of Lydia's life remain lost, presumably for ever. But through our computer screens and high-resolution scanners, our algorithms and our search engines and databases, we have a greater ability to find and collate the traces that Lydia Harvey has left behind, more ways to unravel archives and connect their threads to others. These new ways of searching digitally help us better access the rich details hidden in the physical archives that house the ledgers from courts, the schedules from censuses, the telegraphs that travelled along wires beneath oceans, the fingerprints and photographs and criminal records that were part of a great traffic in paper at the dawn of international policing. Stitching together thousands of these precious details, I have tried to reconstruct Lydia's life. I have attempted to understand – amid all the stories that other people had told about her – how she saw herself.

In Lydia's incredible journeys across two oceans and in the tangled streets of three cities, her life became inextricably entwined with the lives of others. Some of these men and women – the police officers, the social workers and the newspaper reporters who became involved in her case – helped to shape a response to trafficking and prostitution that has echoed down the years, and which profoundly impacts upon women, not so dissimilar to Lydia Harvey, in the present day. Others left almost as small a mark on the historical record as Lydia herself did: the man and the woman who coerced her into selling sex in Buenos Aires and London, who brokered her travel, abused her and pocketed her earnings. This, however uncomfortable it may be, is their story, too.

Why should we listen to any of these voices: the powerful and the powerless, the criminals and the victims? Because they provide a panoramic view of profound but incredibly complicated social problems, whose parameters, causes and solutions look different depending on whose eyes we see them through. These interconnected narratives are a speculation on what might be gained when we consider more than one perspective – when we seek to understand in the round. It is a polyphonic history that makes visible the range of forces that shaped Lydia's story, and thousands of other stories like hers. This historical collage enables us to explore different avenues of thought, discover the many ways people had of living their lives and understand the complex networks of hearts, minds and money that spanned the globe. Each unique standpoint creates a new window through which we can view the early twentieth-century world.

Together, Lydia's story and the stories of those whose lives briefly entangled with hers illuminate some of the darker corners of the dawn of the twentieth century, a period that witnessed the beginnings of many of the laws, ideas and institutions that shape our lives in the present day. It was an era that was hungry for social reforms, better laws and more effective justice, but also one in which more and more power to surveil, identify and incarcerate was put in the hands of the state, and when the poorest and most vulnerable were pushed further to the margins. It was a society in motion, a better-connected planet, a land of commerce and opportunity; but it was also an era that was laying the groundwork for the systems of draconian border control, globalised capital and militarism, exploited labour and organised crime that we still live with. It was a world where working-class women dreamed of better and fought to attain it, but where aspiration could turn to exploitation in the blink of an eye.

The six lives found in this book were lived at a moment of transformation, and their experiences illuminate the profound changes the world was experiencing as the new century dawned. Between the lines of this forgotten trial and the stories that spun out of it lies a history of globalised crime and international policing; of revolutionary social reforms, unprecedented global travel and harsh new migration restrictions; of exploited labour and sexual labour; and of the world-changing rise of modern media. Lydia Harvey's story unfolded against a backdrop of a world in flux, a world that working, travelling, aspiring young women helped to build, often at great cost. This book is a history of the dawn of our modern era, narrated through the perspective of a nobody named Lydia Harvey, and written in the shadow of all the girls who really have disappeared. In telling her own story, under great duress and after great hardship, Lydia Harvey left one small but unforgettable mark on the historical record that has helped make visible her world. She didn't change history. But the story of her ambition, her exploitation and her determination can change which histories we believe to be important.

CHAPTER ONE

THE DISAPPEARING GIRL

Lydia Harvey wore her nicest dress underneath her only coat. It was blustery and wet that autumn evening in May 1909, but the weather was forgotten as she and her sister joined the crowd pouring into the grand foyer of Oamaru's white stone opera house. A brand-new programme of films by Pathé Bros had come all the way from Paris and London to be shown in this small New Zealand town, and after the show the winner of the *Oamaru Mail* beauty contest would be announced. Lydia shrugged off her coat among the other eager patrons and pushed towards the edge with her sister: there, on the foyer walls, were photographs of the contest participants. Lydia walked past images of Oamaru girls looking sweetly into the camera until she found the one of herself, a week or so shy of her sixteenth birthday.[1] The girls in the foyer shifted nervously, giggling with their sisters and friends, wondering who in the crowd had cast a vote in their favour and guessing which one of them would win that evening.

The bells rang and the crowd filed into the theatre. Lydia Harvey took her seat underneath the plaster ceiling and crystal chandelier. The building was only two years old, and everything felt grand and new. The curtains parted and the crowd hushed as the films were thrown onto the screen.[2]

12

Flickering images of a London street played before her, as real as if she were there herself. Women in the finest dresses walked with gentlemen through the Bois de Boulogne in Paris. Next came a film in bright colour, with fairies dancing, framed by enormous flowers. She watched as the fairy's gentleman-suitor transformed into a grotesque faun and then disappeared in a puff of smoke.[3]

After the final film, the curtain closed and the presenter appeared, ready to announce the results of the beauty contest. The girls waited, holding their breath. The winner, he declared after a dramatic pause, was Miss Nellie Mathie. The nineteen-year-old arrived onstage, smiling, and was awarded a gold bangle, an accessory that was all the rage, popularised by an Australian singing idol. Nellie slipped it onto her wrist while the others swallowed their envy.

There was only one more prize-winner to call. The girls in the audience hushed again, swallowing their disappointment and hoping to hear their own name this time. And the runner-up – another agonising pause – Miss Lydia Harvey. Walking through the applause, she joined Nellie onstage to accept a silver purse. The packed house gave them both an exuberant ovation. Lydia was probably so excited by the time she took her seat, her heart still pounding, that she could barely pay attention to Madame Carswell, the ballad singer, who continued to entertain the crowd. When she and her sister Clara went home that night, fighting the wind and rain, to her family's little bungalow in Chelmer Street, they likely talked of little else. But their mother soon put them to work. With twin five-month-olds and a three-year-old to care for and clean up after, there was surely little time for leisure.

Lydia shared the small house that she called home with her mother, Emily Louisa Badeley, and six sisters. It was, by any measure, a large family, made all the more unusual by the fact that there was no father in sight. Lydia was the eldest of these girls, and the most reliable evidence tells me she was born on 3 June 1893 in the town of Dunedin, on New Zealand's South Island. Nothing was written about this event – her birth was not even registered – but we can presume that Lydia Harvey, like most babies, came into the world with little fanfare and some wailing. The year, on the other hand, was (according to the pre-eminent New Zealand historian Guy Scholefield) 'epic'. 'Eighteen-ninety-three glowed pink with the glow of promise,' he wrote. The promise was that of social progress: the year witnessed major reforms, including land ownership and Temperance, and, most epically, was the year that New Zealand became the very first country to grant women the national vote. Lydia Harvey was born into what promised to be a better world.

She arrived, in the parlance of the time, a bastard; born in the house of her mother's guardian, Jane White, who lived in Dunedin's well-to-do suburb of Roslyn with her bank-clerk husband, on a ridge overlooking both the city and the sea. The Whites had taken in Lydia's mother Emily and her two brothers after their mother's death, when Emily was only nine months old. Emily's father, Lydia's maternal grandfather, hailed from a well-to-do English family, but after his wife's passing had left his children with Mrs White in Dunedin and opted for a life of financial fraud and an early death in Tasmania.[4] The Badeley family's ancestral home is now a listed building in Berkshire, England.

The suburb of Roslyn was, both physically and

metaphorically, well above the rougher parts of the South Island's largest and most economically unequal town. It is unlikely that Emily Badeley ever set foot in Dunedin's 'devil's half-acre', the slumland in the city centre known for its crime, violence, alcoholism and illegitimate children.[5] It is therefore difficult to say what the respectable Mrs Jane White made of the trouble her youngest ward had got herself into, when Emily's belly began to swell at the age of twenty-one. She was by this point a talented musician, a young piano teacher and concert performer, and had caught the eye of a local solicitor, Harry George Cannon Harvey, who worked as a clerk for Justice Joshua Williams and was part of a local cycling club with Emily's older brother.[6] We can presume this fateful meeting transpired at least nine months before 3 June 1893, when his unacknowledged, unregistered daughter was born.

Many young women, poor, abandoned and pregnant out of wedlock, gave birth in mother-and-baby homes, whose benevolent overseers compelled them to give up their children into care or adoption; but Emily Louisa Badeley kept her baby. She and little Lydia continued to live in Dunedin with the Whites for a year or so, probably until Lydia was weaned, when mother and baby chose (or were forced) to leave and return to Oamaru, where the Badeley children had been born to their ill-fated parents in the 1870s. It made sense: Emily's elder brothers had both already moved there with their families and there were cousins for baby Lydia to grow up with.

There may have been another motivation as well: the solicitor Harry G. C. Harvey had opened offices in Oamaru a year or so before. As a small-town solicitor, he performed the usual legal paperwork for property sales, wills and civil cases, and represented both plaintiffs and defendants in court. But by the time he set up his own legal practice in Oamaru, there were intimations that he engaged in more unsavoury dealings. In her final public statement the notorious Minnie Dean, who had been accused of baby-farming and child murder, named Harvey. He was a broker, she explained, who sometimes managed the money when a parent or guardian brought her an unwanted child to foster and to put out for adoption. She protested her innocence to the last, explaining that the children died accidentally, but the infant skeletons in her garden damned her both in the press and in the court. Justice Williams sentenced her to death by hanging, and she remains the only woman ever executed in New Zealand's history. Harry G. C. Harvey – as he was in the habit of doing, when it came to unwanted children – escaped with his character unscathed.[7]

Oamaru was a small but curious town, known for its main streets' unexpectedly grand buildings, an 'architecture of prosperity' that made the most of a nearby quarry of pristine white limestone to mimic in miniature the style and grandeur of Britain's noble Victorian capitals.[8] Most streets were named after British rivers, and Thames Street, on which the brand-new opera house stood, was the widest in the whole country. Emily and Lydia found accommodation in Yare Street, in a tiny bungalow on a road that rose steeply just to the north of the centre. It was not the best part of town.

Oamaru had been founded in the 1860s as a service centre for the North Otago goldfields and the vast farmlands that surrounded it and, like many of these gold-rush towns, went 'from quarry to street in a single generation'.[9] Its large harbour had wharves and long jetties, built in the last decades of the

2: A view overlooking Oamaru, Lydia Harvey's hometown in New Zealand, around the time her family moved there from nearby Dunedin. The grandeur of the white stone buildings contrast with the smallness of the place.

nineteenth century, which had transformed a dangerous coastline into one of the country's busiest deep-sea ports. By the time Lydia Harvey moved there the town would have boasted one of the world's first meat-freezing plants, which enabled North Otago to ship lamb and mutton, as well as butter and cheese, to British markets. Indeed, the town boasted all the modern conveniences: in addition to an opera house, there was an Athenaeum, offering books, periodicals and lectures to educate the working classes, a railway line and shops with imported goods.

However, the town's prosperity and grandeur often did not go much deeper than the buildings' facades. In the late nineteenth century Oamaru was known as a rough and booze-soaked place, where a population of just over 6,000 people kept twenty hotels, two breweries, thirty-two 'sly grog' shops (the Australian and New Zealand term for unlicensed bars) and twelve brothels busy.[10] But as the twentieth century dawned, children like Lydia encountered a quieter, more respectable, more regulated municipality. Temperance campaigners had succeeded in getting the place voted dry in 1905, and the raucous hotel bar rooms of Oamaru grew sedate with the sound of teacups. Growing up in such a town in the hinterlands of the settler colonial empire was probably safe but unexciting: for all its homage to London, London it was not.

Lydia was baptised on the corner of Thames and Tees Streets, almost two years after her birth, on 20 March 1895, in St Luke's Anglican Church. Only her headstrong mother Emily stood as a witness, unapologetically alone.[11] The looks that her swollen belly may have received were never recorded in the baptismal register. Three months later, Lydia's sister Clara was born. This sister took her mother's maiden name, Badeley, suggesting that Harry G. C. Harvey was not the father. A few years on, in 1900, another daughter, Lynda, joined the still-fatherless family. Emily took out advertisements for piano lessons at 'rates moderate' and probably gave the children to her sister-in-law, who lived nearby, when she had a pupil.[12]

Lydia's father made himself scarce soon after the birth of Lynda – a hint, alongside their similar names and the fact that both she and Lydia are missing their birth registration, that he may have been the father of this child as well. In 1901, when Lydia was eight years old, Harry Harvey left Oamaru to take up a job as a solicitor in Christchurch and married Agnes Montgomery Ingram, the respectable daughter of a respectable man. Using money inherited from his late father,

3: Avon Lodge, Lydia Harvey's father's thirty-two-room mansion
outside of Christchurch, New Zealand, in which he died. Lydia
herself never set foot in the house, nor did she see any of the
profits from its sale. She may not have even known it existed.

the district court judge George Harvey, he also bought a very
respectable house: Avon Lodge, a thirty-two-room villa in
the suburbs of Christchurch.[13]

Emily Louisa Badeley had no intention of letting Harry
Harvey shirk his paternal responsibilities so easily. In April
1904 she took him to court in Oamaru, on charges of bastardy. In doing so, she joined hundreds of other women in
the province of Otago who brought the 'putative fathers' of
their children to court. Many of them were pressured to do
so by the local Benevolent Institution, so that these fathers
(and not charity) would see to the financial support of the
child. Many were successful – up to 76 per cent of these
women were granted maintenance orders. Others managed

to successfully negotiate maintenance payments privately, which is probably what Harry Harvey had initially agreed. It was only after he stopped these payments that Emily turned to the justice system.[14]

Emily Badeley's case was adjourned twice, but in May 1904 Harry G. C. Harvey was ordered to pay 10 shillings a week for maintenance – a high figure that supports the theory that she was seeking maintenance for both Lydia and Lynda. The short entries in the Oamaru magistrates' court charge book tell a clear story of the highly charged dispute, marked by his evasion and her tenacity. On 22 June 1904 she dragged him back to court on the charge of non-payment of a child maintenance order, Harvey paid it and the charge was withdrawn. Then in June 1905 she brought him to court again, for disobedience of the order. This time Harry G. C. Harvey did not show up in Oamaru until, in October 1905, Emily took him up on the charge again and he paid the £8 owing for that year. The same thing happened in 1906, and he was threatened with prison. Not deigning to leave his mansion in Christchurch, he sent the £9 10s owing by cheque.

Harry G. C. Harvey was not the only man Emily Badeley took to court in these years. In 1904 she laid similar charges against Edward Towsey, a tobacconist in Dunedin, most likely the father of her second-eldest daughter, Clara. Towsey's solicitor came out swinging, saying that his client did not recognise the child and that anyway she had many children by other fathers. Emily's solicitor's firm replied calmly: Miss Badeley had evidence that Mr Towsey had admitted parentage to others, and that 'the question about any other child our client may have does not affect your client's obligation to provide for the child of which he is stated to be the father'.[15] Towsey, like Harry Harvey, was ordered to pay child maintenance. Then, in 1906, Emily took a third man to court on bastardy charges, and after that the court records no longer survive.[16]

Lydia had four sisters by the time she reached her teenage years: Clara Kathleen, born in 1895, two years younger than Lydia; Lynda, born in 1900, and with whom she possibly shared a father; Gertrude Mildred Hawthorn, born in 1903; and Doris Winnifred, born in 1906.[17] All of the children, with the exception perhaps of Lydia and Lynda, appear to have had different fathers. This was extremely unusual in early twentieth-century New Zealand society, but Emily Badeley did not seem willing to conform or repent. And despite the social and financial pressures that all these illegitimate children must have brought with them, her name never once appeared in the records of the Benevolent Institution. Between her music lessons and the money from her children's fathers, Emily made do.[18] The wolf was probably never far from the door, and sometimes the residents of Yare Street were disturbed by the drunken curses from a troublesome neighbour, but, as one early twentieth-century Otago mother put it in her memoir, the Badeleys could count themselves among 'the not so poor'.[19]

The small wooden bungalow on Yare Street in which Lydia spent her early years was crowded with girls, until it grew too small and they moved to Chelmer Street, just down the hill. Saturday mornings were spent doing chores, and the afternoons passed with play in the parks, meadows and the little river. They rode their bicycles down to the beach, played with their cousins, went to church on Sunday (perhaps) and watched the town slowly change. The first motor car drove down the street in 1900, when Lydia was seven years old. The opera house opened in 1907, just in time for the teenage Badeley girls to swoon over the visiting performers and the films that were shown there.[20] In the evenings they would gather round their mother's piano and sing together.[21]

Oamaru Middle School provided Lydia with a basic education and, because she was a girl, with lessons in cookery, sewing, knitting and childcare. The boys, because they were boys, learned military drills, especially after the Boer War swept the country with a bellicose imperialism. Once a year the class of future wives and soldiers was ushered into the yard and made to sit and stand in rows while a man behind a camera snapped a photograph.[22]

Lydia and Clara, like most of the children, appear neat and tidy in their 1907 school photo, but because the list of names is incomplete, I do not know which girls they are. Laurel Badeley (the daughter of Emily's brother, who was the same age as Clara) is identified in the photograph as the second girl from the left in the third row from the front, with a wide collar and a glum expression. The rest of the class list is patchy – only about half the children are named. Somewhere in the photograph is twelve-year-old Clara and fourteen-year-old Lydia.

It is the only picture of her that still exists, so far as I can tell. It is both poetic and frustrating that we cannot know which girl she is. The possibilities can be narrowed down, however, if the pupils who are named are eliminated, and only the girls whose hair could be described – as Lydia's later was – as 'mousy brown' are included. Could Lydia be the second girl from the right in the third row, with long hair

4: A class photo from Oamaru Middle School in 1906–7. Lydia Harvey sits somewhere in this photo, but we cannot know which girl she is.

and a friend's hands upon her shoulder? Or is she just to the right of this, with lighter, messier hair, a girl who has been caught, it seems, in slight motion? Lydia could be the girl in the floral-print dress, missing an apron, in the second row, whose hair is slicked back and who wears a sardonic expression. The girl who sits fifth from the left in the second row is also unnamed. She has dark hair, a dark complexion and a bow placed just like Laurel's, in the row above. Could it be Clara? The last unnamed, brown-haired girl sits fourth from the right in the second row from the front. She is taller than the rest, and her dark hair looks like Laurel's. She is certainly pretty – a descriptor that everyone who encountered Lydia used. Her head is turned a little to the side, but she looks directly into the camera, as if daring the viewer to call her by her name.

Lydia did well enough in school, but did not distinguish herself as a scholar. And then, in 1909, when she was sixteen and finishing her schooling, her mother felt the familiar flutter in her belly once again. In May that year there would be twins, Annie and Evaline.[23] Lydia was the eldest of what were now seven daughters, and a set of twins meant that she would practically be the mother of at least one. More nappies to boil and peg out on the line, more pots to scour, more mouths to feed, more bodies crowded into her bed.[24] She loved her sisters, but if she stayed, she would surely disappear.

The beauty contest sponsored by the *Oamaru Mail* promised, however briefly, to take her miles away from the washing, the nappies and the chores. These contests – much to the chagrin of moral reformers – had rapidly become a regular feature of early twentieth-century girlhood, and small towns like Oamaru were no exception. Some contests required the girls to appear onstage, to smile and wave and show their figure, but most were based on submitted photographs, which would then be displayed in theatre foyers and voted on by concert-goers. Lydia used a little pocket money to have her portrait taken at a local photography studio and posted it to the paper.

Lydia Harvey's beauty-contest photograph, like many of the films that she might have watched that May evening, no longer survives, but this brief adolescent moment reveals precious details about her life and the world in which she lived: isolated in one way, marvellously connected in others. Lydia may have been living in a small town far-flung from the great seats of the European empires, but the technological changes in transportation and communication that swept the globe from the mid-nineteenth century meant that the world was at her doorstep in a way it had never been before. New film technologies meant she could practically reach out and touch a London omnibus. Improved telegraph and postal systems meant she could read the latest news from England. Richer young women – those who had wealthy fathers who recognised them, and who enjoyed life in the upper crust of New Zealand society – could even send a message instantly to friends abroad, or use catalogues to order clothes, creams and other luxuries from around the world. Poor young women like Lydia were left to imagine doing the same. Steamships were faster and more comfortable and, just as importantly, cheaper than before. Travel lay just within or just beyond the grasp of the average working person, depending on their luck and circumstance. It was easy for Lydia to dream of setting off on one of these 'floating cities'. This was her mobile world.

But it was also a world that seemed to slip further and further from her reach, not least because her mother's newest babies were far from the only calamity that year. Up in his thirty-two-room villa outside Christchurch, Harry George Cannon Harvey felt a sudden and terrible pain in his chest. He died instantly.[25] There would be no more maintenance payments sneaking out of his account. He died without a will, but even if he had written one, it is highly doubtful it would have included Lydia. His widow, Agnes, swore in her affidavit to the lawyers that she and his mother were Harvey's only surviving kin. There was no mention of a child.[26] It seems it was easier for me, as a historian a hundred years later, to find a record of his 1904 bastardy order issued in Oamaru than it was for the solicitors administering the intestate probate to find it back in 1909, only five years after he had last been ordered to pay child maintenance. No one, it seemed, thought to pry into the past of such a wealthy, respectable man.

In a house with rent owing, filled with girls who needed school clothes and with babies that needed changing and nursing, Lydia's mother broke the news. Lydia was unlikely to have felt much sorrow at the death of her absent, virtually unknown father, but she was old enough to understand what the loss of 10 shillings a week would mean for her family. And even if she didn't, her mother soon made it clear: Lydia would have to leave school and go out to work.

She could have found something relatively close to home: the local newspapers regularly posted Wanted advertisements for domestic servants in town and in nearby Dunedin, and for girls for the woollen mill in Oamaru.[27] Maybe Lydia was thinking of the women in the omnibus, the crowds bustling through the big city. Maybe she wanted to get away from the little house on Chelmer Street, its front room nightly cramped with one adult, five children, two babies and a piano. Maybe she couldn't bear for the people of Oamaru to see her, the pretty girl who had just won a silver purse in a beauty contest, as a lowly maid-of-all-work. Or perhaps she began to see a way to escape at last the looks that she got on the streets of Oamaru. It was a small town, for all its white-stone splendour. There was little chance that the well-to-do people who ran the place did not talk in hushed tones about Miss Badeley the music teacher, who had just had a sixth and seventh baby girl with no husband in sight. Her daughters – however well they did in school, however tidy their hair bows, and however many beauty contests they won – would still be greeted by a certain look sometimes: the Badeley family had a reputation.

It wasn't long before an opportunity arose. Mrs Batson, a local singer, hairdresser and entrepreneur who moved in the most respectable Oamaru social circles, was said to be looking for a girl to travel with her, her husband and their four children to Wellington, where Mr Batson, a clerk at the Loan and Mercantile Bank, had been promoted to manager. It was to be, Mrs Batson proclaimed, 'easy work for a smart girl'.[28] Miss Badeley, a piano teacher, surely knew Mrs Batson well, and perhaps even accompanied her singing, though as an unwed mother of seven she surely moved in less superior circles. Perhaps Mrs Batson, with four young children herself, saw Miss Badeley and her family as a charity case. Amid a countrywide domestic-labour shortage, such charitable sentiment was also very useful to the servant-employing class. A girl in such desperate circumstances would likely prove a dedicated and amenable domestic worker, and probably a cheap one too.

And so in August 1909 the Batsons and Lydia Harvey departed together on a coastal steamer bound for Wellington. After what was surely a tearful farewell with her mother and sisters, Lydia boarded the ship with the four Batson children in tow, newly sixteen and only a child herself. She was anxious, excited and under the watchful eye of Mrs Batson.[29] After short stops in Timaru and Lyttelton, the ship continued on to New Zealand's North Island, to arrive in the capital of Wellington. Lydia would have helped to herd Mrs Batson's children, and would have joined her fellow passengers as they rushed to the deck when the ship arrived in the city's broad and beautiful harbour, eager to catch a glimpse of her new home.[30]

She was one of millions. The late nineteenth and early twentieth centuries were a period that witnessed an explosion of working-class migration and, like those women on the London omnibuses, a greater and greater proportion of those who left home and travelled for work were single women travelling without their families. By the turn of the century, imperial expansion, urbanisation and high-intensity resource extraction had all fuelled demand not just for male labour in mining, farming, forestry, manufacturing, service and transportation, but also for the female labour that made it possible: in domestic service and other cleaning and caring work; in the new factories, shops and offices that were expanding in cities; and in the sexual labour market that underwrote this new global economy. Many made short journeys, as Lydia Harvey did, from a smaller town or rural community into the city, but many also crossed oceans and continents for work. Young women poured into the world's metropolises and urban centres in this period and were called many names: modern girls, factory girls, shop girls, domestics, prostitutes.[31]

The Batsons, their four children and Lydia disembarked, and a porter found them and their baggage a driver, who took them along a newly built road to the house the family had taken in a wealthy new Wellington suburb. Lydia's meagre box of possessions rattled in the back. Her heart must have sunk as the car travelled further and further away from the bustle of Lambton Quay and the shops on Manners Street, up the steep, winding roads on the outskirts of the city, until at last Wellington harbour slipped from view and they reached a hanging valley in which the suburb of Karori sat. Down in the valley among the hills, you couldn't even see Wellington proper.[32] Instead of bars and shops and people, Lydia looked round to see quiet streets with bungalows and vegetable gardens and, beyond that, sheep and the bush stretching out.[33] It felt even smaller than Oamaru.

Lydia had to be up in time to wash and feed herself and start work by seven o'clock in the morning. The first week was exhausting, with a flurry of unpacking, and after that life settled into an equally exhausting list of endless daily chores. She lit the fires, prepared the family's breakfast and washed up the dishes. She scrubbed floors, polished silver and, once a week, stripped the beds and washed the sheets and hung them out to dry, alongside the household's clothing. She served lunch to her mistress if she was at home, and minded little Violet Batson, who at the age of four was not yet in school. She dusted books, swept the steps and made dinner in time for Mr Batson's arrival from his job at the Loan and Mercantile Bank. She washed up the dishes and washed the children. She folded down the beds, got a small supper for herself, banked the fires and, taking a lonely candle through the darkened house to a little room built off the back, fell exhausted into her bed at 10 p.m., looking forward to nothing other than the next fifteen-hour working day. She was awake before the sun was up and getting the family's breakfast by the time the racket of birds declared the morning.[34]

The next weeks continued much the same as the first. Lydia was lonely and while she was accustomed to helping her mother around the house, she didn't know much about maintaining a full middle-class household. She missed her sisters desperately, and caring for the children of her social betters was nothing like caring for her own relations. Mrs Batson, as a woman who ran her own business in Oamaru, performed onstage and cared for four children, expected no less energy from the 'smart' and 'respectable' girl she had hired. Perhaps, with Lydia's unrespectable mother in mind, Mrs Batson wasted no time in telling Lydia about the things she had done wrong.[35]

A few weeks in and Lydia's hands were dry and chapped, and her knees and lower back ached. Her black-stuff dress smelled under the arms and puffed out at the shoulders in a most unstylish way, and her white apron was stiff and warm.[36] She was miles away from anything fun whatsoever. She ate her meagre dinners alone in the kitchen to the sound of the clock ticking, and she leafed through magazines and catalogues, with all the lovely clothes and advertisements for trips abroad. 'This is essentially an age of advertisement,' the Travellers' Aid Society wrote in its annual report in 1910, noting how many girls were lured away from good positions with the promise of a better post and a life of luxury far away.[37] Or, as the American feminist Jane Addams put it, of the young women who struggled to hold places in domestic service, 'the long hours, the lack of comforts, the low pay, the absence of recreation, the sense of "good times" all about her which she cannot share, the conviction she is rapidly losing health and charm, rouse the molten forces within her'.[38]

Pay day came, and a pittance went into Lydia's silver purse. At last it was Sunday and she got her half-day off. It was all she could do not to run to the tram stop, where she paid her halfpenny and travelled into the city to see the shops and restaurants and the comings and goings of people at last. Once a week for a year she would make this hour-long journey by tram, and in this way she made friends, visited tea rooms, window-shopped and lived the life of a teenage girl, for seven hours on Sunday.

It seems, though, that she made the wrong sort of friends, at least in the eyes of Mrs Batson. A few months into her post, as winter gave way to spring and summer, Lydia began going out in the evenings after her work was finished. By early December she was staying out long into the warm night, coming back to her little room in Karori as late as midnight or one o'clock: the molten forces in her had been roused.[39] After many heated conversations about the declining quality of her work and her unrespectable behaviour, on New Year's Day 1910 Lydia took pleasure in announcing to Mrs Batson that she was taking her box and leaving the house and going to live at Mrs Logan's boarding house in Ingestre Street. This was – to a nice suburban family like Mrs Batson's – the seedy part of town, known for its brothels, its socialists and its drunken nightlife.[40] Mrs Batson immediately wrote to Lydia's mother to tell her of her daughter's unmanageable behaviour. She herself must have despaired, reflecting no doubt on a truism from the age of the 'servant crisis': good help was difficult to find.

Lydia did not see it that way. She had, through her own resourcefulness, made a move that many young women were making in this period: away from live-in domestic service and into shop work. She had found a job as a photographer's apprentice at a studio in Lower Hutt, a town that, like Karori, lay a short commute from Wellington. Unlike Mrs Batson, however, Mr Harlow did not require her to live there: she could return to the city every evening by train, and he would give her 7s 6d a week in wages and 4 shillings besides, for her room. It was more than double what Mrs Batson had paid her, and she had swapped scrubbing floors for learning an interesting trade.[41]

As Mrs Batson's letter travelled by coastal steamer to her mother in Oamaru, Lydia Harvey grew more 'independent' – a criticism often levied at girls by moral reformers. Her new lodgings on Ingestre Street (which has today become part of Vivian Street) were around the corner from the bars, cinemas and brothels of Manners, Dixon and Cuba Streets. The area was filled with single young men who talked radical politics, and with what seemed to Lydia the most modern of modern girls. She stayed in a room with other untethered single young women who were in the habit of keeping bad company. The shop windows showed her items she could not afford, despite her pay rise, and at the Queen's Wharf sat steamships that could take her to Sydney or even London, if only she could afford a ticket. Lydia went to dance halls and the cinema, loitered in the streets and went out with men, unchaperoned.

Mrs Logan's boarding house was, according to reports, 'respectable'.[42] What precisely made a boarding house respectable was a matter of interpretation – for instance, Lydia was staying in a mixed-sex boarding house, instead of a women-only hostel, which would certainly have shocked Mrs Batson and many other respectable young women. What made boarding houses definitely unrespectable, on the other hand, was much more obvious. Aside from the usual advertisements for rooms, boarding houses made it into local and national newspapers – especially the sensationalist and incredibly popular tabloid the *New Zealand Truth* – when they were home to fights, murders and suicides or operated as 'sly grog' shops. Above all, boarding houses (sometimes even the respectable ones) had a tendency to 'be engulfed by flames', owing to often being constructed entirely of wood, with no corrugated-iron fire-walls.[43]

But however much these places furnished the sensational-ist press with headlines, they remained an essential fixture of working-class rural-to-urban migrant life. Not only did they offer affordable accommodation, but they were also a substi-tute for the family life that so many rural-to-urban migrants had left behind. In their cosy, if shabby, common rooms, young men and women chatted over cups of tea, ate their dinners together and shared the news of the day. Lydia made friends with a girl named Doris Gray, who knew a lot more than she did about men and clothes and money, and they went out together at night, after Mrs Logan had gone to bed. One time, in a fit of giggles, they sneaked out of their bedroom window. Gentlemen callers could knock for the girls who stayed there and take them out on the town. Soon a young man by the name of Tom Robinson was knocking for Lydia. It was a million times better than her fifteen-hour workdays and her lonely back room in Mrs Batson's suburban house.[44]

Lydia Harvey's brief romance with Tom Robinson left little mark on the historical record: no marriage or bastardy charges resulted from their short time together. Yet it does seem that he knocked on her Ingestre Street door often, and perhaps even stayed in her room.[45] What happened behind this closed door, away from the prying eyes of both the boarding-house matron and the historian, is anyone's guess: the level of sexual knowledge and sexual activity among young working-class women in this period was extremely varied. While some young women regularly engaged in pre-marital sex, many others did not realise what sexual intercourse was until their marriage night. It is unlikely Lydia was so ill-informed: after all, her mother had clearly had sexual relationships with several men, quite possibly in the family bungalow. But this doesn't mean the act itself wasn't still shrouded in mystery. For young women, to 'be with a man' may have meant penetrative sex, but it could just as easily have meant kissing, necking or clumsy fumbling over clothes.[46] Moral reformers, and Mrs Batson, may have fretted about how easily a girl's complete innocence could turn to total ruin, but Lydia, with Tom Robinson at her side, was probably discovering a range of experiences in between.

Even some of the most conservative moral reformers of the day acknowledged the unfair dichotomy of innocence and ruin that young women like Lydia Harvey were forced into, by a patriarchal society that recognised neither their sexual desire nor their right to deny or withdraw consent. 'Many girls,' wrote the prominent anti-prostitution campaigner Ellice Hopkins, 'get into mischief merely because they have in them an element of the "black kitten" which must frolic and play, but has no desire to get into danger. Do you not think it a little hard,' Hopkins asked, 'that men should have dug by the side of her foolish dancing feet a bottomless pit, and that she cannot have her jump and fun in safety ... without a single false step dashing her over the brink, and leaving her with the very womanhood dashed out of her?'[47]

Lydia's 'false step' came one evening in early January 1910, about five months after she first arrived in Wellington. She had returned by train from another long day at the photographer's studio, arriving in the city just in time for the boarding-house dinner. Perhaps she had seen a particularly well-dressed client at the studio that day, who had made her feel poor and unfashionable; or perhaps she was chatting with a family who had just returned from a trip abroad and were developing the film from their new Kodak Brownie camera.[48] Her experience in the camera shop, which afforded her glimpses into other, wider worlds, would have made even her new, independent life in Wellington feel small. That evening across the dinner table sat a new lodger, a handsome man with a thick accent, who spoke of his European adventures. Lydia complained to him that her longest journey had been from the South to the North Island. He smiled at her and asked her if she would like to meet people who could help her to travel. 'Yes, very much,' she replied.[49]

They finished the meal, and while the charming man continued to regale her with more stories of steamships and far-away cities, they took a short walk together down Ingestre Street, around the corner onto Tory Street and then to College Street, where they came to a stop at number 24. It was a small wooden bungalow like the others in the neighbourhood, with a veranda with wooden lacework, and simple curtains drawn across the windows. It seemed like any other family home or boarding house, except for a feeling of bareness, a sense that no one really lived there.

The man knocked and the door was opened by a striking young woman, just a few years older than Lydia herself, looking as poised and fashionable as a dancer in a Pathé Brothers' film. The woman had dark eyes and dark hair in a French style, with soft pinned curls framing her face and neck. A beauty spot was carefully painted onto her smooth cheek, and a heart-shaped pendant was set against her lacy white blouse. A dark skirt cinched her waist, emphasising the curve of her hips. She smiled.[50]

'This is the lady you are going to travel with,' the man

who had brought Lydia there said, though Lydia had not yet agreed to anything.

'We are delighted to meet you.' The woman spoke with an Australian accent. Smiling, she invited Lydia inside and bade the foreign man farewell for the evening.[51] It is difficult to know why Lydia stepped across the threshold, but the fact that it was a well-dressed, pretty young woman who invited her in must have helped to set her at ease.

The room was not nearly so well put together as the woman to whom it seemed to belong. Lydia noticed that it was untidy and gloomy, the curtains already drawn against the growing darkness. But in the low light she could see all sorts of trinkets: silver plates ringed with flowers, silks with swirling patterns, fans printed with faces and birds.

'What shall I call you?' she asked the woman.

'Just call me Marie,' the woman replied.

Marie invited her to sit in the front room and took her own seat beside Lydia. 'I have been looking for a nice young girl for some time to travel with me,' she said. This was not so unusual at the time, and many wealthy married women regularly contracted the help of a travelling nursemaid for their children, when they took long holidays or accompanied their husbands on protracted work trips, temporary placements or even permanent relocations. This was the main way in which young Indian women, called ayahs, first travelled to Britain, engaged to care for the white children of British families who had been stationed in the Raj, but it was also common for white working-class girls to be hired in similar roles.

Lydia could immediately see that there were no children in this strange house and perhaps she thought Marie required a lady's maid instead, and maybe she grew excited at the thought of boarding one of the steamships in the harbour, and at getting to touch all the fine objects that a rich, stylish woman would own. Or perhaps she began to wonder what was really going on, looking round at a messy, dark room that fell rather short of her expectations of the sort of middle-class home that would be inhabited by the kind of woman who would need a lady's maid. Mrs Batson probably wouldn't have even deigned to sit down.

Lydia wasn't left to wonder for long. Marie's pretty face grew serious as she spoke again. 'You know if you come with me, you will have to do the same as I do?'

'What is that?' Lydia asked.

'See gentlemen,' Marie replied and, unsure if Lydia quite understood, she added, 'Have you ever been with a man?'

'With a sweetheart,' Lydia replied, thinking, perhaps, of fumbling in the dark with Tom Robinson.

Marie fetched a pair of stockings that had been haphazardly strewn across a chair and handed them over. Lydia felt the fine silk, like butter, in her hands. 'You will have nice clothes, you won't want for anything and will be quite happy. These will be yours and we will buy you more things.'

Lydia heard a footfall on the veranda and the door opened, and Marie rose and smiled and kissed the newcomer on the cheek. He was tall and slim, with a carefully curled moustache and a long, narrow face. His suit looked expensive, and he had a pearl tie-pin. Compared with other men she knew – her uncles in Oamaru, Mr Batson the bank clerk, Mr Harlow the photographer – this man looked quite the dandy: handsome and strange.

'Here is the young girl who is going to come with us,'

Marie told him, escalating the plans still further, though Lydia still had not said she was going to come. But this was the way she, and most other girls, had been socialised: agree, behave, aim to please. She must have felt a strong pressure to comply.

This man, Marie explained, was her husband; and, without further ado, he smiled and clapped his hands and came over to where Lydia was sitting and made a show of sitting in her lap. She probably couldn't help but laugh.

'I am Signor Cellis,' he told her, taking Lydia's hand theatrically and kissing her on the cheek, speaking with a lyrical accent. 'You are a very nice girl.' He gave her no time to react to his boldness. 'You come with us and you will have no trouble or worry and be very happy.'

She noticed that his eyes were different colours: one deep brown and the other light blue. They twinkled playfully. Marie explained that Mr Cellis was a commercial traveller from Italy who had many investments in Australia and New Zealand; they had done well in Wellington and now planned to go into business in Buenos Aires.

Another knock at the door. Marie answered and a man's voice spoke from the veranda; she told him that she wasn't working that evening, and to go and see her friend, 'Tit', up the street. She came back to the sitting room, where Signor Cellis was now in his own chair, and suddenly everyone became more serious.

'Do you know what it is that I do?' asked Marie yet again – keen, it seemed, to make sure she had been understood. But again Lydia was given no time to reply. 'If you come with us to Buenos Aires, you will do the same and see gentlemen. Don't worry, it will be no different to what you've already done with your sweetheart.' Marie laughed and delivered one last compelling line. 'It is silly to do it for free, when you can make good money.' Lydia certainly didn't want to be thought of as silly.

As if to prove the point, Mr and Mrs Cellis led Lydia upstairs, where they showed her silk underwear, fine dresses and plush red-leather boots, and encouraged her to touch them, to try them on. Even Mrs Batson wouldn't have had such nice things, or at least nothing so modern and colourful. 'If they fit you, you may have them,' Mr Cellis told her, seeing Lydia admire a pair of red leather boots that sported delicate laces and dainty spool-heels. Pulling them on, she found that their tops came up almost to her knee.

Marie lifted more silk under-things from the chest. 'You will have to wear them when you are in the business,' she explained.

Lydia looked round the room and noticed the pictures on the walls. The women were fully nude.[52]

'You see how well I've set up this house for Marie?' Mr Cellis asked her. 'You too can have this, if you come with us and work hard.'

'You'll have many pretty dresses,' Marie continued, repeating herself. 'You'll not want for anything and will be quite happy.'

Lydia felt the silk of the underwear in her hands, saw the shine of the plush boots that would cost six months' salary from the photographer's studio, and felt surrounded by the ostentation of worldly travel. These things spoke to her more loudly than Mrs Batson's words of disapproval; more clearly than the worries of her now-distant mother and sisters. She agreed to join the Cellises.

They appeared delighted, and instructed Lydia to collect

her things together at the boarding house in Ingestre Street and they would have them brought to Marie's friends' house down the road. But they cautioned that there was a need for discretion. 'If you see me in the street, do not recognise me,' Marie cautioned, 'on account of the police.' The Cellises gave her some of the clothes and even one of Marie's old hats, much nicer than her own, and sent Lydia on her way.

She returned to Ingestre Street with her parcel of items and went up to her room. What must it have felt like to slip on the clothing they had given her, and to feel the soft, light fabric of crêpe de Chine or chiffon against a skin that was used to wool and cotton? To dress better than Mrs Batson, who anyway wore boring clothes; to dress like the women in the Bois du Boulogne? Such things had a worth that Lydia intrinsically understood. Her friend Doris Gray understood them too, and looked at her with admiration when she told her where she'd been. A couple of days later Lydia packed her trunk and settled up with Mrs Logan, then bade Doris and Tom Robinson farewell.

That day she did not make her usual journey to Lower Hutt and the photographer's studio, leaving Mr Harlow to wonder what had happened to her. Instead she returned to College Street, to the house just down the road from Marie's. She was greeted by the woman they called 'Tit', who was French. Marie herself, and her Italian husband Mr Cellis, soon joined them, expressing great delight at her return. Lydia was shown to a room in which she would stay until she departed for Buenos Aires.

Over dinner she learned that Mr Cellis's name was Aldo, and she was served a wine made from grapes that, like Tit, had come all the way from France. They ate vegetables marinated in a strange, grassy oil and seasoned sliced meat. She never saw the bottom of her wine glass. Everyone acted very interested in her, and told her all about the arrangements that had been made to get to Argentina. Lydia, through a cloudy head, was told that she would stay at Tit's for a few weeks, and that Marie and her husband would leave on an earlier ship. She would travel alone – this was because of the police, they said – and they would meet her at Montevideo, the bustling port capital of Uruguay and a gateway to South America.

The wine bottle was emptied and another was opened, and Lydia was given a pen and paper and told to write to her mother, saying that she was going to London to work as a nursemaid for a respectable couple named O'Conner, whom she had recently met when the family came to get their photograph taken at Mr Harlow's. Aldo Cellis took the letter and placed it in an envelope while she dictated her address. He said he would see it posted the very next morning. It arrived, we can only presume, at Miss Badeley's home in Chelmer Street shortly after Mrs Batson's letter, putting Lydia's mother's mind at greater ease.

The dinner ended and the Cellises took their leave, to return to the bungalow at number 24. Lydia was not to speak to them in the street, they reminded her, on account of the police. They would depart in a few days. They bade her farewell with more theatrical kisses. A few days later, Tit handed Lydia a third-class ticket, booked under the name Doris Williams, on the SS *Ruahine* of the New Zealand Shipping Line, departing on 10 February 1910 for London on the Pacific route, via Montevideo, where she would alight.[53]

Lydia Harvey had made a decision. She may not have fully understand what selling sex meant, but she probably had some inkling of what Mr and Mrs Cellis were getting at, when they handed her silk underwear and knee-high boots and told her she'd have to wear them for work. She could not have missed the suggestion that what was happening was illegal – both Aldo and Marie repeatedly told her to say nothing to anyone, in case it got back to the police. She was not kidnapped or coerced into the sex trade. But she was also sixteen, alone, work-weary and starry-eyed. She decided to take a risk in the name of luxury and adventure. It was the kind of decision that many people made, and a courageous one; but because she was poor, and young, and alone, and a woman, this risk-taking was significantly more likely to have dire consequences.

It was not just Mr and Mrs Cellis who played on the aspirations of the world's female working poor. This was an era when employment agencies, especially domestic-service agencies and theatre-recruitment companies, actively sought out young women who were willing to be sponsored to migrate to far-flung corners of the world. Working alongside the business interests of steamship firms, these employment agencies (often government-sponsored) took out ads in the newspapers emphasising the myriad opportunities that were open to the mobile young woman. 'New Zealand wants domestic workers,' proclaimed one government poster that was plastered around the overcrowded working-class neigh-bourhoods of England and Ireland, for 'good homes and good wages'.[54] Popular culture, letters home from those who had already emigrated and enticing travel writing under-scored these advertisements, and few people in the early twentieth century had not been exposed to the romantic idea of building a new life abroad.

The employment agencies that peddled this narrative were totally unregulated in most countries, meaning there were no rules concerning how much commission they could charge their recruits, how much they could require in repayment for passage or what they would demand as the terms of the contract. Employment agencies were regularly prosecuted for 'fraudulent inducements to emigrate', and the exploitation of women's physical labour lay at the heart of these agencies' businesses: more than 70 per cent of employment agencies' worldwide activity comprised the finding and placing of domestic workers, usually in very demanding, unregulated and low-paid positions.[55] The same was true of private advertisements. When Mrs Batson hired Lydia Harvey, she was not beholden to any minimum-wage laws or rules about working hours. Indeed, the same year in which Lydia met Mr and Mrs Cellis, a newly formed domestic workers' union in New Zealand launched a campaign to fix their work week at 'only' sixty-eight hours. They were unsuccessful, and the government took the first opportunity to disband the union.[56]

Despite the risks and demands of the labour, young women kept migrating for this kind of work – many of them successfully. Many cabaret and dance-hall workers saved money, saw the world and then married. Domestic servants sent remittances back to poor families and were often socially mobile. Sometimes these women exploited their employers, taking the money for their passage, but running away to a better post before it had been repaid.[57] Many women in the sex industry saved immense amounts of money and reinvested it into licit businesses and real estate, securing for themselves levels of life-long independence that few other working-class women could achieve.[58] This – the romance, the risks and the rewards – was the context in which Lydia Harvey made her choice to head to Buenos Aires.

And so, in early February 1910, she boarded the SS *Ruahine*, a brand-new refrigerated steamer, alongside a few hundred other passengers, 6,000 carcasses of lamb and 600 pounds of butter destined for the English market.[59] She lay low in her bunk when the steamer made a mail stop in her home town and prayed that no one she knew came aboard, wondering if Clara had ridden her bicycle to the dock to see the fine new steamship in port. Eventually, and surely with relief, she heard the ship's horn and felt its engines hum as it pulled away from the dock, and pictured the limestone buildings and deep harbour of Oamaru growing smaller and smaller.

When Lydia Harvey boarded the steamship to make her trans-Pacific voyage, she joined thousands of other emigrants who were temporary residents of these 'floating cities' in an age of unprecedented travel.[60] For some, this travel was part of a luxurious and itinerant lifestyle, in which they travelled in first- and second-class cabins and played the tourist in ports around the world. For others, this travel was part of their work, or part of a rare and long-saved-for holiday, taken infrequently. For others still, especially those who filled the third-class berths in the lowest and most uncomfortable part of the ship, this voyage was seen as a one-way trip.[61] They had answered recruitment ads to become farmhands in the Argentinian pampas or the Canadian prairies; to become mine-workers in the American Midwest or the Australian outback; to cut sugar cane, build railways, dig canals; to be domestic workers, governesses and factory girls in cities around the world.[62]

The first leg of Lydia's solo journey took fifteen days across the enormous South Pacific, until the rugged islands of Chile's long southern coast appeared on the horizon. Lydia probably passed the time playing cards with her fellow passengers, taking the air on deck and fighting off or succumbing to seasickness (third-class berths were located in the forward or aft of steamships, areas more susceptible to rough seas). She surely joined the other single young women in their flirtations with the young men, despite the efforts of the ship's matron to prevent it.[63] The ship then entered the narrow Magellan Strait, and Lydia enjoyed stunning views of glaciers and dramatic coastline off both port and starboard for the next few days, followed by another week of travel within sight of Argentina's wild southern coast at the height of summer. The air grew increasingly humid and warm as they travelled further north, until at last they reached the sweltering port of Montevideo. She packed her box, fixed the hat that Mrs Cellis had given her to her loosely pinned brown hair and bade farewell to her new London-bound friends. After an immigration inspector and a health inspector had boarded the ship, checked all the papers and looked for signs of communicable disease, the passengers were free to alight.

How did Lydia Harvey feel as she walked down the gangplank onto that foreign shore? Was her sense of adventure running high, her heart racing with excitement? Or had the gravity of what she'd done begun to set in, amid the swirl of strange faces and unknown languages in Montevideo's old and overcrowded port? Working-class men and women on the dockside sought out the employers who had contracted them and who had, in many cases, paid their passage. Indent agents met customs agents and negotiated to receive their goods. Chorus girls looked for the theatre managers' representatives; farmhands sought out the men that the rancher had sent; domestic servants scanned the crowd nervously for their new mistresses. Some young women experienced a rising panic upon discovering that their arranged contact was not on the docks.

Was Lydia's panic calmed at the sight of Mr Cellis, who waited, smiling and waving, handsome as ever, amid the crowd? He tossed his cigarette aside and greeted her exuberantly with kisses on her cheeks, explaining that Marie was already in Buenos Aires and was eager to see her. But then his voice grew quieter. 'We will not travel at once to Buenos Aires,' he explained, 'as your fellow passengers who have travelled from New Zealand with you might think something.' Lydia instinctively looked round for anyone she recognised in the crowd. 'If any questions are asked of you, say you are going to your married sister and brother-in-law in Argentina.'[64]

The next morning they made the trip by river steamer up the estuary of the Rio de la Plata. As they approached Buenos Aires, Lydia joined Mr Cellis on the deck with the rest of the passengers, who found they could see little of their destination but an expanse of muddy water. Cellis assured her the city would soon come into view and, sure enough, as the boat navigated the narrow space between the buoys that marked where a quagmire lay just below the surface, and turned into the port, the vast city appeared. Lydia could see brick-built factories and squat warehouses on the shoreline, and hundreds of other vessels. She thought the ship was going to run headlong into another; there were more vessels here than she had ever seen: ships moored to other ships, stacked two or three deep along the wharf, the smoke from their coal engines spewing into great clouds, the masts of the smaller sailing vessels tangled together in the sky.[65]

There was an enormous metropolis stretching out from this crowded port at the end of the muddy estuary. It was home to more than 1 million people, and up until a month ago Lydia had not even known it existed. It seemed a thousand times bigger than Montevideo, which had, just yesterday, been a source of wonderment to her.[66] The wharves were teeming with men, women and children; with boxes and chests and laden porters; with horses and carts and the occasional motor car. They had to wait for the health inspector and immigration inspector to board the vessel, but these men passed over them without notice. Their things had to go through customs, Mr Cellis explained, and then they could be on their way.

Marie was waiting on the docks, perfectly groomed as usual. She kissed Lydia and welcomed her, and merrily suggested that they all have their picture taken. The trio posed, as though they were tourists or a reunited family. This photograph, found in Cellis's suitcase and entered into police evidence in London, has long since disappeared, so we are only able to imagine the captured moment. Did Lydia look happy, beneath the brim of Marie's hand-me-down hat?

Lydia, Marie and Aldo were three of the almost 3 million immigrants who arrived in Buenos Aires's Puerto Madero in the years between 1887 and 1911. This was Argentina's golden age, a period of economic and population boom, fuelled by foreign investment in transport, agriculture and industry, and by territorial and imperial expansion. All over Latin America, in fact, the labour market had expanded rapidly. Immigrants – especially Spaniards, Italians and Eastern European Jews – flooded into the cities and towns, and huge building projects and massive territorial conquest created demand for an enormous manual and agricultural workforce. In Panama the boat-trains carried passengers, soldiers and sailors from one ocean to the other, while the nearly completed canal project attracted thousands of single male labourers. In Argentina the violent seizure of indigenous land by the state had opened up the pampas, the fertile grasslands of the interior, to a new style of ranching and farming that hungered for seasonal male labour, at exactly the same time that advances in refrigeration on steamships meant that fresh Argentinian beef and pork could reach the tables of Europe and the Pacific.[67]

With this huge rise in migrant male labour, it is no surprise that the commercial sex market was also booming. Buenos Aires was one of the epicentres of the global intersection of labour, entertainment and sex. The Argentine capital had been famous for its association with open prostitution since at least the 1870s, and pimps and prostitutes of various nationalities had flocked there, attracted by the high ratio of male occupants, a huge population of men who came occasionally into the centres from rural and isolated sites, an enormous immigrant and transient population, and an urban tourism centre renowned for its modern, exciting and racy nightlife.

Amid perennial debates about the best way to manage commercial sex, venereal disease and criminality, Buenos Aires had by the late 1880s become home to one of the most infamous regulated prostitution systems in the world. This was the most common way for states to respond to the problem of prostitution in the second half of the nineteenth century. In Buenos Aires, as well as France, Germany, Italy, Russia, various sites in the British Empire and more, women working as prostitutes were required to register with the morals police, submit to regular medical inspection and attend venereal-disease hospitals, pay fees and operate in designated areas – namely, state-regulated brothels. Being a brothel-keeper was legal, and police officers in Buenos Aires were notoriously corrupt, turning a blind eye even to those operations that did not quite follow the rules. And no wonder, since the incentives were strong: around the turn of the century the municipality could expect an incredible 20 per cent of its licensing-fee income to come from these legal bordellos, and police were said to supplement their low salaries with bribes from those who chose not to register officially. Underage prostitution, unregistered brothels, pimping, bribing and street- and club-soliciting were all extremely common. As further attempts were made to reform this imperfect system of regulation, more space was created for third parties to operate illegally.[68]

It seems that Mr Cellis intended to join the clandestine world of unregulated commercial sex in Buenos Aires. After their arrival, Aldo and Marie took Lydia to two furnished rooms with communicating doors, which he told Lydia was called a *pensión*. One of the rooms was meant to be hers. The next morning Marie took her out walking around the buzzing new city and bought her a dress and her own hat. Buenos Aires was magnificent. Huge buildings, each one grander than the grandest limestone building in Oamaru, lined the plazas, and palm trees and fountains dotted the streets; and on every building were strings of electric lights, so that the

5: Buenos Aires in 1910, in the midst of its centennial celebrations with its iconic electric lights on display. This idealised image, produced for a postcard, was likely not representative of the city Lydia Harvey encountered when she arrived with Antonio Carvelli in February of that year.

whole city looked as if it was in the middle of a celebration.[69] Lydia watched in amusement as Marie bought a parrot on a whim. It was a pretty, sad little thing that hopped about on the perch in its cage.

'Your hair is too mousy,' Marie remarked as they shopped. The following day a woman visited the apartment and bleached Lydia's brown hair blonde with peroxide. That evening she was styling her new hair and putting on her new dress in her room when Mr Cellis pushed open the door and came in. He touched her and kissed her in a way he hadn't done before, and the playfulness in his mismatched eyes no longer charmed her. 'He tried to seduce me,' Lydia later explained, 'and after a while I gave way.' It was an ambiguous statement, and one in keeping with the normalisation of coercion and sexual violence that was a feature of many women's sexual encounters in this period. Lydia Harvey's account of the sex she had with Aldo Cellis could be interpreted as her initially feeling pressured, but ultimately consenting; it could also be interpreted as her resisting and eventually physically, or psychologically, having to surrender. She made no further mention of her feelings about the encounter, and she did not explicitly call it rape. Reading her account from the perspective of the twenty-first century, it is easy to identify sexual assault; but what Lydia experienced in her own terms, and in terms of the period in which she lived, based on one line of testimony, is far more difficult to define.[70]

When he had finished having sex with Lydia, Mr Cellis rearranged his clothes and left the room. Soon afterwards Marie, who had sat – so far as Lydia could tell – dispassionately in the next room while her husband had sex with another woman, called through the thin door to get ready: they were going to the Casino to look for men. She gave Lydia paint and powder and showed her how to make up her face: despite her life as a 'modern girl' in Wellington, putting on make-up was a skill Lydia had not acquired. As she applied rouge, powder and lipstick to Lydia's face, Marie gave her further instructions: 'Do not drive right up to the door of the apartment,' she cautioned. 'Always get the money first' and 'Make sure the man leaves a few minutes before you.' This last caution she added because she knew that if the police were watching, seeing a woman enter and exit the building with more than one man during the night would be used as evidence in prosecuting an unregistered brothel. By contrast, Marie offered no advice on avoiding disease or violence from clients: her primary concern appeared to be keeping herself and her husband out of legal trouble.

They took a taxi a short distance to the Téatro Casino, a wide building with a wrought-iron balcony and hundreds of lights on strings that shone into the narrow street. It was a famous Buenos Aires establishment into which the male population of the city poured nightly for gambling, music and sex. The French journalist Albert Londres, in his exposé of 'white slavery' in Buenos Aires fifteen years later, wrote that women selling sex on the Casino's third-floor prom-enade were packed as tightly as 'four hundred sheep on an Algerian cargo boat'.[71] Other reports confirmed that the mezzanine was nightly filled to over-capacity, with up to 150 women soliciting at this 'cheap variety theatre'.[72] These crowds were thicker still than those who swarmed the streets of London in the film Lydia had seen, back in Oamaru with her sister and the familiar faces of the town, in what must have seemed a lifetime ago. Around her now stood strange men from all walks of life: ranchers and ranch-hands, clerks and labourers, criminals and minor politicians. Men both young and old drank heavily, danced, watched the cabarets, gambled and did business. They also bought sex.

Marie continued her training, leaning close to Lydia to be heard over the music and the roar of the tightly packed crowd. 'If a man looks at you, just tilt your head and smile. Being so young, you are sure to attract attention.' She had good reason to think so: regulated commercial sex markets, like those found in Argentina, were well known for their thirst for young girls, and for their demand for a constantly changing rota of young women to keep clients interested. This demand

6: The Téatro Casino on Calle Maipu in Buenos Aires, infamous as a major site of the city's clandestine sex trade. Lydia Harvey and Marie Vernon solicited clients here in early 1910.

motivated pimps and traffickers to recruit 'greenies' – a slang term for very young, inexperienced women – to work for them.[73] Lydia was clearly seen by Mr Cellis as his 'greenie' or, as another slang term put it, 'lightweight baggage': an underage prostitute, imported into a lucrative market.

But Lydia, however young and new and green, failed to solicit a man successfully that first night. 'I was thinking too much of home,' she explained later. She was doubtlessly also reflecting on her sexual encounter with Cellis, which may well have hurt her physically as well as psychologically. It was Marie who took a man home that night, slipping back to the *pensión* and, just as quickly, returning to the Casino. 'Have you not found anyone yet?' she snapped at Lydia, seeing her still standing amid the throng. 'You shall soon get used to it,' she told her then, perhaps a little more softly.

'Did you enjoy yourself last night?' Mr Cellis asked her the next morning as she walked to the bath. There is no record of Lydia's reply. The three had breakfast and lunch together, then Aldo went out on his own. That night it was back to the Casino, with Marie taking charge. She approached a 'gentleman' (Lydia's words, and the parlance of the time), saying, 'This is my little friend, a very nice girl, quite young. Why not take my little friend?'

'She is too young,' the man replied. And she was – four years younger than the minimum registration age for prostitutes in Buenos Aires, which was twenty-one.

'Well, take both of us,' Marie said with a laugh, and off they all went in a taxi to the apartment. Lydia was horrified: 'The man was old, dirty and very repulsive to me,' she later explained. When they arrived at the flat she said she did not want to go with him, and went to her room. 'You have to go with him,' Marie said, following her in. 'I am too tired,' Lydia told her. But Marie pressed her and, again, she 'gave in'. This moment of confessed surrender was less ambiguous than the first. It is clear that she did not want to have sex with the client, and that Marie forced her to, with threats and coercion. Lydia crossed back into the other room.

The man had sex with Marie first, while Lydia was in the room, and then went with Lydia, while Marie stayed to watch. When he left he handed Marie some money, but Lydia could not tell how much. 'Give half to your little friend,' he instructed. But the older woman pocketed the lot. The man left and the women stayed in for the rest of the evening, it being now quite late. Lydia returned to her lonely room and was still awake when Mr Cellis returned from his night on the town.

The sparkling electricity of Buenos Aires grew sinister. Lydia hardly saw the city in the daytime at all, and by night the stone-and-cement houses that lined the noisy streets seemed empty, with their round-arched doorways gaping like dark mouths.[74] Nothing seemed finished. There were holes in the streets filled with pipes, and piles of dirt on the pavements. In her own misery she probably noticed the misery of others more acutely, as well: the child beggars with their filthy bare feet, the women with dark, sunken eyes and flyaway hair, pouring out of meat-packing and cigarette factories at dinner time.[75] She saw the meagre washing strewn across the courtyard balconies of the places they called *conventillos*, which seemed like large-scale versions of the rundown tenements in what Dunedin called its 'devil's half-acre'. In the shadow of the shining chimney stacks of the newest steamships, families lived in shacks of salvaged lumber and galvanised steel, foraging in the dump for food.[76]

'This life went on about a fortnight,' Lydia later recalled, although she wasn't sure. It was as though the trauma had disassociated her from the regular passage of time. They woke up, had breakfast and lunch together, and then Cellis left to carouse and shop, and go to the racetrack. She and Marie would leave the *pensión* at nightfall and head to the Téatro Casino to smile at men. There were ranchers in from the pampas, businessmen in suits, men from the factories with dirty faces, men from the slaughterhouses who still smelled of blood.[77] She took several more men back to the apartment alongside Marie. 'She usually put the old ones on to me,' Lydia recalled bitterly.

Marie and Aldo, insensitive to Lydia's obvious fear and upset, continued to attempt to train her. Marie would explain the different ways to pleasure men, over the noise of the Casino: under the arm, between the breasts, in the mouth. She told her that she could charge £3 for the 'back passage' – an incredible amount of money, equivalent to about a month or more of domestic-service wages – but Marie warned Lydia it had hurt her when she tried it, and she didn't do it again. One morning Aldo joined Lydia and Marie in her bedroom and asked Marie to perform fellatio on him. They told her it was the 'French way'. Lydia watched with disgust as Marie knelt before him. 'Would you know how to do it now?' Mr Cellis asked her afterwards. 'Yes, but I shall never do it,' Lydia replied. Several clients suggested 'the mouth thing' to her later, but she always refused them.

On another occasion Cellis came home early and demanded that this time Lydia perform oral sex on him. Again she refused, and he had sex with her – in her words – 'in the proper way'. Afterwards he explained things called 'French letters', which Lydia had never heard of before. Why the man had taken so long to introduce her to condoms, in a world where syphilis and gonorrhoea were epidemic, is difficult to say. It is clear that he cared little for her well-being, but a 'greenie' with venereal disease was a costly problem.

After three weeks everything changed. The police raided the building where they had been renting rooms, and the landlady was forced to shut it up. Desperate, Cellis brought them first to a municipal building, where they were made to put their names in a ledger; and when she approached the counter, Lydia did as she was told and said her age was *veintiuno*. Then Aldo took them to a large house with other women and, speaking in a foreign language to the madam, found them rooms. Mr Cellis then left, saying to Marie that he would 'see how things went'. Lydia was introduced to eight other women – 'all prostitutes', she explained; it was the first time she had used that word.[78]

There were no more trips to the Casino. This was a registered brothel, and the women there would sit in the main parlour and wait for men to push aside the beaded curtain in the doorway and choose one of them. These establishments dotted the Buenos Aires cityscape, deliberately dispersed by the regulation rules, so that no one neighbourhood would become a notorious 'red light' zone. Being put in this brothel meant that Lydia Harvey's name was placed on the municipality's official register of prostitutes. The lists of names no longer survive, but the official report from that year gives us a snapshot of the women she may have met in such a house. In 1910 the city registered more than 1,000 new prostitutes: 252 from Russia, almost all Russian Jews; another forty women from Austria–Hungary were likely similar. There were 230 women on the list from Uruguay, and 160 from Argentina itself, some of whom were second-generation migrants, and others who were displaced indigenous women seeking work in the city. Of the women from Western Europe, the vast majority were French: 226 women in total claimed this nationality when they registered. There were ninety-one Spanish women, seventy-six Italians, fourteen Belgians, ten women from Germany, six from Turkey, two from England and five 'miscellaneous.'[79] Lydia, as probably one of the only New Zealanders ever placed on the city's prostitution lists, was likely one of these final five.

She was beginning to feel unwell and did not receive any

men during the two days they stayed at the registered brothel. 'You owe Aldo money for your passage,' Marie would hiss at her as they waited in the parlour while men came and went. 'And he paid five pounds to the man who brought you to College Street.' So that was how much money exchanged hands that evening. It seemed a lifetime ago now.

The doctor arrived on the second day, on his usual brothel rounds. He discovered that one woman was suffering from syphilis, and injected something into her veins right there in the parlour while Lydia and Marie watched, horrified. Cellis visited the following day and Marie laid into him, saying that the place was horrible and demanding that they leave. Aldo placated her by telling her that he was making plans for them to go to London and would be back for them soon.

Another two days went by, and when Cellis finally returned to see them, a dark cloud surrounded him. He complained angrily of a break-in at the *pensión*. Someone had made off with his clothing and jewellery. Lydia began to feel heavy, languid and very ill, and he took her to a doctor who could not speak English. As a result, she probably did not understand when she was diagnosed with gonorrhoea and scabies; nor did she know what was in the pills she was given, or the creams that were handed to Cellis to administer to her. He cursed the city and told the women they would move on to London, seeing as they had had such 'bad luck' in Buenos Aires. He bought three tickets for second-class travel on the SS *Asturias*, bound for Tenerife and Southampton in a few days' time. They travelled as Mr and Mrs Collis, with a young girl named Doris Williams in tow.

The SS *Ruahine* and the SS *Asturias* were similar ships: both were newly built, for long and comfortable voyages across the world's great oceans. Yet there must have seemed to Lydia a chasm between her experience on the ship that brought her to South America and the one that carried her away. This time there was no excitement at travelling, only the misery of feeling ill and alone, and the torturous itch of scabies. There were no card games with fellow travellers or flirting with young men: Cellis insisted that both women stay away from the other passengers and often locked them in their second-class cabin, lest their presence with him alert the authorities. Cellis, when he deigned to leave the second-class lounge and return to the cabin to administer her cream, told Lydia that she had cost him a fortune and that, when they got to London, he would have to put her in a hospital and 'that would be more expense'.[80]

After two weeks their ship arrived in the port of Southampton in April 1910. They alighted and transferred their luggage onto the boat-train for London. The port and the railway-station noticeboards that Lydia passed were covered with posters from employment agents, steamship companies and the Travellers' Aid Society, which countered the other inducements to travel with what they called a 'frank warning' to girls against:

> going to London or other large towns, or abroad, without being in communication with some SAFE HOME where they can lodge until they obtain EMPLOYMENT ... they are SPECIALLY WARNED not to accept offers of help from men and women who are UNKNOWN to them, or to go to any situation they have obtained through ADVERTISEMENTS without first assuring themselves of their RESPECTABILITY.[81]

There may also have been National Vigilance Association volunteers in the station, wearing distinctive armbands and searching for young women in precisely Lydia's predicament. As ever, the girls most in need of help were also those least likely to know what those armbands meant. Lydia, like many others, walked right past them, following the Cellises because she had nowhere else to go. They had not given her a cent of the money she had earned in Buenos Aires and they continued to remind her of her debt to them. Besides, Mr Cellis was right: if she went to the police and told them what had happened, they would put her into a reform home for wayward girls and she would have to go right back into domestic service.

The boat-train from Southampton pulled into Waterloo Station a few hours later, and Lydia walked along the platform while black smoke filled the peaked ceiling of glass and steel high above her head. She'd never seen a station like it, and beneath an enormous clock swarmed a sea of horses and carriages and humanity. She followed the Cellises outside to a street that was even noisier than the station, and they hailed a cab that travelled over Waterloo Bridge and into the West End. Lydia looked out the window and saw the city stretching out like a picture in her school textbooks: the Houses of Parliament, the dome of St Paul's, Tower Bridge in the distance, spanning the churning brown water of the Thames. She thought of Thames Street, Oamaru, on the other side of the world.

The taxi pulled up in front of the Piedmont Hotel, in Frith Street, Soho. They slept there and the next day Aldo went out, looking for a friend, he said, and brought someone he called Alex Berard back to the flat. Lydia instantly disliked him, but he and Aldo appeared to be old pals. Other men came and went, all foreign, but Lydia was told not to go out. She watched from the window as Soho transformed from a daytime place of residence and business, with children playing, food cooking and people shopping, into a night-time place of pleasure. Well-dressed people went to European restaurants and cafés; groups of men disappeared into clubs and theatres; women walked in uncomfortable-looking shoes on their way down Shaftesbury Avenue, smiling and propositioning male passers-by. And even later at night, in the neighbourhood's dark brick doorways, a few shabbier women stood and, when they found a man, they did not get into a taxi or walk to a room, but instead had connections right there in the shadows.

Lydia's first real-life glimpse of London's vice-district was short-lived. On Monday, Cellis took her in a taxi directly to the Female Hospital at 283 Harrow Road, Paddington.[82] This and similar hospitals, formerly called 'lock hospitals', were established in every major town by the 1860s, when the UK had experimented with its own form of regulated prostitution, imposing Contagious Diseases Acts in ports and garrison towns that forcibly registered suspected prostitutes, subjected them to medical inspection and incarcerated them, if they were found to be suffering from VD.[83] Before the Contagious Diseases Acts were repealed in 1886, these hospitals functioned as virtual prisons for women, but by the early twentieth century they had become specialist voluntary hospitals for venereal disease, though they were still frequently complicit in detaining women who had been determined an infection risk. Many of the inmates in the Female Hospital by 1910 were either married women, who had caught diseases from their husbands, or their children, who had contracted sexually transmitted infections *in utero* or in the birth canal. A similar male hospital operated in Dean Street, Soho.[84]

Four years later, when war mobilised thousands of troops and accelerated the syphilis epidemic, these hospitals would be full to bursting. But in 1910 the Female Hospital's bleach-clean wards were mostly quiet, especially at night. Lying under the bed's starched white sheets, with the itch of the scabies-mite infestation still torturing her, Lydia was surely struck by the loneliness of the place – but perhaps she found some comfort as well, in the nurses and ward maids who tended to her in a space where Cellis was not. He had threatened her again before he left, telling her that if she said anything, the police would be notified and her parents would hear about what she had been doing, and the police would throw him in gaol and put her in a home, and then she would have to 'work for other people' – that is, go back into service. Cellis kissed her and told Lydia to tell the hospital staff that he was her boss.[85]

It was an effective threat, made sharper by the revolver she had seen beneath his pinstripe-suit jacket. Lydia did not breathe a word to the ward nurses or the superintendent, and when Marie turned up each Wednesday afternoon to visit her and remind her of her debts, Lydia told the staff she worked as the woman's maid. If anyone were to ask her about us, Marie told her, 'Say you are here to be cured and not questioned.' And they did ask. The secretary of the hospital came to her bedside, showing Lydia news stories about other girls who had disappeared. He told her that after she was better, they could help her. She could go and live in the building next door and do the hospital's laundry in exchange for room and board and, if she was a very good girl, she would get a reference to go into service. 'I am here to be cured and not questioned,' Lydia replied.

After a month of treatment that included very painful urethral irrigation, Marie came to fetch her.[86] It was 25 May 1910 – Lydia marked the date well, because it was three days after her sister's birthday, and she would be celebrating turning ten years old 12,000 miles away in Oamaru. Marie had brought Lydia a dress, but it was plain and brown, a far cry from the nice dresses she had been promised back in Wellington. She packed her bags under the suspicious glances of the ward nurses, but they did not intervene.[87]

Marie took her to a flat in Soho, and the strange faces that came and went disoriented Lydia. There was another foreign girl, who was introduced as Marie's maid. Aldo was there with the man Alex Berard, who had with him a young girl called Marguerite Carl. Other men came and went, but she did not catch their names, only sensed their coldness.

'You've cost me a pretty penny, and now you will have to make it up to me,' Cellis told Lydia. 'You can't stay here,' Marie explained, 'because there will be two women in the house.' She was referring to the 1885 Criminal Law Amendment Act that had outlawed brothels, which were later defined, in case law, as a place where more than one woman practised prostitution. So long as women worked alone, they and their landlords were largely immune to prosecution in the UK.[88] 'I will give you some clothes and you will go to a different flat,' she told Lydia.

Marguerite Carl, in a moment out of earshot of the cold and dangerous men, told Lydia that the man called Berard was bad news. She heard that he had hit a girl named Florrie on the way to Buenos Aires and had nearly got them all arrested. She had seen him beat his wife Annie when she did not bring home enough money, and the woman had run away from her husband back to New Zealand.

Lydia dined with Cellis and Alex Berard, and after that they carried her box down the stairs and looked around for the police. Determining that the coast was clear, they all got into a cab and drove to a flat in Winchester House, a nearby apartment block in St Giles High Street, Bloomsbury. Lydia protested that Marie had not given her the clothes she said she would, and that she didn't have the clothes to receive men in. 'What you have will have to do,' Cellis told her. 'Here you charge fifteen shillings.' It was a low price. A few days later Alex Berard returned, showed her some porno-graphic photographs and asked Lydia to come away with him. She refused, grateful for the French girl's warning. A few days after that Marie turned up, telling her that she was leaving.

'Do you not intend to leave me any money?' Lydia asked her.

'Aldo will see you settled,' she replied, and took her leave. It was the last time Lydia would ever see her.

Still more foreign men and women came and went. Aldo next took Lydia to a flat in Wells Street, off Tottenham Court Road. There he introduced her to another man whom she agreed to go with, just as she had gone with Mr Cellis. What choice did she have? 'I had to accept the conditions offered by Cellis,' she later explained. 'Because I had no money and no proper clothes.' Cellis told her he could not give her any money or pay for her passage home, because he had to pay the rent instead.[89] She never named the man who bought her from Aldo Cellis, but whether this was because she respected or feared him more than Cellis, we will never know.

For the next few weeks Lydia Harvey solicited on the streets near Piccadilly Circus. She walked and walked because she was told by other girls that if she didn't keep moving, the police would arrest her. She went out as the sun went down, dodging the splashes sent up on the pavement by the omnibuses. She stayed out all evening, walking beneath the electric lights of Leicester Square and the theatre foyers on Shaftesbury Avenue. She had the shops and the theatres, and the plays they were showing, practically memorised. Crowds poured out of *The Dollar Princess* with Miss Lily Elsie, which was playing at the Pavilion, while *The Arcadians* was the newest hit at the Shaftesbury Theatre and told the story of people from a pure and innocent mythical island corrupted by the pleasures of London.[90] The Alhambra, where Ethel Levey was headlining the varieties, was Lydia's typical destination and she was grateful for its overcrowded and overheated balcony. The streets were so cold! Why was London so cold, even in the summertime? On 3 June 1910 she turned seventeen and, back in Oamaru, her mother probably began to worry. It had been months since she'd heard from her eldest daughter.

More days and evenings passed. Lydia walked and walked. Her feet ached and her back was sore. She was still wearing the same brown dress. Whenever a man responded to her lame entreaties, she took him back to Wells Street and charged 15 shillings for what they called a 'short time'. Her brown roots now stood out against her dyed-blonde hair. Cellis and Berard were nowhere to be seen, and someone told her that they had gone to Paris. Having long since given up on getting any of her money back from them, Lydia probably wished they'd stay there. But towards the end of June, Alex Berard – or whatever his real name was – turned up like a bad penny. He introduced her to another French girl, who looked even younger than Lydia herself. Her name was Mireille, but she said it in a way that Lydia couldn't pronounce. Lydia told her that her name was Doris Williams. She didn't give the lie a second thought; besides, she may well have felt that Lydia Harvey had disappeared. Mireille didn't speak a single word of English, so Lydia couldn't even explain what the other girl had told her about Berard. Mireille would discover it for herself before too long.

Berard asked Lydia to show Mireille where to walk to find men for a 'short time', so they headed off from the flat down Tottenham Court Road to Charing Cross. She showed Mireille with gestures where to go. When they arrived at the Alhambra, she showed the other girl what to pay to get up to the balcony, and in the crowded bar showed her how to smile at men, just as Marie had showed her in Buenos Aires. She leaned over the railing and listlessly watched the varieties below. The place was a thousand times more ornate than the Oamaru opera house, with dark wood and exotic tiles, and tier upon tier of seats looking down on a richly appointed stage far below. But after several trips up the stairs to the Alhambra's balcony, Lydia had begun to notice the stains on the seats, the scuffs on the woodwork, the broken tiles. She looked over to see that Mireille had caught the attention of some man. Another man approached Lydia and she asked if he wanted to go with her for a short time. They walked back down the stairs, found a cab and went back to the flat, where the man finished his business in record time. He gave her 15 shillings and she walked back to the Alhambra. Mireille had also returned, and Lydia mimed leaving to get some tea. They sipped their cups at the Hotel d'Europe in silence, watching the crowds pass by outside. Afterwards they parted ways, and Mireille melted into the London night.

Back on the street, another man approached Lydia. He was middle-aged, wearing a suit and an overcoat and a smart-looking hat, with a notebook tucked into his pocket. She asked him if he wanted to go with her for a short time. He refused her offer, as so many did, but appeared to want to talk. Did she know anyone by the name of Aldo Cellis or Alex Berard? Yes, she replied, her heart probably lurching.

'I am a police officer,' the man then told her. 'And I would like you to come with me.'

CHAPTER TWO

THE DETECTIVE

It was a story that played out dozens of times a night in Picca-dilly. Illuminated by the lights that spilled out of the theatres and restaurants and cafés, a plain-clothes police officer watched a young woman walk alone along what was known as 'the wickedest pavement in England'.[1] It was the last day of the bank holiday, Easter Monday, 28 March 1910, and the streets were busier than usual. Once, twice, the constable saw her solicit men. On the third occasion he nodded to his uni-formed partner, who approached her. 'I am arresting you for being a common prostitute behaving in a riotous or indecent manner,' he told her. The young woman spoke little English and did not protest when the officer asked her to walk with him up Regent Street to Marlborough Street Police Station. In the charge room, she gave her name as Marguerite Leroy and said that she was from France.[2]

She had no money for bail, so she was brought through the station into the adjoining court, where, in the dark back corner, stood the police cells. She sat on the short wooden bench beside the commode as the lock clanged noisily shut. She waited for hours in the tiny cell, illuminated by the dim light of the electric bulb that shone through a small transom window above the heavy metal door.[3] At 4 a.m., by this time surely exhausted and distressed, she asked the officer to send word to a woman named Marie Balandras, who lived at 40a Wells Street in the area known as North Soho, in order to bring her money for bail. Once found, Balandras said she did not know the name Marguerite and refused to come. And so the young woman curled up on the cell bench and watched until a sliver of dawn's light crept through the transom and the noise of the court began. She was handed some soap and water and told to wash. At midday it was time for her case to be heard.[4]

Detective Inspector Ernest Anderson, a Criminal Investigation Department (CID) officer attached to C Division, Soho, had just arrived as the court began to come alive. The remands were heard first, and then the sorry lot known as the 'night arrests' were brought in through the wooden door that led from the cells into the large mosaic-floored court waiting room.[5] There were the familiar faces who had been arrested for begging and street betting; and a half-dozen drunks who had been arrested on the final night of the bank holiday blinked blearily in the light that poured through the grand glass ceiling. They received the usual fine. One had been in such a 'state' the night before, according to the prosecuting constable who stood in the witness box with his police notebook, that he had been reciting Shakespeare in the police station.[6]

Next, a string of weary-looking women waited to answer one of Soho's most numerous charges: 'disorderly prostitute'. This was not, in fact, an actual charge. The real law read: 'being a common prostitute behaving in a riotous or indecent manner'. But the court's clerk, and the police, had long since fallen into expediencies when it came to the women who sold sex in the West End of London. Mr G. L. Denman, the magistrate who sat at the long wooden bench on the dais at the court's back wall, dealt with almost every case in less than three minutes – the women all pleaded guilty, and he handed out a fine here, a remand there. It would go on like this for the rest of the morning.

Marguerite Leroy was the sixth case of the day. She stood in the dock before the bench in the noisy, crowded court. 'How do you plead?' asked the magistrate. 'Guilty,' said the young woman with a thick French accent. 'And how did you come to this country?' Denman continued. Marguerite told him that she was born in Rouen, but that her parents were both dead. She had come to England as a nursemaid the year before but, after losing her position, was destitute and took up prostitution. In France she had worked at her aunt's laundry. 'I sentence you to a fine of forty shillings,' Mr Denman said, 'and I shall bind you over into custody until the fifth of April, at which time I will consider an expulsion order.' The court's clerk marked 'French' in red beneath her name in the court register.[7]

Inspector Anderson, waiting in the court to give evidence in another case, noticed that there was a group of men in the gallery who appeared extremely interested in the outcome of what was otherwise an ordinary story of a 'common prostitute' in Soho. He saw them whisper fiercely among each other in a language he couldn't understand. They were visibly angry. They left the court quickly as Mr Denman moved on to his seventh case.[8] Marguerite Leroy was taken away by the bailiff to have a mandatory conversation with the police-court matron, who would offer her opportunities to reform herself before she was deported under the auspices of the

Aliens Act 1905, which allowed for the expulsion of any woman found guilty of a prostitution offence.[9]

In the meantime Anderson, following a hunch, went to find Marie Balandras, the woman whom Leroy had unsuccessfully named as a bondswoman, at 40a Wells Street, North Soho, a short walk away from the court. The middle-aged French woman ushered her daughters away and invited the inspector in, when he knocked on her door. The family lived and ran a small tailoring shop on the ground floor, she explained, and rented out six upper rooms to lodgers. Anderson, suggesting that Madame Balandras surely did not want to make trouble for her husband or her daughters, encouraged her to tell him more. She admitted that she was aware these lodgers engaged in the traffic in women, and that their leader – a man she called Max – often stayed in the house. She had found a letter the poor girl had written, torn but unburned, in the grate after the men had gone out for the day, and had carefully pasted it back together. She showed it to the inspector, eager to appear cooperative.

'*Chère Maman*,' Marguerite had begun, and then explained that she was very well. She had a grand flat, she told her mother, and proceeded to itemise the things that made the flat extravagant, in the eyes of a former laundress: a servant, two bedrooms, a kitchen, a bathroom and a dressing room. 'I have always dreamed of this,' the young woman wrote. 'And now it has come. I have found a young man, very rich and tall, though' – and here the letter became more sinister – 'I think you would not want to know any more.' They were soon to leave for South America, for Buenos Aires, where it was warm, and she would not see any of her family again. '*C'est la vie d'une princesse*,' the letter concluded.[10] The life of a princess, in a rundown flat in North Soho.

Inspector Anderson stood in the empty room, with its shabby bedstead and scuffed furniture. Dust motes swirled in the bright sunlight that poured in through the window.[11] He could picture the man standing at the elbow of Marguerite as she wrote her childish letter – a man who was almost certainly one of those he had seen at the police court the week before.

The detectives and constables of the Metropolitan Police took a surprisingly sympathetic view of most criminals. They respected the gangsters who adhered to their own kind of code of honour. They pitied the drunks, the beggars and the gamblers who couldn't seem to make good. They accepted the women who nightly paraded around the streets near Piccadilly as an inevitable presence, so long as men were there to buy what they were offering. They shook hands with known thieves in the streets, celebrating their release from prison even as they were sure they would soon see them back there again. They had a dark admiration for the murderer who was clever enough to get away with it; they understood the killer who, in a fit of passion or rage, took a life.[12] But no such respect, pity, acceptance or understanding was felt by the police for traffickers and pimps: the men who lived on the earnings of women who sold sex. They were, in the policemen's eyes, the most despicable of criminals, 'the lowest form of animal life on the criminal scale'.[13] Ernest Anderson surely felt no different. Placing the pathetic pasted-together letter from the young woman into a fresh evidence folder, he resolved to open an investigation.

In doing so, he was probably motivated by more than

personal feelings or a collective antipathy towards pimps. As more and more stories appeared in the newspapers about innocent country girls who had disappeared on the streets of London, Paris and New York, the police were coming under increasing pressure to find these girls – and the people responsible for their alleged disappearance. 'For God's sake *do something*,' General Booth of the Salvation Army had famously exclaimed when the first sex-trafficking scandal broke back in the 1880s; and by the early twentieth century 'the traffic in women and children' had become a cause célèbre. In the last decade of the nineteenth century, campaigners met in fancy hotels and palaces to hash out international agreements to stop 'the immoral traffic'. In 1904 the first international agreement was signed, requiring signatory states to pass laws against trafficking, establish a central authority to monitor such crimes, surveil ports of entry for suspected traffickers and assist any of their victims who wished to return home.[14]

It fell to the police to head up the fight. Yet instead of being heralded for their successful prosecutions, the Metropolitan Police had been shaken by scandal after scandal. Cases of wrongful arrest, police extortion, abuse, blackmail, harassment and fully fledged corruption had plagued the force – and C Division, Soho in particular – for years. A successful investigation into a real case of 'white slavery' would not only strike a blow against the 'nefarious traffic' in England, but would also look very good for the Met.

The men with whom Anderson served were as well equipped as any in the world to take action against potential traffickers. C Division had a score of officers who did little else but work the vice-cases of the West End – arresting prostitutes, watching suspected pimps, undertaking surveillance on dodgy clubs and suspected brothels. From this group, Anderson chose PC William Mead, a thirty-year-old man who had a decent reputation. Like many officers who frequently went out in plain clothes, there were rumours that Mead's behaviour was not always above board. But it was difficult to find a straight cop who worked these cases; being a little too friendly with the club owners, prostitutes and brothel-keepers of Soho was viewed by most of them as a necessary part of the job. To his credit, Mead had a good memory and could write a clear report, and he had received a medal a few years before for rescuing a woman from a burning room in the police district.[15]

On 5 April 1910, the date of Marguerite's remand case, PC Mead arrived at the court mid-morning to watch the usual parade of drunks and ne'er-do-wells. The London police courts were the backbone of the metropolis's justice system, and all criminal cases – large and small – passed in front of the magistrates' bench. From there, they were either dealt with summarily, with the magistrate handing out fines, short prison sentences and remands into custody, or they were referred to a higher court. The police courts, scattered all over London, also provided rich entertainment, both to the readers of the police-court report columns of local and national newspapers and to those who attended the court's gallery itself.[16] Constable Mead joined them, acting as though he was just one of the dozens of people who had come for a morning of free theatre. Marguerite Leroy's case was called at a quarter past twelve, and the expected expulsion order was handed down. She was to be escorted to the boat-train headed for Dover on 20 April and would remain in prison on remand until that date.

As soon as the decision was handed down, an old man who 'looked French' slipped quickly out of the courtroom. Mead rose and followed as the man left the building and, turning into Poland Street, made his way through the tangle of Soho. Up Broadwick and across Wardour his quarry went, past cobblers and grocers and pawnshops and cafés, until he arrived at Old Compton Street and made his way to where it intersected with Dean Street, where he met a well-dressed man who also 'looked French'. Mead ducked into a doorway and watched them carefully. When this well-dressed man received the news, he passed the old man from the court some coins, and the messenger disappeared into the lunch-hour crowd. The well-dressed man scowled and gestured to another man across the street, who joined him. They talked and gesticulated and appeared angry, though Mead was not close enough to hear the words. Three more men joined them, and a heated discussion ensued.

Soon the first pair of men were on the move again. Mead spent the day and night shadowing them. He followed them to the Café Henry on High Street, Bloomsbury, a well-known haunt of pimps and criminals, where they appeared deep in conversation; then to a restaurant on Old Compton Street and another on Frith Street; and finally to the Admiral Duncan public house on Old Compton Street again, where Mead watched them enter with a woman he recognised as a 'common prostitute'. He slipped in behind them and took up a spot at the wooden saloon bar. 'The prostitute paid for the drinks,' he noted in his report.[17]

The next day PC Mead handed his report to Inspector Anderson, who, now convinced that he had found a gang of foreign traffickers, hurried to Scotland Yard. Passing under the brick archway at Whitehall, he arrived at the central nervous system for the Metropolitan Police. He asked the constable at the desk for the assistant police commissioner Frederick Bullock, who had been appointed the central authority on matters related to 'white slavery' in 1905, a position that all signatory countries to the 1904 International Agreement for the Suppression of the 'White Slave Traffic' were required to create.

Fred Bullock, who had been actively involved in the anti-trafficking movement for the majority of his police career, took this role very seriously. He looked through Mead's and Anderson's reports and agreed with the inspector's appraisal: this could be the biggest case of 'white slavery' the Met had yet seen: a real opportunity to prove their mettle, in the face of what people believed to be a growing problem of global organised prostitution. Bullock immediately gave Anderson the go-ahead to pursue the case, and authorised him to recruit a police constable and a police sergeant to help him by doing 'plain-clothes' duty – when ordinary constables discarded their uniforms and donned streetwear to keep suspects under surveillance.

Anderson quickly assembled his small team to 'aid the CID'.[18] He decided to keep William Mead as a plain-clothes constable on the case. Mead was a Londoner, familiar with the streets of Soho, where the case would likely be tracked. He had been born and raised in Delhi Street, just beside King's Cross; his father was an engine driver for the railway and William himself had worked as a railway fireman before joining the Metropolitan Police in 1902, at the age of twenty-two. Three years later he had married Eleanor Keep, the daughter of a farrier, and they had two children.[19] Mead projected the image of a respectable married man and an experienced police officer, despite rumours about his less-than-respectable actions on the beat.

Inspector Anderson then chose Walter Burmby to be the police sergeant on the case. Burmby, known to be fastidious, thorough and professional, had been raised around police work: his father James was a police inspector, and every household on the Pimlico street where he grew up was headed by a policeman. This must have given him an immense advantage over fellow recruits to the police, not least because there was no formal training for police officers until 1907.[20] Burmby had joined the Met in 1904 when he was twenty-one years old and was made a sergeant only six years later.[21] Anderson must have recognised some quality in these two men, and took this chance to test their characters and their potential to become future detectives themselves: it was a common practice to select such promising-looking constables for plain-clothes duty.

Both men probably welcomed the opportunity. The pay was as bad as it would be had they stayed in uniform, but it was a clear chance to prove themselves worthy of commendation and promotion. Plain-clothes officers could also boast of a freedom above and beyond that of the uniformed beat officer. Unlike the morally upright image of the bobby, the plain-clothes man had to deliberately lower himself to the level of the criminal, to 'mix with all types of shady characters', and yet never become a criminal himself. It is no wonder it was widely acknowledged that men had to be 'specially selected' for this kind of work.[22]

As for the man who headed up this new trafficking investigation, Inspector Ernest Anderson had been a young detective himself, joining CID as a detective sergeant and reaching the rank of detective inspector in his second decade with the force. Like many Metropolitan policemen of earlier generations, Anderson was a recruit from the provinces. He was born in Eynsham, a small town to the north of Oxford, in 1867, and grew up as the youngest in a family of three sisters and two brothers.[23] At the age of twenty-one he noticed the posters outside his local police station announcing that a recruiting party from the London Met would be at the Shire Hall.[24] He signed up in June 1888, when the whole force was in the throes of Jack the Ripper chaos. By the time he took on the Marguerite Leroy case, he was forty-two years old and had remained unmarried. This was not untypical of CID men, who worked long and irregular hours and were often bound more firmly to the work of the department than to anything else in their lives.[25] Anderson lived alone on Thomas Street, near Grosvenor Square and Oxford Street, in a building owned by the Artisan Dwelling Company, which – thanks to its very reasonable rents for such a central area – was very popular among police officers. Constable William Mead and his family lived in another Artisan Dwelling Company flat around the corner.[26]

There is much that we cannot know about Inspector Anderson and the officers who worked beneath him. Unlike many of their colleagues, none of these men penned a memoir or autobiography in their retirement years, nor were they the subject of anyone's reminiscences. The dozens of books written by former Met officers help to reconstruct their worldview and the kind of work they did, but do not tell us what each individual man felt about the police service, or about the policeman's role in stopping the trafficking in women and applying the law against prostitution. Indeed, most police officers – including those who did write books – chose to remain silent on the question of prostitution and trafficking, preferring to outline the murder cases they had worked on, or the conmen and thieves they had outsmarted. Prostitution and trafficking were stickier and more complex problems. Women who sold sex were arrested over and over again and regularly occupied what, for the sake of a tidy narrative, should have been contradictory positions: victim and criminal. Crimes against them were rarely solved, and the whole thing was seen by the average man as a 'necessary evil'. It didn't make for a good drama, and it rarely ended with a story of justice fairly served. Coppers turned crime-writers, like journalists and moral reformers, wanted to tell simpler stories.

And yet trafficking was instrumental in shaping policing worldwide at the dawn of the twentieth century. 'The traffic in women' was the first – and for a time the only – global crime that required police forces around the world to establish a central authority in each country, in charge of coordinating the national and international efforts to combat it. Discussion of 'white slavery' dominated early international police conferences, and the problem of sex trafficking was instrumental in establishing what would later become Interpol. In short, concerns about border-crossing traffickers and the 'foreign prostitutes' they brought with them ushered in a new era of international crime control.[27]

This era of international policing and border control coincided with – and fed and was in turn fed by – the revolution in modern communications and transport that reached new heights in the early twentieth century. Police stations were linked more effectively by motor cars, and although it would be 1928 before police call boxes became an iconic feature of the London landscape, all stations had installed telephones by 1910, and most detectives had them in their homes as well. 'In less than half an hour,' wrote one early police historian, '20,000 men can be informed of the particulars of a crime.'[28] By the turn of the century, telegraph cables and the wireless telegraph increased the speed, spread and ease of communications. And when paper – fingerprints, photographs and original records – had to be sent, it could be dispatched on steamships that were twice as fast as those three decades earlier.[29] These material records (fingerprints and other biometric information, past criminal records, registers of known criminals) were becoming more and more standardised and reliable. Scotland Yard was at the forefront of these developments. Its organisation and its ability to communicate, it was said, enabled it to 'pluck the murderer from his fancied security at the ends of the earth'.[30]

But this time the CID registers came up empty: no one matching the descriptions of the men that Marie Balandras called Leon and Max were found in their walls of filing cabinets. So in mid-April Anderson sent Mead and Burmby out once again to 'keep observation' – the ubiquitous term for surveillance – on the gang of suspected traffickers. It was not difficult to find them: they were sitting yet again in the dark saloon bar of the Admiral Duncan public house on Old Compton Street. Mead and Burmby went in and ordered a drink.

Max and Leon were joined by a third man, whom the officers would soon identify as Charles Peneau, a French teenager. Two other men walked in a while later, looking like typical pimps: 'little, loudly-dressed braggarts with cold and vigilant eyes', as one former detective described them.[31] The first was of average height, with very dark hair and olive skin. He wore a velvet-banded bowler hat and a dark pin-stripe suit. The second was taller and fairer and equally well dressed. He sported a large dark moustache. Had the officer been able to get closer to him, he would have seen that his right eye was brown and his left eye was blue.

Leaving Max, Leon and Charles Peneau at the Admiral Duncan, Mead and Burmby followed the two new men into Bloomsbury to the Café Henry and then to a flat off Charing Cross Road, where they re-emerged with 'a tall French woman'. After a short drink in a theatre bar, they returned to the flat and collected another, shorter woman. The two women walked ahead of them down Charing Cross Road to Leicester Square, the man with the bowler hat and the man with the moustache following them, with the plain-clothes police officers bringing up the rear.

Burmby and Mead knew these streets like the lines on their hands. They had both been walking them as uniformed officers for almost ten years. They knew the pubs where pimps and bookmakers gathered, the cafés and bars where prostitutes stopped for refreshment during their night's work, the pawnshops where fences bought stolen goods, the public toilets where men engaged in 'gross indecency', and the restaurants with rooms for rent by the quarter-hour upstairs. They had a mental map of the inner world of the West End and saw the beggars, kerb salesmen and gutter musicians who passed through the jostle of the crowds and traffic 'like a wick through a candle'.[32] This was, as one former detective described it, 'the skein and thread of the web that makes up of the secret life of London'.[33]

Mead and Burmby also knew the women who called these streets their workplace. By name or by face, they recognised the women who sold sex nightly on the classic circuit of Shaftesbury Avenue, Leicester Square, Piccadilly Circus and Charing Cross Road – a route that also formed one of C Division's main foot-beats. Some women were there, day in, day out, for years. Some women trailed 'protectors', who followed them on their usual routes, while others worked alone. Some moved on to nightclub work, where they could solicit indoors; or took up work as maids in brothels, got another kind of job or left when they married. Others became landladies and business owners, investing their earnings. Some simply disappeared.

The police and these women were locked in a futile customary battle. The women would solicit, the police would tell them to move on. They would move on, but if seen again, they would be arrested by the police. A night in a police cell, sleeping uncomfortably by the light of the transom window, a morning at the police court, a fine of 40 shillings quickly paid, and then the woman was back on the streets, being asked to move on by the police the next night. It is difficult to say what Mead and Burmby thought of them. Detective Frank 'Nutty' Sharpe called them 'poor little devils', noting how they were easy prey for murderers and other violent men. 'The easiest murder to commit and the hardest murder to solve is that of the street girl,' he explained.[34] But the pity only went so far. 'They are most distinguished liars,' Sharpe continued. Superintendent Robert Fabian was much stronger in his condemnation: 'The whore is a bad apple,' he wrote in his second memoir, 'there is a big brown bruise on her soul, of self-indulgence and selfishness ... They are hard as nails.'[35] Between the attitudes of the average police officer and the laws that forced women to work in isolation, it is little wonder that crimes against women who sold sex were so rarely investigated or solved.

Most police officers considered arresting women for soliciting to be the most unpleasant part of their duties, and many quietly supported regulation in the form of a laissez-faire attitude to brothels and other off-street premises that operated quietly. Other police officers were more zealous and were committed – like Frederick Bullock – to doing their part to rid the streets and buildings of London of the moral evil of prostitution. Yet others saw opportunity, knowing that brothel and club owners would rather pay a little protection money to a copper than find their licence revoked by the London County Council for 'irregular' activities. Just because the government refused to regulate prostitution didn't mean that a man couldn't do a little regulation himself. While corruption scandals of this sort wouldn't break in the newspapers until the 1920s, former officers and journalists intimated that this sort of behaviour was rife in certain divisions – none more so than C Division – long before then. There were rumours, in fact, that Constable William Mead supplemented his earnings with notes and coins slipped to him across bar counters and on street corners: from prostitutes, pimps and café owners hoping he would look the other way.[36]

PC Mead probably felt it was no more than he deserved for the hard work he was doing. For seven days in mid-April he and Burmby continued to keep observation. They followed the well-dressed suspected pimps around Soho, North Soho and Piccadilly, watching them as they 'stalked'

– these are Burmby's words – the women who were working for them. The tactic called 'for quick wit and a fertility of resource', explained one police biographer. 'A detective may pose as a drunken man, a street hawker, a milkman. He may use a small mirror and keep in front of his quarry, or he may outguess the latter's intentions. It is a high art when it is properly carried out.'[37]

Mead and Burmby left no description of the costumes they donned, but they began their observations around midday, the time when the women 'for whom lunch was breakfast' usually emerged.[38] They watched as the man with the moustache and his associate shadowed the tall, dark-haired woman and the shorter girl as they solicited in Piccadilly Circus, carefully recording the raised voices they heard when the men accused the women of wasting time; noting down each time they saw money change hands; reporting on the constant string of pubs, cafés, music halls and restaurants that formed part of their nightly circuit. Fuelled by cigarettes and tea from the police canteen and street stalls, they tailed the men and women from the afternoon until the wee hours of the morning, when at last the gang made their nightly journey back to their rented rooms. The officers waited until a light turned on in an upstairs window and then was eventually turned off again, before finally returning to the station at Marlborough Street, where they would fill out their diary and their daily expenses, perhaps soak their aching, blistered feet in the station's ablution room and then drag themselves home for what was left of the night.[39]

These thirteen- or fourteen-hour workdays were not uncommon for police officers, and in early 1910 the men of the Metropolitan Police would have to wait another few months before, at long last, a rest-day per week was introduced into their schedules.[40] Even then, detectives and ordinary officers on special duty could expect to be woken by a telephone call in the middle of the night summoning them to the station. Being very well acquainted with the people involved in the West End's commercial sex industry (with whom, after all, they shared a workspace), these men also knew full well that the 'common prostitutes' they were arresting made on average ten times what they did in a week, for less than half the hours of work. It would be another forty years before police would get paid overtime for appearances in court, or for work outside their scheduled hours. These working conditions played no small role in the corruption scandals that would plague the Met in the subsequent two decades, and led to a strike in 1918.[41] It is no surprise that many officers could not sustain this kind of relentless working life without seeking its illicit rewards.

Charles Peneau, the youngest of the pimping gang, made an easy first target for Anderson's investigation. After Mead and Burmby witnessed him taking money from Vera Wilson, a 'known prostitute', they arrested him and charged him with 'living off the earnings of a prostitute' under the 1898 Vagrancy Act, and hoped they could press him to squeal on other, more established pimps. But when he was charged, his 'respectable' parents rushed from France to their son's aid, claiming that it was the prostitute Vera who had led their sweet boy astray. Charles escaped prison time and was deported.

No one was more surprised that Inspector Anderson when, a few days later, Vera Wilson showed up at Marlborough Street Police Station. She was, she explained, incensed at the way she had been characterised by the judgemental

Peneaus. Anderson showed her into the inspector's room and, in 'a fit of indignation', she told him that 'she knew a great deal if she cared to speak'.[42] Taking out his police notebook, Anderson invited her to continue.

Vera Wilson joined a long list of people upon whom the police silently relied to help them solve crimes and prosecute offenders: 'the squealer', 'the police spy', the 'copper's nark', the 'nose', the 'grass', the police informer.[43] These informers are hidden in the pages of thousands of police reports. 'I learned,' an officer might write, or he might explain that he had acted 'from information gathered'. 'The officer is generally proud of his knowledge and does not leave lines down for other people to pick up,' a police historian explained.[44] But this obliqueness was not just about protecting one's sources, who might end up with their cheeks slashed with a 'nark's mark' if they were caught by the underworld.[45] To divulge the identity of police informers would be to admit that the greatest source of information used to catch criminals was provided by criminals themselves, and sometimes by the semi-criminal acts of police officers.

Vera proved to be a font of information. A man named Leon Brieux had trafficked the woman that police knew as Marguerite Leroy, she explained. He had been planning on taking her to Buenos Aires, but had recently made himself scarce. Max Kassell, who was known as 'Red Max', was the leader – he organised the scene in North Soho and he always carried a gun. And the men who were seen in the Café Henry with her darling Charles Peneau, the men who had been stalking the women who worked for them up and down Shaftesbury Avenue? Their names, as far as she knew them, were Aldo Cellis and Alex Berard.

At last Anderson had something to go on. But he knew that he did not have enough evidence to prosecute Cellis and Berard, neither under the 1898 Vagrancy Act for 'living on the earnings of prostitution' nor under the more serious 1885 Criminal Law Amendment Act for 'procuring a woman or girl for the purposes of prostitution'. The tall, dark-haired woman who was seen giving money to Cellis was their best chance of getting the necessary evidence for a charge. Inspector Anderson began personally to keep her under observation. He watched her go in and out of pawnshops, sip coffee at the Hotel d'Europe and solicit men. He saw her meet the man Cellis for dinner, for which she paid; and then he saw her go back out on the street again. She was fashionable, composed and took the harsh words that he saw Cellis speak to her in her stride.

Then, on 27 May, Anderson followed her as she left a flat off Charing Cross Road in the company of Cellis, the younger man Berard and the other shorter and younger-looking woman. They boarded the Central London Railway's underground train at Tottenham Court Road and travelled to Liverpool Street, with Detective Anderson in the next carriage. From there, the Metropolitan Railway took them to docklands and a waiting ship, the RMS *Tainui*. Anderson enquired at the ticket office and was told that the vessel was bound for Wellington, New Zealand, and ports in between.

He took his new Kodak Brownie camera from its bag and played the role of a tourist, managing to snap some furtive surveillance photographs: a dark, blurry image of the two men beside the ticket office; and one of the two women on the gangplank. The tall French woman turned back towards the other woman as the shutter flicked open and closed, her dark features caught in profile. The valet came behind them

7: Veronique White (far left), aka Marie Vernon, boards the RMS
Tainui in London, alongside an unidentified woman (going by the name
Marguerite Carl) in May, 1910. The image was taken by an undercover
detective, Inspector Ernest Anderson, to accompany his report. A valet,
unwittingly caught up in the surveillance, follows with their baggage.

in a crisp white uniform, carrying a suitcase and a parrot in
a cage.[46]

Cellis and Berard accompanied the women on board
the ship, and Anderson went back to the ticket office and
demanded to see the manifest. The women had boarded
under the names Miss Williams and Marguerite Carl, both
listed as dressmakers. The two men had no tickets and, sure

enough, left the ship before it sounded its departure horn. The RMS *Tainui* steamed slowly down the Thames, taking with it Anderson's best shot at a prosecution. A few days later Burmby and Mead reported that Aldo Cellis and Alexander Berard also appeared to have left the city. The case, it seemed, was dead in the water. It was only a matter of time before another nosy newspaper man or zealous moral reformer accused the police of sitting idly by, while traffickers operated with impunity.

Then, on 16 June, another tip came Anderson's way: Alexander Berard had been spotted back in London. Anderson sent PC Mead and PS Burmby back out into the streets and they quickly found Berard in his old haunts, this time in the company of a very young-looking French girl, a new face on the scene. This clear link to the Parisian underworld prompted Anderson to return to Frederick Bullock and ask for one more police officer to work the case: Detective Sergeant George Nicholls, known for his meticulous work and, crucially, for his ability to speak French. Nicholls had been born in Islington in 1877, the son of a glass warehouseman. Like Burmby, Nicholls was thus far enjoying a stratospheric rise through the ranks. He had joined in 1901 at the age of twenty-four, and by 1910 had made detective sergeant, working as a clerk for Frank Froest, the soon-to-be retired cop turned crime-writer who was then head of CID.[47]

With four officers now on the case, observations were stepped up. Alexander Berard couldn't buy a newspaper without a policeman watching. Inspector Anderson and George Nicholls followed Berard and his associates, while Mead and Burmby were assigned to keep an eye on the young French girl. For several nights they followed her as she made her way from Marie Balandras's flat at 40a Wells Street down Tottenham Court Road, past the theatres and bars of Shaftesbury Avenue, until she reached Leicester Square, where she would attempt to solicit men. On 17 June they noticed that she was with another woman, a very young-looking girl with peroxide blonde hair, who seemed to know the streets better than her companion. They watched as the blonde girl described the route the other must walk using gestures, and surmised that the former could not speak any French. The pair of young women eventually made their way to the Alhambra, the famous music hall that stood in Leicester Square. They paid their five-shilling admission for the balcony, which had been known since the theatre opened back in 1858 as a place where prostitutes met their clients.[48]

Burmby paid the admission and climbed the stairs to the theatre's highest floor. The place was filled to capacity this Friday night in June. Close to 200 bodies on the balcony alone created a hot and humid atmosphere. The air was prickly with tobacco smoke and thick with perfume, which hid the smell of stale beer.[49] On the stage, far below, played the usual weekend 'varieties': comedy acts and musical numbers, ventriloquists and dancing girls.[50] Burmby got himself a drink and pretended to watch the show, but instead watched the women, every last one of whom, he surmised, was 'of known immoral character'. He gave his eyes a chance – a turn of phrase used by coppers across London – and they lit upon the little French girl and her young blonde companion. They 'patrolled' the balcony looking for clients, and the French girl soon departed with a man in tow. At ten minutes to ten the blonde girl also found a man who wanted a 'short time', and they left the balcony together At ten o'clock Anderson and Nicholls arrived with PC Mead. But their quarry – Alex Berard – made no further appearances that evening, not even to shout angrily when the two girls, reunited after finding clients, had coffee at the Hotel d'Europe when they were meant to be out soliciting on the streets.

The next day it was back to the tedium of keeping observation for Mead and Burmby. They positioned themselves carefully outside the house and waited for the suspects to emerge for the day. Then, around noon, a taxi pulled up in front of the house, and out stepped none other than Aldo Cellis himself, freshly returned from Paris, with two more French girls and a pile of luggage in tow. He greeted Berard at the doorway.[51] The two men wasted no time. Mead and Burmby watched as they took the girls for lunch in Soho and then, without further ado, showed them the circuit they were to walk to solicit men. Burmby, watching from afar, noted the circular arm gesture: Shaftesbury Avenue, Piccadilly Circus, Leicester Square, Charing Cross Road and then back down Shaftesbury Avenue again.

Anderson, Nicholls, Mead and Burmby kept up their intensive observations of the group for two more days. Money changed hands. Voices were raised in anger. Trinkets were bought in pawnshops for the three French girls. Finally Mr Muskett of the police solicitors advised that he thought they had enough evidence for a charge under the 1885 Criminal Law Amendment Act for 'procuring for the purposes of prostitution', so long as, after the charge was laid, the police could prove that the men's victims had not already been 'common prostitutes or of known immoral character'. As the law saw it, you could only traffic an 'innocent' girl.

A warrant was issued. On 23 June, while Nicholls was

watching the young women solicit in Piccadilly Circus, Anderson and Burmby staked out Terroni's restaurant on Old Compton Street, where Cellis and Berard were enjoying a long, late Italian lunch. They emerged and made their way towards Wardour Street, straight into the path of the two officers. Anderson stepped forward – they had them at last.

'We are police officers,' he said calmly, 'and I am arresting you on a warrant for procuring, or attempting to procure, three French women whose names are unknown to become common prostitutes.'

'What for?' asked Cellis, with a tone of studied incredulity.

Inspector Anderson handcuffed him and, searching his person, found a loaded revolver. Exchanging a glance, both officers stepped up their guard. Burmby quickly came forward, took hold of Berard's wrist and suit jacket and handcuffed him, but found no other gun.

'What is this for?' Berard asked.

'For procuring three French women for an immoral purpose to become common prostitutes,' Burmby repeated, getting the wording of the law wrong.

'I don't know any women – where are they?' Berard asked snidely, as passers-by began to stop and watch the scene.

'Those three French girls at 40a Wells Street,' answered Burmby, seeing realisation dawn on both men's faces. They had thought they were cleverer than the police. Anderson and Burmby surely relished their disillusionment.

Denial now seemed their only defence. 'I don't know any girls. I have only just come out of Terroni's restaurant,' Berard protested.

Impatient to make their long-awaited arrests, and uninterested in standing on the street listening to drawn-out lies, Anderson and Burmby didn't let Berard get any further. They marched both men back to the charge room at Great Marlborough Street Police Station, fingerprinted them, wrote their names in the charge book and threw them in cells. The next morning the magistrate bound the two men over into custody, giving the police a week to find more evidence in the case against them.

Detective Anderson had obtained a search warrant for the men's rooms and had seized their possessions. As the two men sat and waited in the cells, refusing to speak and waiting for their solicitor, he went through their suitcases and itemised what he found. There were photographs of Cellis on the dock of Buenos Aires, with two young women on his arms. One was clearly the tall dark-haired woman whom Anderson had photographed leaving on the RMS *Tainui* in May, and the other was a younger girl with mousy brown hair. Also among Cellis's possessions were some bankers' drafts from Paris, Buenos Aires and Wellington. There was also a collection of obscene photographs: many pimps doubled as obscenity dealers, importing illegal postcards and books from the Continent, which their girls would sell to clients. Anderson then skimmed through letters between Berard and Cellis, between them and other pimps and traffickers, and between them and the women who worked for them, which described in explicit prose their intense and torrid love affairs.[52] Caught up within this distasteful correspondence was a letter from a man named Luigi Carvelli, whose address was 8 Devonshire Place, Brighton. The writer addressed the man as Antonio.

*

Meanwhile, down in Piccadilly Circus, DS Nicholls waited until a constable ran down from Great Marlborough Street Police Station to give him word that the two traffickers had been brought in. Knowing that the men were in custody, he now approached the two French girls who were soliciting in broken English on the pavement in front of the Pavilion Theatre. In fluent French, he explained that he was a police officer and needed them to come back to the station with him. Nicholls left no indication in his report of whether they welcomed his help or whether he threatened them with arrest for soliciting. Either way, by dinnertime he had a seventeen-year-old girl called Mireille Lapara and a nineteen-year-old called Marguerite Bescançon in the inspector's room at Great Marlborough Street Police Station.

Nicholls conducted the interviews in French, with Inspector Anderson as a witness. Their questions, unrecorded, can only be inferred from Mireille Lapara's replies.

'What is your occupation?'

Mireille told them she was a dressmaker – which was both typical work for working-class French girls and a common cover-story for women who sold sex.

'Do you have any family living?'

'My mother and father are both dead,' she answered. She had no one in the world except a ninety-three-year-old grandmother, Adèle, who was in a nursing home in Bordeaux. Mireille had left that city three years before, when she was only fourteen years old, and had gone to Paris. Since then she had moved from firm to firm as a dressmaker – so many that she had difficulty remembering the addresses.

'And how did you come to meet Alexander Berard?'

She had been entering the Métro at Les Tuileries, she told them, when Berard had invited her back to his large hotel – '*très chic*', she added. At this hotel she had met Aldo Cellis, who was already there with Marguerite Bescançon and another girl called Victoria Bricot. Aldo told her she would be '*très content*' with Berard. They invited her to come with them to London. They told her to leave all her things with her friend – they would give her new items when they arrived in London.

'Did they tell you what you would be doing here?'

'He said he worked at London, but he did not say at what trade ... Two days after I had arrived here he told me to go out in the streets and take men home to 54 High Street, and to bring him the money that I earned. I told him that I would not do it, but he said I should soon get used to it.'

Nicholls encouraged Mireille to describe her life in London. She told them about the restaurants, the flats, the trips to the Alhambra and the men she had solicited. 'I walked about very miserable.'

And then the crucial questions. 'Have you ever worked as a prostitute before you came to London?'

'*Non*.'

'Had you ever had sexual intercourse with a man?'

'*Non*. Not before Berard. I have always earned my living by working.'

Nicholls and Anderson had got what they needed from her.[53]

While there is an extensive record of her words, there is no record of Mireille Lapara's feelings. She must have been frightened, disoriented, on her guard. It would be good to think that Nicholls spoke to her with kindness, but the goings-on in inspectors' rooms were notoriously hidden from public view and from the historical record.

After Mireille, it was Marguerite's turn to be brought from the station waiting room to the interview room, where she told George Nicholls that she was an orphan who had grown up in a convent until she was sixteen. She came to Paris to stay with her sister, then bounced around in different jobs and accommodation. Her story of being groomed – or 'procured', as the law put it – was strikingly similar to Mireille's. She was between domestic-service posts when she met Aldo outside his hotel. He invited her to go to London with him, and she said she would like to. She had not slept with him, and had only been soliciting in London for a few days. Marguerite seemed to find the interview deeply upsetting. Being asked about her family caused her great distress, because she wanted more than anything else – more even than being able to get away from her traffickers – for the stigma of prostitution not to follow her home. She refused to say anything until she was assured that her sister would not hear of what she had been doing in London.

Nicholls pressed on with the key questions.

'Did you act as a prostitute before coming to London'.

'*Non.*'

'Had you ever had sexual intercourse with a man?'

'A few. The first one about a year ago.'[54]

Did Marguerite feel shame or resignation? Was her tone defiant? In any case, with this statement Marguerite became a near-useless witness. Her admission that she had had 'a few' sexual partners meant that Cellis and Berard's defence solicitor would have no trouble proving that she was 'of known immoral character'. It was now imperative that the police find more of their victims, in the hope that one of them could better play the role of the innocent 'white slave'.

They located a third young woman the next day. Victoria Bricot sat hostile and uncooperative, but was eventually threatened or cajoled into telling the officers her life story – or a version of it at least. Her parents were both living and ran a *crémerie* in Chantilly, not far from Paris. She had worked there as a shop girl, before a 'difference with her mother' had caused her to leave home just two months before. She was unemployed in Paris when she met Aldo Cellis at a restaurant near the Gare du Nord. They walked in the Bois du Boulogne and he asked her to be his mistress. He bought her tailored clothes and asked her to come to London.

Victoria agreed. 'I thought he had the means to keep me as his mistress,' she explained. 'He did not tell me he was bringing me to London to send me onto the streets.' She had only solicited one man since she had come here, who gave her a sovereign, which she put in a box, intending to start saving. 'Although I have had sexual intercourse with a man before Aldo, I have never been a prostitute.' George Nicholls, judging her by her confident words and her savvy way of saving her money, had his doubts.[55]

Despite their imperfections in the eyes of the law, these were the witnesses Anderson's unit had. And so they went ahead, and the case appeared before G. L. Denman at Marlborough Street police court on the last day of June. The men, who stood in striped prison uniforms rather than tailored suits, were formally charged with 'conspiring with a woman unknown to procure Mireille Lapara, Marguerite Bescançon and Victoria Bricot to become common prostitutes'. This provoked Cellis. Turning to where Anderson sat in the inspector's box, he shouted, 'You must prove it!' This was met with delight among the police-court audience who enjoyed the drama, and with fury from the magistrate, who called the court to order and remanded the prisoners back into custody, buying the police more time.

Anderson probably remained stoical under Cellis's attack. He had every intention of 'proving it', but he must also have been aware of the challenges he faced in trying to build a convincing case of 'procuring for the purposes of prostitution'. Anderson, like most police officers, was well aware of the story told by the judicial statistics. In 1909 fifteen cases of 'procurement' were reported to the police forces around England and Wales, but only seven of them were seen as having enough evidence to go to trial. Of these seven cases, three ended in acquittal; and of the four men who were found guilty, only one served a sentence longer than a year. In the meantime more than 11,000 arrests were made in 1909 of women committing solicitation offences, almost 10,000 of which ended in conviction, with 2,500 prison sentences.[56]

There is no record of what Inspector Anderson thought about the iniquitous operation of the criminal-justice system when it came to prostitution, or of what his role may have been in seeing some of these thousands of women charged and prosecuted. For the present, he was chiefly concerned with the women in the case as key witnesses; and once their statements were tucked safely in the folder in the inspector's room, he had to find a safe place to put the women themselves. It would be at least a week before the next court date, and quite possibly several more weeks before another one. If the police were successful in having the charge proceed, the girls would be in London for possibly two months or more before they testified at the Central Criminal Court trial. If the police lost track of them – if they absconded from their 'protective' custody and returned to their traffickers, or slipped back to France, or found new contacts in the sex industry – the case, which was, as Anderson's superiors reminded him, 'of the highest public importance', would be lost. It was imperative that the women be kept under close watch.

Anderson rang William Coote at the National Vigilance Association, the largest anti-vice organisation in Britain, and arranged for the women to be placed in what were called 'rescue homes'. But these plans were disrupted when one of the homes telephoned Anderson at the station: upon admission there, it was discovered that Victoria Bricot was suffering from venereal disease; she could not stay. Anderson had to collect her and take her to the Harrow Road hospital at once.[57]

Bricot was tight-lipped as the cab travelled north to Paddington, and Anderson, unable to speak any French, communicated with gestures when they arrived. As the secretary of the hospital recorded her name in the register and saw to her admission, the inspector told him in hushed tones how Victoria Bricot had come to suffer from her disease. A man by the name of Aldo Cellis had brought her from France some weeks back, he told the man, and she was now a key witness in the case against him. She must be watched carefully to ensure she did not leave the hospital, and that no man or woman came to fetch her.

The secretary appeared thoughtful. 'I know that name,' he said. 'He brought another girl here a couple of months ago.'

After a long day in the courtroom, and driving back

and forth across West London, Ernest Anderson probably rejoiced at this potential break in the case, which offered one last chance to find a solid witness who could bring these 'despicable ruffians' to justice. It was, perhaps, a long shot. Still, he got back in the cab and went straight to Great Marlborough Street Police Station, collected the photographs he had found in Cellis's suitcase and then returned to Harrow Road.

The secretary, Robert Eddison, fetched the sister in charge of the ward, Mary Alice Wood. Anderson showed them both the photograph of Cellis. 'That is the man,' they confirmed. He showed them the photograph of Marie boarding the steamship with the parrot, and the one of the younger woman, who went by Marguerite Carl on the manifest. 'That tall woman came the next day to check on the girl,' the nurse told him; but the other woman's face was too obscured to identify her.

They spoke in hushed tones in the sterile hallway. Mary Alice told the inspector that she had seen the man in the hospital on 11 April. His eyes, she explained, were very memorable. He had said he was the girl's employer and that she was the governess of his children, but before he left he had kissed her intimately, and the nurse's suspicions had been raised. The young woman gave her name as Doris Williams and refused to say any more. Anderson showed Mary Alice the picture of Aldo Cellis on the Buenos Aires docks. Yes, the nurse said with confidence, it was that girl there, but her hair was lighter when she came here, having clearly been bleached blonde.[58]

Doris Williams: another witness, who might still be in London. Anderson returned to the station and summoned

William Mead and Walter Burmby and showed them the picture. 'I've seen that girl before,' Mead said. He had a very good memory for faces. She was the one in the Alhambra that night, he told his superior: the blonde girl who was showing Mireille Lapara around. Mead and Burmby left the station that afternoon with orders to find her, hoping that she hadn't yet disappeared.

While they spent more days and nights searching London's 'square mile of vice' for any trace of the missing Doris Williams, Inspector Anderson travelled to Brighton, to chase up the man who had written the letters he had found in Cellis's suitcase. The train travelled through Surrey and into Sussex and, alighting into the fresh sea air that was a welcome change from London, he walked from Brighton railway station to 8 Devonshire Place, the address on the envelopes. A housekeeper opened the door. Maestro Carvelli was at home, she confirmed, and showed the inspector into the sitting room.

The house was filled with instruments. A grand piano crowded the corner of the reception room, a cello sat nearby. A beautiful French horn was beside it, and the shelves were crowded with the uneven pages of sheet music. An older man stood as the inspector entered, shaking his hand and introducing himself as Luigi Carvelli, explaining that his English was very poor.

Anderson showed him the picture he had of Aldo Cellis and explained the charges slowly, saying that he had found a letter from Luigi in the man's suitcase. Confusion and distress swept over the older man's face, and he confirmed that the man Anderson had in custody was not really called Aldo Cellis. His real name was Antonio – Antonio Adolpho

Carvelli. He was born on 13 February 1879 in Turin and was Luigi's firstborn son.

'He lived with me and his mother at Via Saluzzo, number 9, until he was eighteen years old,' Luigi explained. His son had shown promise: he was a talented musician, and had joined a prestigious military regiment after he left school. He returned home for a few months three years later, then left for Australia. A letter or two came, but after that 'he did not continue to correspond with me'. Luigi left Italy himself a few years later, taking a job as first horn with the Brighton Municipal Orchestra.

His son had come to Brighton for one night in early June, about a month ago; it was the first time Luigi had seen Antonio for ten years. As far as Luigi was concerned, his son had been working in Western Australia for the French consul. During their brief reunion Antonio had said that he had recently taken a job as valet to a millionaire in New Zealand. Yes, Luigi had questioned why Antonio was using an alias, but had accepted his son's explanation that it was 'for business purposes'.[59]

Luigi had must have felt a mix of emotions: shame for having been made a fool; horror at the revelations of the policeman; and panic lest anyone find out. The musician told Anderson that he was very anxious that his friends and colleagues did not discover the truth about his son. Anderson assured Luigi Carvelli that he would do his best to keep the maestro's name – and his son's real name – out of the press.

Learning Cellis's real name unlocked a rich potential network of information about the man, his movements and his past crimes. Armed with this crucial knowledge, as well as the date and place of his birth, Anderson set about sending

8: Antonio Carvelli (middle, with binoculars) and Alessandro di Nicotera (right) watch a horse-race in Wellington, New Zealand, sometime in 1909. The photograph, later sent to the Metropolitan Police in London to aid their investigation, was taken by Wellington Police, who were keeping the pair of suspected pimps and traffickers under observation.

telegrams to police forces around the world. He telegraphed the police in Wellington, New Zealand, who wired back telling him that the man Aldo Cellis was a known associate of the prostitute Marie Vernon, who ran an imported-goods shop – a thin front for a brothel – on College Street. And he was always seen in the company of one Alexander Berard. They were forwarding copies of photographs taken of the two men at the horse-races, and the New Zealand police assured the Met that they would track down Marie Vernon, who had recently arrived back in Wellington from London, as well as another prostitute, Annie Sawyer, who had also returned from London a few weeks earlier and was known around those parts as Berard's wife.[60]

Meanwhile, authorities in Italy reported that Berard's real name was Alessandro di Nicotera, who, after a decade of petty theft in Belgium, had been drafted into the Italian Army. He was currently wanted for desertion, to serve his outstanding sentence of two years in military prison.

Next Anderson telegraphed the authorities in Western Australia, where Antonio Carvelli's father had said he had been working for the French consul. Their reply confirmed this to be true, but they added that Aldo Cellis had also been a bludger – their word for a pimp – in the goldfields, and had stood trial for 'living on the earnings' back in 1908. He skipped out on the charge and had not been heard from since.[61] The South Australia, Victoria and New South Wales police all told a different tale. In these states, Carvelli was one of the many small-time thieves who worked the streets of Adelaide, Melbourne and Sydney in the years between 1901 and 1908, but he had never been prosecuted for pimping. They had no idea what had become of him.[62]

Finally, Anderson also heard back from the *questore* of Turin, who reported that a young Antonio Carvelli was still wanted on a warrant for offences in his home town committed back in 1900.[63] The then twenty-one-year-old had run away to parts unknown before his appearance in court. Carvelli was, as a newspaper would later call him, a 'versatile rogue'.[64]

While Anderson was discovering the history of Antonio Carvelli and Alessandro di Nicotera, and Mead and Burmby continued to scour the streets for the blonde girl calling herself Doris Williams, George Nicholls travelled to Paris to uncover what he could about the past lives of the men's French victims. In doing so, he was trying to get ahead of Cellis's and Berard's wily defence lawyers, who intended to argue that the women in question could not have been procured because they were already 'common prostitutes' in France before they arrived in England.

Nicholls arrived in the French capital on 3 July 1910 and began to follow leads. He retraced Mireille Lapara's precarious employment history as a young dressmaker, which led him around the north-west of Paris. She worked first at Paquin's on rue de la Paix; then at a large costumier on rue de Rome; and finally at another place on the boulevard des Batignolles. Girls under twenty often changed jobs every few months, he learned from the managers, because they were not permitted to work late at night, like older women, and in any case the work was very precarious. Mireille and Marguerite were two of a small army of Parisian girls who sewed, beaded and laced the prêt-à-porter women's clothing that was pouring out of Paris and into catalogues and shop windows around the world. Their wages and hours rose and fell as the companies bid for contracts, eager not to be undercut by those in New York that, with access to a huge surge of desperate immigrant labour, could impose pay that was lower still and conditions even worse.[65] Only a few short months after Nicholls interviewed Mireille's former bosses in Paris, the world woke up to the news that 146 people – the vast majority of them Jewish and Italian girls under the age of twenty-three – had burned to death at the Triangle Shirtwaist Factory in Greenwich Village, New York. The doors and stairwells had been locked, as was customary, to stop theft and unauthorised breaks.[66]

In the aftermath of the fire, in angry speeches and pamphlets, women labourers and socialists in the United States called for workers to unite and demand their rights. The fight for workers' rights in the textile industry raged in Paris as well. The very year that Mireille went to London, Paris garment workers undertook the second of three significant strikes.[67] Mireille's own protest against the conditions of her labour was quieter. She quit. She took a risk and agreed to go with a strange man to London, who promised her good money and a steady job. Detective Sergeant Nicholls probably knew little of the conditions of Parisian garment workers, but what he did realise was that this spotty work history could be used by the defence to spin a tale of dressmaking by day in the rue de Rome and soliciting in Montmartre, just a short walk away, by night.

Next, Nicholls checked the registers of the Parisian morals police for the three names, especially Victoria Bricot's, and was told that she had 'been in the hands of the Paris police for prostitution'. It was precisely what he didn't want to find. He went to her last address on the rue Buffon, which ran alongside the Jardin des Plantes on the left bank of the Seine, but no one knew her there.

From there it was off to the suburbs, to Le Pecq, where Marguerite Bescançon had worked as a servant, and then to Saint-Germaine-en-Laye, where she worked at a stationer's. Then back to the north of Paris and a café on the rue de Clichy, then to a house where she worked as a servant on boulevard d'Opéra, around the corner from Mireille Lapara's first employer. Finally Nicholls went to the rue Rodier near the Gare du Nord and sought out the hotel where Cellis and Berard had been staying. He returned to London the following week with little more than a story about three poor young French women who, like so many in that era, changed jobs every few months, fell into unemployment and fought to survive entirely on their own. In a city where women's work was poorly paid and came with no guaranteed hours, and where social welfare fell to a network of private charities, this bid for survival often included making acquaintances and transactions with better-off men. 'The class of woman and girl we've had to deal with,' as the prosecuting solicitors later put it, made the case very difficult. They were far from the ideal 'white slaves'. The search for the mysterious Doris Williams became all the more urgent.

As Nicholls retraced the working lives of disappearing girls through the broad avenues and cobbled streets of Paris, Burmby and Mead were combing the streets of Soho, North Soho and Piccadilly for any sign of the blonde girl identified by the VD hospital nurse as Doris Williams. On Saturday 9 July they were 'giving their eyes a chance' in Piccadilly Circus when they spotted her, walking along the pavement by the Criterion, shivering in the unseasonably cold evening air, wearing a brown dress that was too long for her.[68] Crowds passed her and most men ignored her quiet 'Goodnight', but some turned their heads. The two officers needed to act quickly, before one of the passing men took her up on the offer of a 'short time'. Burmby sent Mead in a taxi to the station house to fetch Inspector Anderson, and continued to watch her as she spoke briefly to passing men. Anderson arrived quickly and, wasting no more time, he and Burmby approached the young woman with the faded blonde hair.

As they came through the crowd, they would have

appeared like any other men out for a stroll that evening. Noticing their focused gaze, the young woman pegged them as potential clients and smiled shallowly, greeting them with a 'Goodnight' and asking them if they were interested in a 'short time'. 'I am a police officer,' Inspector Anderson replied, and explained that he would like her to come with him back to the station, to answer some questions about a man she knew as Aldo Cellis. They knew they had the right girl when they saw her reaction to the name. Her face had frozen at Anderson's first words, but now she became nervous and flighty, her eyes scanned the bustling, noisy crowd.

Anderson persisted and eventually 'induced her to come', as he put it.[69] What did this 'inducement' entail? A gentle entreaty, born of pity for the girl, who was clearly so young and so far from home? A threat of arrest for soliciting, 'to the annoyance' of passers-by? A firm hand gripping her elbow – a subtle reminder that she would be coming with them, one way or the other? Ultimately, for the police, the method mattered little: they had finally found their missing witness.

At the police station Anderson invited the girl to sit in the stove-warmed inspector's room, and he used the telephone to contact the lady assistant, Miss Eilidh MacDougall, asking her to attend to take a witness statement. She arrived shortly afterwards in a taxi, unfazed by the late hour. But even with the comforting presence and open, friendly face of Miss MacDougall, the girl was cagey. She told them she was nineteen, and that her name was indeed Doris Williams. She recounted the story of being induced to go to Buenos Aires by 'Mr Cellis', as she called him, but equally implicated 'Mrs Cellis', his supposed wife. It was Marie who had made the false promises; Marie who had really convinced her to leave

New Zealand. 'I was surprised when Mrs Cellis told me the life I was going to lead,' she explained to Miss MacDougall and Inspector Anderson, 'but she said I should have an easy life with nice dresses, and it was that that induced me to go with them and I was also glad to be able to travel.'

She signed her statement in a shaky hand, and Inspector Anderson sent her away in the care of Miss MacDougall, who was to take her to the newly opened Metropolitan Police Home for Women and Girls and see if she could get any more information out of her. Doris Williams, both the inspector and the lady assistant agreed, was certainly not her real name.

On 13 July Miss MacDougall brought the girl back to the police station and into the inspector's room. She was cleaned up and dressed in the hand-me-downs of some benevolent lady's daughter, and looked even younger than she had on Saturday night. They were back to give a further statement, Miss MacDougall explained.

'What is your correct name and age?' Miss MacDougall asked, taking out her pen.

'My correct name is Lydia Rhoda Harvey,' the girl replied. 'My correct age is eighteen on the third of June last.'

Miss MacDougall began to write.

Chapter Three

THE NEWSMAN

Guy Scholefield made the same journey every morning. Leaving the New Zealand Press Association offices that he shared with the *Daily Mail* on Fleet Street, he headed down the Strand, which surged with its typical tangle of horse carts, carriages, bicycles and motor cars. Above his head hundreds of banners rippled in the wind, advertising clothes, creams and foodstuffs, while at his feet lay the detritus of the immense human traffic that travelled back and forth along the pavements every day. London's busiest street was crowded with coffee stalls and food stands, taxi ranks, flower sellers, shoe-shiners and newsagents; and people ducked in and out of its shops, pubs, offices and restaurants. It was a cacophony of sights and sounds, and Scholefield, the unassuming newsman, was in the middle of it all.

Reaching the imposing facade of Charing Cross Station, he took the junction that brought him to Trafalgar Square. As a self-defined 'imperial nationalist', thirty-two-year-old Scholefield was surely thrilled to find himself on this daily journey through the very heart of the Empire, under the gaze of Nelson and alongside the colonnades of the National Gallery, with Whitehall stretching to the south.[1] And if the stern-faced, well-dressed newsman saw the other side of

9: Guy Scholefield, journalist, archivist and renowned New Zealand historian, pictured here in 1929 in his early fifties. Almost twenty years earlier, as a young reporter in London, he broke the story of Lydia Harvey (aka Doris Williams) for the New Zealand Press Association.

London – the beggars on the Strand, the men who slept rough on the stone benches around Nelson's Column, the women who asked him for a 'short time' near the station – he did not recall it for the readers of the missives from 'our own special London correspondent' back in New Zealand.

Passing by the building site for the enormous Admiralty Arch, he made his way down The Mall. The bustle of the city was forgotten by the time he reached leafy St James's Park, where a stroll beside the lake brought him to the hoardings around the soon-to-be unveiled memorial to Queen Victoria. On Victoria Street he arrived at the offices of the New Zealand High Commission, his daily destination.

He had come to London primarily as a journalist for four

associated newspapers back home, but when he had left Wellington for London he had also been appointed a justice of the peace, in order to be of assistance to New Zealand visitors and residents of the capital. Usually the high commissioner, William Hall-Jones, had some affidavits for him to witness or other documents to sign, but this morning, around 11 July, it was a different matter altogether.

William Hall-Jones looked strained. He had just opened a dossier, he explained, for a most unpleasant case. As high commissioner, he was charged with brokering various diplomatic issues between the new Dominion of New Zealand and the United Kingdom, and with lending aid (often in the form of repatriation) to any New Zealanders who found themselves destitute or in crisis. Unlike the commissioners and consuls who worked for countries with huge waves of out-migration and in countries with volatile economies, this particular aspect of Hall-Jones's work did not keep him particularly busy. It was a far cry from European consuls' experiences in Buenos Aires, whose cabinets were filled with the sorry tales of washed-up migrants stranded in what had promised to be a better land.

But London was not without its drama, and this case certainly threatened to become a thorn in his side. There was an Otago girl, he explained to Scholefield, as the newsman took a seat in his ornately appointed office – an eighteen-year-old from Oamaru – who had been found on the streets of London, engaged in a most unmentionable activity. She had been brought here, after an ordeal in Buenos Aires, by two continental traffickers in women. She was due to testify against these men at a London police court on 20 July, and the London police had asked him to arrange for her eventual repatriation. She was using the name Doris Williams, the high commissioner explained, but he understood that might be a pseudonym. It was best for Scholefield to watch the case, should the young woman require assistance. And he supposed the trial ought to be reported, in the interest of the New Zealand public.

Guy Scholefield was used to covering high politics and matters of state. He prided himself on his fast transcription of the speeches of prime ministers, and cultivated careful relationships with civil servants and politicians. He had come to London with the intention of informing his newly inaugurated Dominion about the goings-on in the heart of Empire: imperial trade tariffs, the growing diplomatic tensions in Europe and her colonies, the import and export of goods. Stories like Doris Williams's were best saved for the gutter press, which traded in sensationalism. These papers relished the growing panic over what they called 'white slavery', and printed column after column that recounted the horrible experiences of girls imprisoned in brothels, snatched from railway stations and trapped in lives of shame. It seemed there was a new version of the same story every day. But it was not every day that stories like this happened to a New Zealander. And so Scholefield resolved to attend the upcoming trial and to add one more terrible tale to the worldwide obsession with 'the infamous traffic'.

Guy Scholefield had loved the newspapers since he was a boy and passed many happy hours sprawled across his parents' living room, poring over issues of the *Illustrated London News*.[2] Of course by the time it reached Dunedin, on the steamships and clippers that brought it to the other side of the world, this news was a little outdated, but papers like the *Illustrated London News* and *The Times* nonetheless played a vital role in connecting white New Zealanders to the centre of their imperial identity. His mother's family, the Hardys, had been early white settlers on the South Island. His maternal grandfather, John Hardy, arrived in a wooden barque in the 1850s, to farm the fertile land of Otago and raise sheep. Later, when men from all over the world rushed towards 'a gloomy gap in the wintery hills' to pan for 'payable dirt' in the Otago gold rush, his grandfather made out well in a successful claim.[3] Of course women followed too, and the wintery hills of the Otago goldfields became a site of prostitution, but Guy Scholefield, in his autobiographical recollections, did not see fit to include this in the province's brave history.

Guy's grandfather later became a civil engineer and town councillor and, after marrying, moved to Dunedin, joining Lydia Harvey's grandfather, Justice Harvey, among the brightest and best old founding families. Guy's father, John Scholefield, could claim an equally respectable background, with a family full of ministers and Cambridge Greek professors and prosperous shipbrokers. After marrying John Hardy's eldest daughter Marion, he established a pharmaceutical laboratory in Dunedin and taught at a local school.[4] Guy Scholefield, a son wedged between four daughters, enjoyed a prosperous, middle-class childhood.

He grew up amid a communications revolution. He was spellbound by the ships in Dunedin's harbour, which brought him 'letters from strange and distant lands'.[5] Undersea cables stretched across oceans, carrying telegraphic information to every corner of the world. Wireless signals were also improving, enabling those on ships to communicate with those on shore. Steamships carried paper information far more quickly now. By 1885 the *Illustrated London News* reached Dunedin at least two weeks faster than it had when Scholefield's father had first come to New Zealand.

The speed and ease of communication were matched by an explosion in the number of people communicating. The early twentieth century was an era of unprecedented literacy and witnessed an explosion in popular print, as books and newspapers became cheaper to produce and cheaper to buy. Daily and weekly papers and periodicals multiplied in number, and 'illustrated' news appealed to an even wider readership.

From the comfort of his living-room floor, Guy pored over the stories of the brave deeds of major generals who commanded British troops in the Sudan, and gobbled up the tense tales of Cossacks on horseback, as a war with Russia over the Afghan border seemed imminent. Gladstone's election campaigns and Greek plays at Cambridge University, half a world away, felt like they were on Guy's doorstep.[6] The *Illustrated London News* brought the wide world of the British Empire and its sphere of influence to life: from the Caribbean, to Argentina and New Zealand itself.

By the late nineteenth century more and more newspaper magnates in the British Empire and around the world had responded to the tastes and interests of this growing mass readership.[7] There was still plenty of old-fashioned reporting – politics, war, Empire – but there was also more society news and gossip, more reporting on nightlife and entertainment. These papers were staffed by a new generation of journalists, who increasingly believed it wasn't just their job to report the news, but also to make it. This was the dawn of 'investigative reporting', and it opened up a new world where journalism could be used to educate the public about social problems, and to pressure states to fix them.[8]

Then one day in late August of 1885, Guy Scholefield's mother, like all parents around the world, snatched the daily paper from her child before he could read the headlines. 'THE GREAT LONDON SCANDAL', they screamed. Word of the 'Maiden Tribute of Modern Babylon' case in England had reached New Zealand by telegraph, hinting at the horrors that the original articles – on their way by mail steamer to the Antipodes – contained. But long before the physical papers had made it to the other side of the world everyone knew its author's name. William T. Stead, the firebrand editor of the *Pall Mall Gazette*, had just reinvented journalism.[9]

It was like nothing anyone had ever read before in the daily press. A Minotaur, Stead explained, lived in the belly of London, and every night the police and the judges and the brothel-keepers sacrificed white English virgins to its hungry maw. Over several days of instalments, and with a startling new kind of journalistic prose, Stead catalogued the extent of sexual trading in young girls in London, which he dubbed 'Modern Babylon'. The articles were narrated as though they were a report on vice from a 'secret commission', and Stead gave first-hand accounts of his own twisted journeys in London's labyrinth. He described brothel doors that were locked from the outside; explained how girls were 'tied down' and how, thanks to padded walls, their 'screams were not heard'. To prove such crimes were possible, Stead had gone so far as to 'purchase' his own 'virgin', a thirteen-year-old named Eliza Armstrong, handing her impoverished, alcoholic mother £5.

In the newspaper he called this girl 'Lily', to emphasise her whiteness and her innocence. In order to assure readers of her incontrovertible 'purity', Stead arranged to have her forcibly inspected for an intact hymen. He gave little thought to the way that the real girl, Eliza Armstrong, had suffered for his metaphor. Stead had written this earth-shattering piece of journalism as part of an impassioned campaign for legal change, and the cause was more important than any individual girl.

Like many of his allies, Stead was a Nonconformist Protestant and a radical liberal, an iconoclast interested in bringing about real social justice. 'Exploited prostitution' was seen by him and others as one of the most urgent social problems of the day. In the decades leading up to the 'great London scandal', radical liberals, early feminists and anti-vice reformers had been working to raise public awareness of the evils of state-regulated prostitution, the horrors of exploitation in the sex trade, and the traffic in women and children. This traffic, they argued, was fuelled by the fact that the age of consent was inexcusably low: in Britain it was set at thirteen. In the UK bills were put before Parliament, but were stalled by hand-wringing MPs who worried that their sons, out sowing their wild oats, would be at risk of extortion from precocious fifteen-year-olds who looked and behaved far older. What was needed, Stead and his allies believed, was 'justifiable sensationalism': a newspaper exposé that was so shocking that it 'arrests the eyes of the public and compels them to admit the necessity of action'.[10] And so, in the first two weeks of July 1885, William Stead turned the traffic in women and children from a pressing social issue into an international obsession, quite literally overnight.[11]

This 'government by journalism', as Stead described it, seemed to work. By August 1885 Parliament had passed the Criminal Law Amendment Act, which made 'procuring for the purposes of prostitution' an offence, if the girl or woman 'was not already a prostitute or of known immoral character'. The Act also raised the age of consent to sixteen, and made the prosecution of brothels far easier. Anti-vice campaigners, in celebration, held a rally in Hyde Park that drew a crowd of up to 300,000 – testament to the degree to which Stead's exposé had truly rallied the public to the cause. A parade of reformers, with banners blazing, wove their way through the enormous crowd. There were anti-vice campaigners, Temperance campaigners and representatives from the women's movement; there were trade unionists and socialists; there were representatives of local and national religious charities, joined by the girls they had 'saved' from damnation. These girls marched, giggling, with white flowers symbolising purity pinned to their dresses. At the centre of it all was William Stead, who opened the ceremony with a rousing speech from a makeshift stage at the Reformer's Tree. More speeches followed. 'All these speakers,' wrote a decidedly unimpressed *New York Times* correspondent, ' ... promptly traced the corruption of young girls back each to his own special grievance against society and then discussed that grievance.'[12] The campaign against exploited prostitution could be turned to many ends.

One of the most significant unintended (or at least unspoken) consequences of the Criminal Law Amendment Act 1885 was an unprecedented crusade against the brothels of London. The Act had made keeping a brothel a non-indictable offence, which meant that it was far easier and cheaper to prosecute it. But it left the definition of a brothel deliberately obscure. In the end, case law defined it as a place where 'more than one woman' practised prostitution. It was a far cry from the image William Stead had painted of large, organised brothels, run by pimps and madams, in which young girls were systematically exploited. But it proved an effective way to crack down on vice.

All around London, women who worked in these so-called brothels found themselves uprooted and homeless after their landlords evicted them, or the police and anti-vice campaigners prosecuted them under the new law. Many were forced to turn to pimps to secure new accommodation, and to pay unscrupulous estate agents exorbitant fees. Crucial safety networks between women in the sex industry, built on shared accommodation and mutual support, were eroded. On this, the newspapers were silent: these women were the unseen collateral damage of the crusade to save innocent girls. Indeed the law, in word and in practice, mirrored the image that the newspapers had painted: drawing heavy lines between innocent girls like Lily, and girls who, in the words of one rescue worker, 'suffered a lasting blight of their moral senses and never again regained their pristine purity of character'.[13]

Any journalist who worked after 1885 did so, in one way or another, in the shadow of William T. Stead, and the 'Maiden Tribute of Modern Babylon' left an immense and global legacy. Some readers were inspired to campaign for more rights and protection for young women, but far more were hungry for the details of their depravity. In Australia local newspapers reprinted Stead's articles in full, and copies sold for as much as 30 shillings – hundreds of pounds in present-day money. By September 1885 these papers had made their way by coastal steamer to New Zealand and were received with both horror and fascination by readers all over the country. According to the *West Coast Times*, it was 'one of the most hellish and infernal indictments against civilization that ever appeared in print ... No more awful, no more sickening, no more horrible record has ever before been even hinted at by gutter novelists past or present.'[14] Guy Scholefield, at the tender age of eight, would never have been allowed to read a word of the 'great London scandal', but its themes of vice, ruined innocence and melodrama would go on to shape and influence the journalism in which he built his career in the years that followed. All the while the lines between justifiable sensationalism and sales-boosting melodrama were growing increasingly blurred.

While Stead's revelations reverberated around the world, Guy Scholefield and his mother and sisters experienced their own smaller, but more closely felt, calamity. The year 1885 was the year that John Scholefield died, and the now-fatherless family relocated from Dunedin to the smaller Otago town of Milton. Here, as he grew into a man, Scholefield witnessed profound transformations in social and political life that were linked to the reformist zeal that had motivated the anti-vice campaigners in London. Just as they were doing in the Empire's metropolis, the Salvationists with their brass instruments marched noisily down Milton's usually quiet streets, demanding an end to the drink trade, and they succeeded. Women, including Guy's mother, demanded the vote and – unlike women in London – got it. Farmers campaigned for more rational and equitable land reforms, and won. In what felt like the blink of an eye, modernity had come to Milton. '1893 dawned pink with the glow of promise,' he later wrote, of what he believed was the start of a more just and more prosperous age. For the rest of his life Scholefield recalled with admiration the cacophony of those Salvation Army bands.[15]

The way in which the immense social changes that Milton witnessed in microcosm were echoed around New Zealand and the world fascinated Scholefield, and when he was a teenager he met the editor of the local newspaper. 'I, who had watched all these things with wonder, was sixteen and wanted to be a journalist, so I asked him for a job.'[16] At first the only work he found was as a print compositor, toiling with ink-stained hands until four o'clock some mornings to prepare the press for the print run, but soon enough he was writing the columns rather than setting them to type.[17] Then in 1899, at the age of twenty-two, he got a job at the *New Zealand Times* in the capital, and left for Wellington 'with the enthusiasm of an explorer'.[18]

There would be no 'justifiable sensationalism' in Schole-field's columns, but all the same it was impossible to ignore the new role that journalists were playing in the public sphere. Throughout the late nineteenth and early twentieth centuries social reformers and anti-vice campaigners worked closely with these new journalists, who were instrumental in raising public awareness about social problems and inspiring popular support for their campaigns. News stories about exploited prostitution not only lined the pockets of the papers' owners, but also encouraged donations to organisations dedicated to anti-vice and rescue work.

Back in England, money poured into the bank accounts

of the newly formed National Vigilance Association, whose morally strident general secretary, William Coote, had made the eradication of vice his lifelong crusade.[19] The NVA, as it was known, alongside other organisations in various countries, launched an endless campaign against what they called 'immorality', and were instrumental in shutting down the two-woman brothels of London. Sometimes a handful of women who were evicted from these premises even accepted their offer of 'rescue'. Vigilance crusaders stormed the basements of booksellers, seizing pornographic books and photos and burning them in bonfires. They prosecuted unsavoury newspapers that printed 'indecent advertisements' for 'masseuses', 'models' and 'women's pills'. They campaigned for councils to revoke the licences of licentious art shows, music halls and mutoscope displays, where the viewer could look through a slit in a spinning cylinder and watch a woman take off her clothes in staccato time.[20] This was the dawning of a new era of what they called 'social purity'.

This was also a new age of internationalism, and the NVA, alongside other organisations the world over, began to work in the name of preventing the trafficking in women and girls. In the closing years of the nineteenth century, anti-trafficking campaigners of various political stripes met at lavish international conferences. In hotel boardrooms they hashed out the terms of the very first International Agreement for the Suppression of the 'White Slave Traffic', which was signed in 1904. It attempted to standardise law and policy against trafficking around the world and required signatory countries to put in place laws punishing traffickers, set up systems of surveillance at ports and railway stations, establish a central authority in charge of monitoring and responding to the traffic and help to 'repatriate' its victims.[21] Far from these boardrooms, NVA volunteers – almost all of them women – worked tirelessly in the name of helping young women who were in danger of being trafficked into prostitution. They plastered railway stations with posters, warning them of the dangers of accepting offers of work away from home. They stationed themselves at ports, wearing distinctive armbands, helping new arrivals safely to their destinations. And they escorted destitute girls back to their homes.

Journalism and moral reform worked in tandem, and whether in the name of social justice or the bottom line, more and more editors encouraged sensationalism, scandal and melodrama, as well as more illustration, advertisements and bolder headlines. Luckily, stories of divorce, murder, prostitution and scandal were in ready supply. When Schole-field was made chief of staff for the *New Zealand Times* he ensured the paper maintained a more serious, and some might say old-fashioned, tone, but newer publications felt no such constraint.[22] In 1905 the *New Zealand Truth* was founded by the controversial, larger-than-life Australian journalist John Norton, who had founded similar publications in Australia. Staffed by socialists and sensationalists, the *New Zealand Truth* quickly became a paragon of the early twentieth-century newspaper, filling its columns with stories of crime, destitution, radical politics, sex and scandal.[23] It had one of the widest circulations in the country, and was joined the world over by similar publications. Back in London, newly founded dailies like the *Daily Mail*, the *News of the World* and the *People* reported the news that the public really wanted to read. And while it would be a few more decades before photographs augmented this growing sensationalism, the tabloid era had certainly dawned.

Four years after the *New Zealand Truth* was founded, on the other side of the world, another journalist was in the process of rediscovering 'the infamous traffic' for a new generation of readers. In November 1909, in the United States, George Kibbe Turner published a shocking exposé in *McClure's Magazine*, another pioneering 'muck-raking' publication. He called it 'The Daughters of the Poor: A Plain Story of the Development of New York City as a Leading Centre of the White Slave Trade of the World'. Turner used his account, about mostly Jewish young women bought and sold in the tenement districts of Manhattan, to illustrate the corruption of the municipal government, and to redeploy the depictions of the sexual underworld that had shocked readers of the 'Maiden Tribute of Modern Babylon' twenty-four years earlier. But Turner went further than Stead and detailed the international spread of the terrible 'white slave traffic' and the terrifying organisation of the traffickers. From Buenos Aires to Paris to the Pale of Settlement; from North Africa to Istanbul to London, men from the criminal underworld were buying and selling the bodies and souls of poor immigrant girls.[24] It was a powerful revelation of what was a very real experience for many women, although these stories overlooked the poverty and inequality that had made them so vulnerable to traffickers in the first place.

Turner's revelations exploded into public consciousness around the same time that Lydia Harvey boarded a coastal ship in Oamaru on her way to Wellington with her employer, Mrs Batson. By 1910, as Lydia Harvey set sail for Buenos Aires, the world was in the grip of a new 'white slavery' panic.

10: Images from three of the dozens of books published in the early twentieth century about what was called 'white slavery'. These, and other similar images, depicted the imagined dangers of urban life and allegorised the kidnap, confinement and ruin of young women who were led astray. These images were also highly racialised, always emphasising the whiteness of the female victim, and often suggesting the Jewish or non-white identity of the trafficker.

In the months that she spent selling sex in South America and London between 1910 and 1911, dozens of book titles appeared in shops and mail-order catalogues with titles like *The House of Bondage*, *In the Grip of the White Slave Trader*,

War on the White Slave Trade and *The Girl That Disappears*. A feature-length silent film, *Traffic in Souls*, in which a Swedish émigré is tricked into prostitution by a pimp in New York, was released in 1913 and made almost $1m. It was one of the highest-grossing films of its era, one of the very first feature-length films ever made and is widely considered the first film in what would become the 'sexploitation' genre.[25]

Newspaper columns, meanwhile, were filled with anecdote and rumour, with stories of girls who had disappeared after leaving their small towns for work in the big city. The typical tale went something like this: a young, naïve woman from a small town accepted a job offer from a handsome man she met at a dance hall or cinema, and then arranged to meet him to take up work in the big city. Or, perhaps, the girl became a victim of her own foolish dreams: as one writer put it, a 'white slave' was often 'a servant girl tired of the tedious round of domestic duties, who thinks she could do better behind the footlights'.[26] Beauty contests, run by the same newspapers that decried the 'white slave traffic', were considered a particular evil. 'Their self-assurance was hideous to watch,' wrote one anti-vice campaigner after an evening spent scowling as pretty girls paraded onstage at a beauty contest at the English seaside, 'and they had already caught all the antics of the tried professional. They minced and smirked and smiled with all the aplomb of an "unfortunate" and worst of all their own parents apparently encouraged them.'[27] According to anti-trafficking campaigners, beauty contestants like Lydia Harvey and Nellie Mathie were dancing on a moral precipice. 'From the beauty show to the devil,' the writer concluded, 'is but a step.'[28]

However she came to be there, upon arrival in the

threatening big city, the girl in the story was drugged, kidnapped and taken to a hidden brothel. If she was lucky, she was found before she could be 'ruined', and in this way the story preserved the rescued heroine as someone worth saving. These layered, repetitive accounts of young, guileless women exalted pure womanhood, fetishised virginity and created an ideal victim of trafficking who was 'pure, innocent, unsuspecting, trusting, and young'.[29] And what of the girls who were not rescued in time? 'Their health is broken down, their bodies are utterly ruined, their minds poisoned and dulled, they are thrust out into the streets to perish there, unless some hospital ward opens its doors to them,' explained one writer. 'What else could happen to them?'[30] Or, as another campaigning journalist intoned ominously, 'The girl who disappears lives on somewhere in the under-world.'[31]

The 'white slavery' panic encapsulated the anxieties of a society where a young woman's roles were rapidly changing.[32] Every city to which she might migrate, and every job she might take, was imagined as a source of potential danger. The theatre recruiter, the employment agent for hotels and shops and the handsome suitor were all potential pimps in disguise. Most of all, the places where she might enjoy herself – the cinema and theatre, the dance hall, the bar and the café – were said to be the hunting grounds of procurers. Young women were told to beware 'dangerous amusements', and their parents were reminded that 'the proper place for the girl is in her home'.[33] 'White slavery' was a fear fashioned by crusading journalists and anti-vice campaigners and taken up by a society that longed for young women to remain in their traditional place, while exploiting them for their cheap and flexible labour.

'White slavery' was a powerful and very troubled metaphor. Initially used by American socialists to describe the poor working conditions and pay of white men, by the late nineteenth century it had, as historian Gunther Peck argues, profoundly and effectively shifted its meaning. In the hands of anti-vice campaigners and journalists, it feminised and sexualised the idea of enslavement, and, crucially, used the threat that white women could meet such a fate to garner support. The fact that black women had been sexually exploited in slavery for centuries – and continued to be in colonial plantations, in the homes of white women, and in unsafe and underpaid factory work – went without mention in these new campaigns, which concerned themselves only with the fate of white women. 'The White Slave Trade,' wrote one campaigner, 'consists of the trapping of young women, who, once "broken in", are condemned to a perpetual servitude, beside which the sufferings endured by the African slaves, prior to their liberation, are as nothing.'[34] Meanwhile black, Asian and indigenous women who engaged in prostitution – often in highly exploitative conditions – were rendered almost invisible by the language of 'white slavery'. And long after the term was changed to 'the traffic in women and children', in recognition of its impact on non-white women, the trope of white victimhood remained.

This erasure of black suffering and the invisibility of other exploited people of colour was unsurprising in a period that embraced racial hierarchies and enforced racial segregation. The idea that a white woman could be bought and sold for sex was especially shocking and abhorrent, because the health of the 'white race' was seen as intimately tied to the sexual purity of white women, and the strength of Western empires was linked to the idea that whites were more civilised and more moral than the people they colonised. 'White slavery' was built on the idea of the fragility of young women, but it was fuelled by the fragility of whiteness itself.[35]

If the victims of 'white slavery' were imagined in newspapers and novels as perpetually white, the 'white slavers' who terrorised them were profoundly racialised. These men were called many names: pimp, ponce, bully, macque, procurer, *souteneur*. They horrified the respectable readers of the newspapers that detailed their crimes, but fascinated them as well. They were 'vampires', 'fiends in the shape of a man', who 'sold women like cattle into a life of shame'. No language seemed florid enough to adequately capture their heinousness and brutality: 'These murderous traffickers drink the heart's blood of weeping mothers while they eat the flesh of their daughters, by living and fattening themselves on the destruction of the girls.'[36]

Most commonly, and in keeping with the pervasive anti-Semitism of the age, pimps and traffickers were imagined to be Jewish men, who usually trafficked Jewish women. But as black migrants arrived in larger numbers in northern American cities, fleeing violence and prejudice in the south, American literature and news increasingly linked the problem of 'white slavery' to black men from inner-city ghettos. Chinese men were also often branded as traffickers, part of the narrative of 'yellow peril' that was sweeping places like Australia, the United States and Canada at the time, who were witnessing large amounts of Chinese migration, not least because of those countries' hunger for cheap labour in mining, railroad-building and canal construction.

But whiteness itself was also racialised and gradated, and

many men who engaged in trafficking were seen as what we might call the 'wrong kind' of white. The depiction of Jewish men as notorious traffickers is the clearest example of the way in which anti-Semitism pervaded the concept of 'white slavery', but this kind of racialisation was also applied to the millions of Italian men who flooded into world cities during an era of incredible out-migration from Italy. These men were often treated suspiciously, branded as criminals, anarchists and carriers of disease. They were portrayed as swarthy, foreign and corrupt. Many newspaper reporters milked these racialised images for all they were worth, playing to an anxious society that agonised over what was called 'national degeneracy'.[37] Women, too, could find their status as victim or criminal determined by their imagined place in a white racial hierarchy that was dominated by Britain and the anglophone world. French women, alongside French pimps and traffickers, were subject to particularly sharp prejudice within the British imagination, which saw them as more sexually immoral and vicious than English-speaking white women from Britain and her white colonies.

It is no coincidence that the anti-trafficking movement was born at the same time as anti-immigration politics were on the rise. In Britain this was mostly precipitated by the arrival of thousands of Eastern European Jews, who were fleeing violent pogroms and destitution in the Pale of Settlement and seeking better lives. These Jews were seen by many xenophobes as an imminent threat: they brought dangerous infections, a suspect religion and backward ways of living; and they were notorious socialists, anarchists and traffickers. But anti-trafficking campaigners were almost equally suspicious of the western and southern Europeans who were coming to London, New York and other Western world cities at the same time. According to William Coote, the general secretary of England's National Vigilance Association, the French, German and Italian migrants turned neighbourhoods of London into foreign countries and brought with them, in Coote's words, 'special forms of vice'. These women, he explained to Britain's Royal Commission on Alien Immigration in 1903, were not victims of 'white slavery', but instead had been 'already debauched in their own countries'. In the boardrooms of international conferences, Coote and his like-minded campaigners proposed measures that would bar foreign women from working in state-licensed brothels, would implement 'compulsory repatriation' for trafficking victims, and would even prevent any woman from emigrating without special permission from her father, husband or the state.[38]

Many of these measures were successfully challenged by feminists and liberals who fought to maintain a place at the table of the anti-trafficking movement in these years, but nonetheless legal measures designed to combat the traffic in women almost always doubled as tools through which states could limit and criminalise certain kinds of migration and could monitor and control the movement of all women. In 1905 the Aliens Act gave the Home Office the power to deport anyone who had committed a prostitution-related offence, however minor, and similar policies of expulsion extended to the British colonies. In the United States a series of Immigration Acts had singled out procurers and prostitutes as particular kinds of unwanted migrants; and in Australia the dictation test that was part of the 'white Australia' immigration policy, introduced in 1901 at the time of federation, was regularly used to prevent 'undesirable immigrants' from entering the country, with suspected prostitutes and pimps as some of their key targets.[39] These deportations, overwhelmingly of migrant women selling sex, rather than of pimps, vastly outnumbered the prosecutions for trafficking in all these countries in any given year. Such ironies of the supposed 'white slave crusade' went unremarked in the papers.

In 1908 Guy Scholefield came to London as the most desirable of immigrants, after he had applied for and been offered the enviable post of 'our own special London correspondent' by the New Zealand Press Association. He and his wife Adela boarded the old-fashioned steamer the SS *Morayshire*, which made the voyage to London via Cape Horn. 'It was not a luxury liner,' Scholefield later recalled, 'but it made us appreciate the comforts supplied when we thought of the tiny sailing ship in which my mother's family had voyaged to New Zealand.'[40] After stops in Montevideo and the Canary Islands, they arrived in London and began to make a temporary home in a large bay-fronted house in the Victorian suburb of Streatham. It was here that the couple's first child, Jack, was born.[41] Two other children would follow before the family returned to New Zealand a decade later, at the end of the First World War.

The London that Scholefield arrived in had been utterly transformed since the days when his father, John, had lived in England in the 1860s. The same drive for economic, social and moral reform that had convulsed the little town of Milton in New Zealand had changed the landscape – physically and culturally – in the world's largest city as well. These changes could be felt most acutely in the heart of the city, through which Scholefield passed on his daily walk to the New Zealand High Commission. The tangle of slum land to the north of the Strand had been razed, and through it had been pushed the modern thoroughfares of Shaftesbury Avenue and Charing Cross Road. Oxford Street had morphed from a residential area into the shopping centre of London, with new department stores offering work for ambitious 'shop girls', who could never afford the wares they sold.

The medieval streets, squares and cemeteries around St Martin-in-the-Fields and Drury Lane become the home of the London School of Economics. Scholefield, who would soon enrol there to take a degree in economics and political science, found the process remarkable. 'For many months I sauntered through the churchyard of St Clement,' he wrote, 'watching industry pushing out vestiges of history – an army of labourers working to prepare a site for the warehouse of WH Smith and Son, publishers. Bones, earth, gravestones and fragments cascaded into the barrows at my feet ... on their way to a new resting place in East London.'[42]

As the maps of the social investigator Charles Booth showed Scholefield, it was East and South London to which poverty and raucous street life had been pushed as well. Compared to a generation earlier, when large groups of 'unfortunate' women would crowd the pavements of Regent Street and the Haymarket, meeting gentlemen from the clubs, central London was 'an open-air cathedral'. Now women solicited furtively and alone, some relying on pimps to keep an eye out for the police. The brothels that had peppered Piccadilly and St James's had given way to single furnished rooms rented from dodgy landlords, tucked down back alleys in Soho. The great war on 'white slavery' and vice may have done little to abolish it, but it had at least helped it to disappear from sight.

On the morning of 21 July 1910, Guy Scholefield did not take his usual walk to the high commissioner's office. Instead, as the high commissioner had suggested, he made his way up through the furnished rooms, cafés and restaurants of Soho to Great Marlborough Street police court. Passing through the stone doorway into the court's busy foyer, Scholefield found Courtroom One and joined the other reporters on the bench. It was the first and – as near as I can tell – the last case of 'white slavery' he would ever cover, a deeply unexpected duty of being the New Zealand Associated Press's 'own special London correspondent', but he took his reporter's notebook from his pocket and prepared to write.

Scholefield would never have counted himself among the ranks of the sensation-seeking 'new' journalists from the 'gutter press'. Though he was dedicated to social and moral reforms like Temperance and welfare, he was conservative in his language and interests and mostly endeavoured to communicate the news factually and without melodrama. Yet as soon as the trial began, it must have become clear to him that sensation would be difficult to avoid.

That summer day in late July began the final hearing to determine whether the case involving the New Zealand girl 'Doris Williams' would go all the way to the highest court. The prosecuting council and the defence rose as the magistrate took his bench, and the prisoners were led into the courtroom from the Black Maria that had carried them to Great Marlborough Street from Brixton Prison. Next to Scholefield, a newspaper artist from the *Marylebone Mercury*

The prisoners: ANTONIUS CELLIS and ALEXANDER BERARD (in circle).

11: An unknown court artist's sketch of the men known as 'Aldo Cellis' and 'Alexander Berard' that appeared in *Reynolds's Newspaper* in July, 1910.

sketched furiously, producing two images of the prisoners in profile. It was a fair likeness, though it emphasised their southern European features heavily: thick brows, Roman noses and dark, sunken eyes. The police detective, one Ernest Anderson, took a seat in the inspector's box. Then the witnesses were led in. They all looked painfully young.

The magistrate, seated upon a wooden dais, called the court to order. He cleared the room of any women who were not witnesses, as was customary, lest their delicate sensibilities be offended by what they would hear. The solicitor for the prosecution rose to give his opening remarks. 'The facts of this case are of a loathsome and disgusting character,' he warned the court. First, the three French girls took turns being questioned, and gave their responses to the prosecutor's questions via a translator. Then the defence stood to question them about their sexual histories. Victoria Bricot proved a particularly untrustworthy witness, refusing, it seems, to play the role of 'white slave'.

Finally the girl going by the name of Doris Williams was called to the witness box, and she made the journey from the side-bench on which she waited. Did she look at the tiles on the floor or the wooden railings? Or was her head high, her face illuminated by the light that poured through the glass ceiling? At last she reached the raised dais, boxed in on three sides. She could keep her hands at her sides to prevent the courtroom from seeing them shaking, but because she was forced to stand, her legs may have betrayed her.

She was good-looking and well dressed, Scholefield jotted down in his notebook. Accustomed to recording, in rapid shorthand, the speeches of Asquith and Lloyd George, Scholefield now scribbled down the stilted testimony of a frightened eighteen-year-old girl. She spoke with the soft accent of his very own South Otago.

'I was eighteen in June last,' she told the court, 'but I met Mr Cellis six months ago.'

She had been working at a photographer's studio in Wellington, she replied after the prosecutor's question, and she used to sleep in a respectable boarding house. She was a hardworking, respectable girl. Her ordeal had clearly interrupted her sense of time, and she was not able to say precisely when she had met Mr Cellis and his wife, Marie: was it January or was it February? In any case it must have seemed a lifetime ago to her. They had shown her high boots and silk underwear, and had told her that she would have to 'see gentlemen'.

The questions moved on to her time in Buenos Aires. We will never know precisely what she was asked or how she answered, but her comments would most likely have outlined the material in her surviving witness statement: soliciting in the Casino, being forced to have sex with old and dirty men, Carvelli demanding oral sex. Even if Scholefield had been the sort of reporter who was unscrupulous enough to write these details, there would be no way it would ever be legal to print them: obscenity law, and the mores of the general public, forbade it. Instead he summarised the young women's ordeal in a single line: 'What took place was of a horrible and revolting character,' he wrote.[43]

Her cross-examination attempted to portray her as less innocent than she claimed. Had she ever been with a man, before travelling with Mr and Mrs Cellis? Mr Newton, the council for the defence, interrogated. She admitted that she had had a sweetheart in Wellington. Mr Newton pressed on. Why had she consented to go with this couple? She replied that she thought she would like to travel. It was a guileless, foolish answer: exactly the sort of story the audience in the courtroom had been taught to expect.

The magistrate, G. L. Denman, had heard enough. He committed the prisoners to trial at the Central Criminal Court, charged with conspiracy and with procuring for the purposes of prostitution under the 1885 Criminal Law Amendment Act. Bail was set at £500 and £200 for Carvelli and di Nicotera respectively: intentionally high, knowing that it was unlikely either would be able to pay it. They were taken back to Brixton Prison in the Black Maria. Scholefield exited the gallery – leaving the police court reporters to cover the next unfortunate tale due before the bench.

Despite the necessary obfuscations, Scholefield's reporting on the case involved some of the most sensational language he had ever employed, and he used the case of 'Doris Williams' to challenge New Zealand's image of itself as sheltered from the darker problems of modern life. 'A startling evidence has just come to light of the terrible reality of the White Slave Traffic,' Scholefield wrote. 'So far as was generally known, the traffic existed chiefly between America, Europe and the Far East, but a very sad case has just come to light which indicates that there are bands of miscreants even in New Zealand procuring girls for the markets of Buenos Aires and elsewhere.' This was a subtle but important critique of a young country that exhibited, in Scholefield's words, 'adolescent nationalism'.[44] New Zealand had only just begun to forge a political identity as a new, independent Dominion that was prosperous, progressive and wholesome.

Scholefield continued, outlining the 'unfortunate girl' from Wellington's shocking downward spiral. She was, like all young white New Zealand women were imagined to be, a 'thoroughly respectable, hard-working girl', but she had been lured away by fine clothes and her dreams of travel. 'The end of the horrible story,' he concluded, 'was that she had become a common woman of the street.' She had been rescued 'by merest luck' from 'the life of shame for which she was dragged away'. Like journalists before and after him, Scholefield justified his brief foray into sensational reporting by the good it might do for society. 'The story,' he concluded, 'though not a savoury one, ought to be told as a warning to other girls who might be deceived in the same way, and to their parents.'[45] Instead of posting the article by steamship to the Press Association's newspapers back in New Zealand, he telegraphed all 500 words from his London office that same day, at significant expense.

For those deeply invested in the image of a moral and orderly New Zealand, Scholefield's unsavoury warning about trafficking in Wellington was seen as a serious threat to their authority and vigilance. For starters, he had intimated that the police had done little to stop this 'band of miscreants' from operating in the capital. More broadly, his article suggested that New Zealand was not immune to the problems of organised crime and trafficking, and that those in power were ignoring these urgent issues. Soon Scholefield had a telegraph from his editor at the *Evening Post*: a judge had issued a suppression order on all reporting of the case, and the newspaper would not be allowed to print his story until it was lifted. All that would go to press on 23 July would be a short paragraph, outlining the basics of the case.

It is clear from the paper trail that survives that the suppression order was an intervention that had come all the way from the top. With journalists temporarily muzzled, the New Zealand prime minister Joseph Ward wrote to the Wellington police and the Department of Justice, emphasising the need to get the story straight before the news broke in the papers. It would be particularly important to prove that the 'unfortunate girl' from Wellington was not the 'thoroughly respectable, hard-working girl' that she – and Scholefield – had claimed her to be.[46]

This was, perhaps ironically, the same goal that Carvelli and di Nicotera's defence solicitor had in mind. Rather than protesting the innocence of his clients, Mr Newton would put all his weight into proving the culpability of the young women – relying on the law's wording, and its vision of what innocence looked like, to undo the case against the two men. The police solicitors, responsible for turning the investigation of Ernest Anderson and his team into a successful prosecution, were worried. The case was, they explained, 'a somewhat difficult and anxious one owing to the class of women and girl we have to deal with'. Mr Newton was a 'doughty opponent', who would not hesitate to introduce doubts about the sexual histories of the young victims in court. Nonetheless, the police solicitors believed it was worth the fight: 'In these two men we have ruffians deeply implicated in the white slave traffic,' they wrote in their notes, 'and it is of the highest public importance that – if possible – convictions should be secured against them.' Inspector Anderson agreed. He was deeply concerned, he explained in a report to the head the CID, that the pair would escape conviction because of the previous histories of the women, and 'be absolutely free to commence their nefarious practices again.'[47]

Sometime in August 1910 it seems that Mr Newton realised the jig was up for his clients. The three young French girls were easy enough to dismiss: they had all admitted loose sexual behaviour, and one of them had been denounced by the Paris police as a prostitute. Not only this, but Newton would have planned to play English prejudices about immoral French women to his advantage. Doris Williams, on the other hand, was another story. She was a white colonial and, other than her Antipodean twang, acted every bit the English girl. Her guileless dreams of travel and fine clothes, and her history of respectable work, played into the expected narrative of 'white slavery'. After a month of considering this, and perhaps after trying and failing to find anything against Doris Williams, Mr Newton decided it would be too risky to allow all the charges to proceed. His clients, it seems, agreed.

They would pursue a plea bargain. They would plead guilty to the first charge – 'conspiring with a woman unknown to procure Mireille Lapara and Marguerite Bescançon, unmarried girls, aged 17 and 18 years respectively, to become common prostitutes' – and the other charges would be dropped. This 'conspiracy' offence was a common-law charge that referred to the conspiracy to commit a crime, not to the crime itself. It meant that the men would be punished and imprisoned, but the more serious charges under the 1885 Criminal Law Amendment Act for the actual trafficking offences would not proceed. The prosecution, still deeply worried that the case would fall apart if it were to rest solely on the evidence of four imperfect victims, reluctantly accepted the deal. If it proceeded, the prosecution ran the very high risk of seeing the men acquitted, even if it knew that, in making a deal, Carvelli's and di Nicotera's sentences would be 'utterly inadequate'. This was the daily reality of work in prosecutions for sexual crime.

It was lucky that Mr Newton didn't read the New Zealand papers. On 30 August the suppression order was lifted and Scholefield's article finally went to print, more than a month after he had sent it. In the intervening time the Wellington police had supplied the prime minister with enough information to enable him to announce in Parliament the next day that the supposedly innocent girl had been 'living an immoral life' in the capital, before she had gone to Buenos Aires. He wanted to make a statement before Parliament, he explained, lest anyone think that 'some respectable girl' had 'been decoyed away'.[48] After all, no police force or prime minister could be accused of ignoring the problem of 'white slavery' in New Zealand if it was made clear that the problem didn't really exist.

Scholefield was made to look a fool for suggesting in his original article that there was a 'white slave traffic' in New Zealand. The *New Zealand Truth*, the country's premier tabloid, relished mocking the up-and-coming reporter and the 'respectable' papers that he worked for. 'The young man who left the staff of a Wellington daily paper to go 'Ome, and there represent the cream of the Dominion's cleanest daily papers as "our own special London correspondent", seems to have badly blundered,' its lengthy article on the case began, calling Scholefield's original report a 'ludicrous sensation'.[49] For the stoical journalist who had dedicated his life to reporting the objective facts, even when he found them uninspiring, this last charge must surely have stung. After these personal attacks, Scholefield may have borne a grudge for the way the politicians had censored and then twisted his work. Many years later, as he reflected on the New Zealand politicians he had come to know in his time as a reporter, he mused that Joseph Ward, the prime minister who had ensured that his own work was mocked, 'lacked the qualities necessary for a leader'.[50]

Scholefield returned to the more usual duties of 'our special London correspondent' after this scandalous trial, leaving the high commissioner, William Hall-Jones, to try and convince Joseph Ward and his government to assist in Lydia Harvey's repatriation. Scholefield reported on Shackleton's next voyage to Antarctica, racehorses that were being sent to New Zealand, and the latest in the campaign for imperial preference tariffs. But before long he found himself a war correspondent instead, covering the battles and deaths of young New Zealand men on the western and southern fronts of the First World War. He received his OBE for the Dominion of New Zealand in 1919, and shortly afterwards he and his family left the privations of post-war London. By the mid-1920s Scholefield had largely left behind the charged and fast-paced world of journalism and had become the official New Zealand parliamentary librarian, as well as the comptroller of its archives, in 1926. It was a role that demanded the utmost political neutrality and absolutely no sensationalism.

CHAPTER FOUR

THE RESCUER

It was around ten o'clock at night on 9 July 1910 when the bells on the telephone box began to ring, making Eilidh MacDougall jump. Unhooking the receiver and lifting it to her ear, she heard the operator tell her she was connecting her to Detective Inspector Ernest Anderson at Marlborough Street Police Station. Anderson's voice crackled on the line. He told her he'd just picked up a girl in Piccadilly who said she was from New Zealand, and who he was sure was connected to a 'white slave' case that he'd been working on for weeks. Could she come up and try to get a statement out of the girl? He was sending a taxicab, straight away.

As she waited for her car to arrive, MacDougall smoothed her unruly hair and finished the letter she was writing, blotted it and recapped the ink bottle. It was another plea for donations for the newly opened Metropolitan Police Home for Women and Girls, which was still missing some essentials: clothes for the residents, books and games, and furniture. The girls who came here, she wrote, had 'all been through some shock or tragedy' and were often 'brought in without anything except the clothes they stand in, they often have no change of linen or clothes'.[1] Once the dramatic news stories of 'white slavery' ended and the traffickers had been arrested, it was women like Eilidh MacDougall who stepped in to actually care for the victims, who so often, and so ironically, became forgotten amid the moral clamour to do something about sex trafficking.

Like many of the women who would come to dedicate their lives to charitable and social work, Eilidh MacDougall came from a wealthy and stable family and could afford to take demanding work for little pay. Her father, the son of a wealthy landowner, was born in Jamaica and christened in St Catherine's church as Alexander William MacDougall in 1837.[2] Alexander's father, William Church MacDougall, was a landowner, and his grandfather (Eilidh's great-grandfather), Alexander MacDougall, was likely the same man who was listed as receiving £100 compensation for the loss of four slaves in 1835. It is impossible to say whether Eilidh knew or was ever troubled by this family history, or was aware of the irony that part of the wealth that helped her save 'white slaves' had come from the exploitation of black men, women and children. It was, after all, a history that many English and Scottish imperial families shared.[3]

In 1862 Eilidh's father left Jamaica, trained as a barrister and married Cassandra Bird, an English woman from Cheltenham in Gloucestershire. The couple had seven children and Lorna Eilidh Louisa MacDougall was their fourth, born in 1871 at the Clan MacDougall's ancestral home in Argyll, Oban.[4] Her childhood was split between Scotland and her mother's home county of Gloucestershire, until the family moved to Oakhurst House in Westcombe Park, Greenwich, when Eilidh was a teenager.[5] Although she continued to make frequent visits to Oban, her working life was spent in London.

12: Eilidh MacDougall, an early twentieth-century social worker
and path-breaking advocate for the rights of victims of sexual crime.
She is pictured here (top: right; bottom: third from the left)
in 1915 with her family (likely her cousins) at Clan MacDougall's ancestral
home of Dunollie Castle in Oban, Scotland. Five years earlier, she took
Lydia Harvey's witness statement and sheltered her while she awaited trial.

The MacDougalls' richly appointed, six-bedroom home in Greenwich was surrounded by the grinding poverty that stretched across the whole of South London. On Charles Booth's map, published in 1898, Eilidh's neighbourhood was marked by the red-and-yellow colour code of affluence; the red houses meant 'well-to-do' and the golden ones meant 'wealthy'. But beyond the ring of streets around Greenwich Park and Blackheath, to the west, lay the neighbourhoods of Deptford, Lewisham, Rotherhithe and Brixton, where the colours grew darker. While some households were 'fairly comfortable' and 'mixed', the majority were 'poor', or worse. Deptford and Lambeth, which lay further west, were two of the darkest spots on the whole of London's map. Here, all but the houses and shops on the main streets were coloured with the markers of want and extreme poverty; and many of the back-alley slums were coloured in black, signalling, in Booth's words, that they were inhabited by the 'lowest class, vicious, semi-criminal'.[6]

This was the world into which Eilidh MacDougall, the barrister's daughter, walked when she left the family home, determined to help the girls and young women whose poverty also rendered them more vulnerable to unwanted pregnancy, abuse and exploitation. She was far from the only woman to be called to such 'rescue work'. This largely voluntary endeavour was the chief way that middle-class women were able to work outside the home and, several decades before social work formally professionalised itself, these women saw their rescue work as a calling or a career. Thousands of middle- and upper-class women like Eilidh MacDougall ran secular philanthropic organisations, volunteered at shelters, sat on the boards of religious charities and metropolitan councils and sometimes, as MacDougall did, walked the blackest streets themselves.

She first started working as a social worker locally, joining the Greenwich and Deptford Workhouse Girls' Aid Committee in 1894. Their records show her as an active member, who was able to garner the support of her extended and wealthy family: she and five other MacDougalls donated more than £30 to the Rochester Diocesan Association for the Care of Friendless Girls that same year.[7] Similar organisations stretched across London, often coordinated by national committees or rescue-work unions. It was a time before state-funded social care and, for the poor and vulnerable, these sorts of charities often represented the only way to survive calamity. This expanding network of rescue and charity organisations ran mother-and-baby homes, homeless shelters, soup kitchens, midnight Bible meetings, children's homes, asylums and rescue homes.

MacDougall worked within a system of such organisations, based in London, that were connected to the Church of England. By 1901, at the age of thirty, she had taken up a new post with the Southwark Diocesan Association in Lambeth, where the social problems and the poverty were even more acute than in Greenwich and Deptford. Her main job was visiting young, pregnant and unmarried women and girls in the workhouse and the local infirmaries. Aside from the relatively rare case of playing matchmaker between a pregnant girl and a young father-to-be, MacDougall's work consisted mostly of helping girls who remained – in the parlance of the time – friendless.

As the Southwark Diocesan Association put it in a plea for funding, Lambeth was a place where girls and young women were 'thrown up upon our southern shore by the need for cheap shelter'.[8] The crumbling casebooks of the Association for the Care of Friendless Girls provide brief snapshots of these castaways. Some women were ill and without any means of subsistence, like eighteen-year-old Maude, who had an epileptic fit after the birth of her baby. Others were bereaved, destitute and mentally ill. Thirty-three-year-old Dora tried to drown herself for the third time in 1902; a woman named Hilda 'seemed very despairing, having been prevented by a policeman from throwing herself over Westminster bridge, the night before'.[9] Twenty-six-year-old Lilian's first baby had died, and she 'was most anxious' that she and her seven-month-old child be helped. A fifteen-year-old's baby was taken into care at the workhouse, but died two weeks later. Her behaviour became so bad that she was forced to leave the maternity home.[10]

Many other young women had been sexually assaulted, abused and raped. Fifteen-year-old Florence 'mixed with bad companions' at an Embankment coffee shop and was five months pregnant, after being assaulted in a flat by an older man named Jack Bates.[11] Charlotte, eighteen, said that her master's brother 'took advantage of her – but he denies it'.[12] Fifteen-year-old Lily was raped by her father and was two months pregnant. When the police went to arrest him, they found he had committed suicide by ingesting poison. Lily was placed in a temporary home, but 'screamed there so much that the neighbours complained'.[13] The sheer magnitude of these offences, reported or otherwise – the quotidian nature of sexual assault and rape – is only just coming to be quantified and understood by historians.[14]

Just below the surface of any given community lay many

such stories. Nellie Mathie, the girl who had won the first-prize gold bangle in the beauty contest at the opera house in Oamaru had, at the age of twelve, been a victim of a violent rape by her aunt's neighbour. The man's breath had smelled of cigarettes, Nellie told the court. She had asked Jesus to help her.[15] In a tangled coincidence of patriarchy, power and proximity, it was Harry G. C. Harvey who defended William Gilchrist, twelve-year-old Nellie Mathie's rapist, in 1899. The girl could not positively identify her assailant, Lydia's father claimed in court. After all, many men in the area smoked.

MacDougall's work with these young women and girls varied according to their needs. Though she was not a lawyer, she used her familiarity with the law to help them pursue justice in the courts, and to pursue the fathers of their babies in order to get formal affiliation orders. At other times, she would help them secure support through more informal means. She made fostering arrangements for their new babies, and found the mothers domestic-service positions after their post-partum confinement. For the large number of girls and young women who had become pregnant through incest or rape, MacDougall also coaxed them into making statements against their abusers. She became a regular fixture at the police station and the police court, often spotted with a distressed and visibly pregnant girl in tow. Once the girl's statement was taken and a charge was made against her abuser, MacDougall very often brought the girl in question back to her own two-bed flat on Lambeth Road. There were few other places for them to go: MacDougall clearly could not bear to place a traumatised pregnant girl in a crowded shelter or punitive workhouse ward.

Her empathy for these women, and her determination to

secure justice for them, permeates the thin archive she has left behind. After almost a decade of informally assisting the police with prosecutions for trafficking and sexual assault, MacDougall was officially appointed by the Metropolitan Police in 1908 as a 'lady assistant': the first woman employed in this capacity with a police force anywhere in the UK, and probably one of the first in the world. Her job was to take statements from women and girls who had been trafficked and assaulted, because the police felt, and MacDougall agreed, that male police officers were ill-suited to this delicate and distasteful task.

When Inspector Anderson rang MacDougall late in the evening of 9 July 1910, it was not an unfamiliar appeal or an unexpected hour. She left her flat promptly and arrived at Great Marlborough Street Police Station by taxicab around half past ten. She climbed the stone steps and walked into a noisy entry hall, which was filled with drunks, men and women with battered faces, grubby children, prostitutes and pickpockets. Uniformed constables came and went, leading a parade of typical arrests: it was Saturday night in the heart of Soho. Anderson, in a detective's plain clothes, found her and escorted her to where a young woman sat in the inspector's room, warmed by a little fire in a grate. She wore an ill-fitting dress and the roots of her mousy brown hair were visible beneath the peroxide blonde. She looked very young.

Miss MacDougall sat down and introduced herself, telling the girl she was there to ask about what had happened to her, and saying that she could help put in prison the man who had misled and harmed her. But the girl was tired, nervous and cagey. She told Miss MacDougall that her name was Doris Williams and that she was from New Zealand. She had gone to Wellington to work as a domestic servant, and then in a photographer's studio. She had met a woman named Marie and a man called Cellis, her husband. Why had she gone away with them? 'They said it would be an easy life with nice dresses, and it was that that induced me to go with them and also I was glad to be able to travel.'

With MacDougall's coaxing, the girl briefly recounted her journey to Buenos Aires, her time in a regulated brothel there and the subsequent voyage to London. She was adamant that before meeting the couple she had never worked as a prostitute and was respectable. She spoke the last words of her statement clearly: 'I have never done that sort of thing for money or presents before meeting the Cellises and I regret that I ever met them.' MacDougall, listening to this line, knew what was at stake. This Doris Williams was an English-speaking white girl from the Dominions, claimed to be sexually inexperienced and her testimony was painfully naïve. MacDougall recorded her responses to the questioning, carefully crafting a first-person witness statement that would be useful for the prosecution. At the bottom of the statement, which was written in MacDougall's distinctive penmanship, the girl shakily signed 'Doris Williams' in her own hand.[16]

Eilidh MacDougall knew it was her job to turn the real, complicated girls she encountered in the police station into the perfect victims that the judge, the jury and the newspaper men were expecting them to be. It required a knowledge of law and jurisprudence, and if she had been a man she would surely have studied to become a barrister, like her father. Years after she left home, she could still often be found in his well-appointed study in his large Victorian house in Black-heath, asking him about the finer legal points of the cases she had encountered. How could she apply the bastardy laws to chase down wayward fathers? What was the burden of proof for a five-year-old girl who had been abused by her neighbour? What powers did rescue workers have to remove children from the home of a sexually abusive father? Did a twelve-year-old's pregnancy count as proof of her assault? What did she need to get a young woman to say in order to ensure that her trafficker was sent to prison? 'He was tremendously interested in my work,' she recalled in 1924, some ten years after her father's death. 'I used often to consult him, and from him there is no doubt I got a good deal of legal training.'[17]

MacDougall also knew that the vast majority of victims did not report the crimes, and were often coerced and threatened into silence, either by their abuser or by knowledge of a criminal-justice system that would offer them little recompense for airing their shame. She suspected that Doris Williams was not this girl's real name, and that nineteen was probably not her real age, but whether the girl would ever be willing to tell her the truth remained to be seen. Many victims refused to speak altogether. The testimony that Doris Williams gave was short, stilted and clearly withheld much. It – like the testimony of so many young women whom Eilidh MacDougall interviewed over the years – represented an attempt by Doris to protect and obscure herself, a narrative woven as a kind of armour.[18] After all, what would be gained from the truth?

Young women like Doris often refused to play along with the expectations of the authorities. As the casebooks of the

Southwark Diocesan Association for the Care of Friendless Girls show, many disappeared after they had been charged with some crime themselves, or after the birth of their babies, unwilling to be helped, monitored or sent off to domestic-service situations. Sarah was 'discharged from the Police Court and has not been heard of since'. Hilda, found in very bad company, 'quite refused to leave the house and said she should go into the workhouse for her confinement'.[19]

Girls like Hilda often came honestly by their disdain for rescue, and rescue workers. Homes were usually punitive, and had as a primary objective the moral and religious reform of young errant women, with all the judgement and condemnation such reform could bring. But they also had an ulterior motive. These homes were places where wayward girls and women were shunted into low-paid, low-status jobs in laundry work and domestic service in order to plug the profound labour shortage in these sectors, and to raise money to run the homes and charities themselves. Babies were a profound inconvenience in these contexts, preventing young women from doing this work, and so their babies were fostered out or adopted by wealthier families. This is where the notorious 'baby-farmers' like Oamaru's Minnie Dean would sometimes come in.

The Southwark Diocesan Association for the Care of Friendless Girls, unlike many other rescue organisations, was adamant that suitable young women should be kept with their newborn babies, because it 'strengthens the sense of parental responsibility'.[20] But the young mothers could not stay with their babies for very long, because the vast majority were forced to go into live-in domestic service after their convalescence, in order to pay for their child's care. It caused Eilidh MacDougall great anxiety to place a newborn baby in a foster home that was not satisfactory, with only the workhouse as an alternative, believing as she did that 'an unloved child never thrives'.[21] Still, she participated in this traffic in babies born of mothers who could not afford, or be permitted, to keep them, as they scrubbed the floors of the comfortable classes in the red and golden houses of Booth's London.

In an era when cheap domestic labour was getting more difficult to find, rescue workers engaged in what the historian April Haynes has called a 'tender traffic': shunting the daughters of the poor 'out of brothels, and into kitchens'.[22] The daughters of the poor, for their part, seemed well aware of these designs. As one feminist writer put it, 'No scheme of rescue appears to have the slightest chance of success while prostitution is not only the best paid, but the only well-paid profession for large numbers of girls ... under present conditions nobody can pretend that a respectable life of work is a guarantee of tolerable comfort and well-being.'[23] It is little wonder that young women often deliberately obscured their identities and intentions under interrogation, and refused offers of 'rescue'.

The idea that women who were in danger of becoming prostitutes needed to be 'rescued', and that those who already had become prostitutes needed to be 'reformed', was a very old one, which had its roots in pre-modern religious penitentiaries. Even in the early twentieth century some homes and organisations still operated under this long, usually condemnatory tradition and required women to live under strict discipline and spartan conditions. While these sorts of institutions were falling out of favour in early twentieth-century

England, the attitude that penitence, self-denial and religious teaching were essential to women's salvation was still a prevailing approach. Some young women may have appreciated this, or at least put up with it, in a period when there were few other options between a down-and-out young woman and starvation. Many others had no choice; rescue homes often operated as an arm of the prison system: young women were admitted against their will and then kept under lock and key.

But the records of these homes also teem with reports of misbehaviour, ingratitude and escape. Young women, it seems, were often highly resistant towards efforts to reform them, and preferred to choose a life of freedom on their own terms. They swore, thumbed noses, stole food and, in the dead of night, climbed high walls and slipped back into the city. Rescue workers emphasised the importance of separating out such women – many of whom had sold sex for money and had every intention of returning to this life – from those who were only 'at risk' of turning to prostitution. These unrepentant women were undeserving of rescue, impossible to reform and exposed the whole rescue-and-reform movement as a failure.

By the early twentieth century the panic over 'white slavery' had added a new urgency, and international reach, to 'rescue work'. And while men were in the overwhelming majority in the ballrooms, palaces and government offices where officials met to sign international anti-trafficking agreements, the foot soldiers of this new movement were women. The National Vigilance Association and the International Bureau for the Suppression of the 'White Slave Traffic' relied upon a worldwide network of mostly female moral reformers and rescue workers, who scoured the sea-ports and patrolled the railway stations of Britain's empire and the wider world.

There was Cecily McCall in Egypt, who did her best to convince the young women who poured in from Eastern Europe and France via Constantinople to choose a more righteous line of work or, better still, to go home and let the local girls, whom she wrote about in deeply racist terms, take over. There was Rosalie Lighton Robinson in Buenos Aires, who lived in the YWCA hostel and travelled down to the docks whenever a ship from Europe was due in. She searched for the girls who looked, in panic, for someone who wasn't there, or whose male companions held their arms too tightly. She helped girls find respectable work and took them to safe hostels, and tried to save the ones she could from the brink of 'white slavery'. In an era with very few central services, women like Lighton Robison must have been a godsend to some stranded women travellers. But when there were no 'white slaves' to save, she spent her days tearing down indecent advertisements in shop windows and informing local police about cafés and *pensións* that were being run as clandestine brothels.[24] Like many other rescue workers, Rosalie Lighton Robinson offered both help and condemnation.

Back in London, Miss MacDougall did her best within a fundamentally cruel system, and tried to make it clear to the girls and young women she encountered that she was truly there to help and not condemn. But we can presume that Lydia Harvey, still pretending to be Doris Williams, was sus-picious of Miss MacDougall. Her hatred of domestic service, which she shared with many other young women, had seen her abandon her post in Wellington for work in a shop. The threat of having to go back into service was used by Carvelli as an effective tool to keep her working for him, and to keep her from talking to the authorities.

When the girl claiming to be Doris Williams proved unwilling to say any more, Miss MacDougall took her back to the newly opened Police Home for Women and Girls. Their taxicab travelled through dark streets that had grown quiet: the lateness of the hour meant that most respectable revellers had left Soho and gone home. Only the homeless, the desperate and the drunk remained, as the bars and restaurants emptied and the electric lights switched off.

A short trip across Waterloo Bridge saw them arrive at the crumbling terrace house at 198 Lambeth Road, which had just opened as the official safe-house for victims of trafficking in the UK. Technically, the signatory governments of the 1904 International Agreement for the Suppression of the 'White Slave Traffic' were responsible for finding a place to keep such women before their trial. But despite the key role British campaigners had played in getting the first Agreement signed, the UK government, like all other signatory governments, had little intention of doing any more than the bare minimum to adhere to its terms. It had fallen to Eilidh MacDougall and Metropolitan assistant police commissioner Frederick Bullock to find the funds to establish a safe-house. Bullock was able to secure £37 per annum from the Home Office, which would come out of the fund set aside to repatriate trafficking victims. A police fund built by voluntary subscription provided a further £20, and Bullock personally donated another £32. The rest was raised by Eilidh MacDougall's wealthy friend Mary Leaf, who established a fund to pay for the rent of a premises and the room and board of a live-in matron. MacDougall's salary, which was paid by the Home Office and only covered her work as a statement-taker, was not supplemented to cover her add-itional duties, so she resolved to run the Home in her own voluntary time. The Home, furnished with donated bed frames and dressers, and boasting 'a little strip of garden', had opened in Lambeth earlier in 1910.[25] Its total annual budget was dwarfed many times over by the money that had been spent on catering alone at the two international conferences on the 'white slave' trade in Paris and Madrid that same year.

Lydia Harvey stepped across the darkened threshold of 198 Lambeth Road that night with only the clothes on her back. She had travelled across two oceans, had been raped and abused and was 12,000 miles from home. This girl was surely one of the people on MacDougall's mind when she penned the Home's first annual report a few months later. 'The difficulties of dealing with these girls will be readily understood,' she explained. 'They come to us from a life of degradation and excitement; both physically and morally they are wrecks.'[26]

Miss MacDougall introduced the girl to Miss Jackman, the Home's matron, who brought Lydia up to a little room with a comfortable bed and a change of clothes. She was shown where she could bathe and was told that she was safe. Whether she truly believed this or not, by the time the sun came up on her third morning in South London, she was prepared to say more. When Miss MacDougall arrived from her flat across the road on 13 July, the girl told her that her real name was not Doris Williams and she had not just turned nineteen. Her name was Lydia Harvey and she said she was eighteen years old. Her birthday had passed in early June, while she walked the streets of the West End.

Miss MacDougall explained that they must go back to the police station to take a new official statement, and somehow she got Lydia to agree. They travelled through the West End in the daylight this time, when it was filled with business-men and shopping ladies, who thronged the now respectable streets. Inspector Anderson met them in the police station's entrance and they returned to the interview room. Off the record, Anderson and MacDougall promised the girl that her real name would not be read in court, and that she would be introduced as Doris Williams. Only the magistrate would be told the truth, before the trial, in chambers. With these assurances, it was time to begin.

'What is your correct name and age,' MacDougall began, her pen poised above the witness-statement form.

'My correct name is Lydia Rhoda Harvey. My correct age is eighteen on the third of June last.'

This next statement was far longer, and far more detailed and explicit. Throughout the difficult interview MacDougall encouraged Lydia to speak of the men she had been forced to have sex with, of being coerced into sex with Carvelli, of watching Marie perform oral sex on him. She spoke of her venereal disease, of her fear and upset, of her worry about having to go back into domestic service and her fear of her mother discovering what she had done. 'He said if I gave information to the police they would put me in a home and then into service where I would have to work for other people,' she admitted, as Miss MacDougall's hand scratched across the page. There are hints that Lydia still held truths back, or that she herself was unclear on crucial details.

According to the most compelling evidence, she had turned seventeen in June 1910, not eighteen. It was fairly common for people to be confused as to their birth year, and Lydia – born in obscurity and unregistered – may have had special reason to be unsure. Or she may have got used to lying about her age. In any case, sixteen pages later, Lydia Harvey signed her real name in a steadier hand.

MacDougall had secured Lydia's full statement just in time for Carvelli and di Nicotera's next police-court trial on 20 July, at which Lydia would have to testify. MacDougall needed to make sure she was well prepared. Do not look at him, she told Lydia; and be prepared to feel nauseous as the trial unfolds. Fifteen years later, Woman Police Officer Dorothy Peto recalled a standard strategy that she shared with young women who were about to testify on their experience of sexual assault: 'when you feel sick, turn your back to the judge, be sick in this envelope, hand it to me – I shall be standing just behind you'.[27]

On the morning of 20 July 1910, Lydia Harvey and Miss MacDougall walked up the stone steps of Marlborough Street police court and into the busy foyer. Those who had made bail were on their way out of the station after a long night in the cells; solicitors met their clients, and court reporters arrived for what promised to be a well-attended session. Anderson appeared and told them what time the trial was scheduled for, and they sat and waited. Soon another woman appeared with the girl Mireille in tow, along with the two other French girls whom Lydia had briefly met on the streets of Soho. Their language differences meant that little was said between them; but perhaps there was also simply little to say.

The bailiff arrived to fetch the four girls and Miss

MacDougall, and they all filed into the courtroom. It was smaller than one might expect, with a crowd of onlookers packed tightly in the gallery, which was so close to the wooden witness box, solicitors' benches and prisoners' dock that those in them could hear the scratching of the court reporters' pens across their notebook pages. Along a back wall covered in books lay a long wooden bench on a dais, at which a stern-looking man in a sombre suit sat in judgement, flanked by a clerk who sat beside a huge ledger, and a bailiff. The whole place had been designed to intimidate the criminals on trial and, as usual, no thought was given to the fact that it intimidated victims in equal measure. When it was her turn to be questioned, Lydia took her place in the wood-panelled witness box, having no choice but to be part of the spectacle.

A trial for 'white slavery' in 1910 was like something out of a salacious novel, and people frequently treated the police court as a cheap source of entertainment. The presiding magistrate, G. L. Denman, had cleared the court of all female spectators, which was the usual practice in cases of sexual crime. As she stood in the witness box, Lydia stared out at a sea of strange faces, and every one – save that of Miss MacDougall and her fellow witnesses – was male. She answered the questions she was asked, and if she was sick, no one bothered to record it. At the prompting of the police-court solicitor, she told her story. She was working at a photographer's studio outside Wellington when a fellow lodger offered to introduce her to someone who could help her travel. The court reporters scribbled furiously.

MacDougall and Anderson were true to their word, and Lydia was permitted to say that her name was Doris

Williams, which was a rare and important concession on the part of the police and the magistrate, in order to protect her from exposure by the press. These 'horrible little papers', as MacDougall called them, often made the victim a spectacle in her neighbourhood and heightened her distress.[28] For the rest of her career, MacDougall advocated for a law or an order that would protect the identity of victims, but she would not live to see it happen. It was not until 1992 that anonymity for victims was secured, almost forty years after her death.

As Anderson had predicted, Lydia Harvey's testimony was the crucial factor in the magistrate's decision to send Antonio Carvelli and Alessandro di Nicotera's case on to the country's highest criminal court, on several charges under the 1885 Criminal Law Amendment Act and the common-law charge of conspiracy to commit a crime. For the police it was a victory, but also a challenge. The trial would take months to be scheduled and, in the meantime, they had four young women who had to be fed, housed and, most crucially of all, kept under lock and key in London. These young women were essential witnesses in the trials against their traffickers, but were very liable to go missing: leaving their furnished rooms without notice, sneaking out of rescue homes in the dead of night. This wasn't the first trial for trafficking that had presented such problems.

Sometimes these women were simply seeking freedom on their own terms. At other times it was the dread of having to testify in court, having to speak publicly about their rape, humiliation and working as a prostitute, that caused them to flee. But in other cases they had been enticed or threatened by their traffickers. They were promised more money and more affection, or were threatened with exposure and harm.

As these young women disappeared back into the labyrinthine streets of Soho and Montmartre, and onto steamships bound for South America, the case that the police had built went with them.

In order to prevent such a thing happening to his case, DI Anderson had asked William Coote of the National Vigilance Association to find a Catholic, French-speaking rescue home or shelter for the three French girls, but this proved easier said than done. Not only was Victoria Bricot denied admission, due to venereal disease, but when Coote tried to place Marguerite Bescançon in a Catholic refuge home run by the Convent of the Good Shepherd in Liverpool Street, she had to be moved 'because of her unwillingness to settle down to the strict rules of the convent'. He had placed Mireille Lapara in a shelter known as the Catholic Settlement, but this proved, somewhat euphemistically, to be 'unsuitable for long-term accommodation'.[29] Finally, he found a place for all three at a Catholic home run by the nuns at the St Margaret of Cortona Convent, all the way out in Canning Town. These women religious appeared able, for the time being at least, to keep Anderson's key witnesses confined and isolated enough to prevent them running off into the streets of London and disappearing.

No record of their treatment there survives, although we can see from extensive historical research that rescue homes run by Catholic nuns were among the strictest and most punitive, maintaining many of the penitentiary aspects of older reform homes.[30] It may be that, like thousands of other young women, Marguerite, Mireille and Victoria had their hair hacked off, ate meagre, bland meals and slept in deliberately uncomfortable bedding. It is very likely they were forced to do manual labour in the convent, such as laundry or cleaning. Escape would have been difficult, not least because Canning Town was, in London terms, in the middle of nowhere. Here, behind the sombre and solid red brick of the convent, they awaited the moment when they would have to give gruelling testimony once more, and could then look forward to eventual deportation under the 1905 Aliens Act as 'undesirable migrants'.

Lydia Harvey fitted the imagined role of ideal victim more easily. She was more sexually inexperienced, and was a white, Protestant, English-speaking young woman from a British Dominion. This status seems to have enabled her to access a significantly more pleasant form of 'rescue'. After she gave her statement, she returned with Eilidh MacDougall to the Metropolitan Police Home for Women and Girls. Despite its progressive and significantly more congenial accommodation, Lydia must have found her sudden change of lifestyle jarring. On 8 July she was soliciting among the crowds of Piccadilly; on 23 July she was sitting in a small parlour, with the rattle of carts outside the window, doing a jigsaw and playing 'other quiet games'. MacDougall's annual reports always requested donations of clothes, storybooks and puzzles. 'It will be remembered that each one has passed through a time of great excitement, or anxiety, before coming to the Home,' she explained, 'and then if she is waiting to give evidence against some prisoner, she is often frightened and needs to be kept amused, and interested in other things.'[31]

It may have been a kind sort of confinement, but Lydia was still a prisoner. MacDougall insisted that residents should never be allowed to go out on their own. Lydia was 'taken constantly for walks and tram rides', but spent many hours in July and August watching the clock tick down to the trial on 13 September 1910, under the watchful eye of the matron, who kept the doors and windows locked.

On the morning of the trial, the Home's matron Mrs Jackson ensured that Lydia dressed the part. She wore a plain cotton dress, a cast-off from some middle-class sub-scriber to the Southwark Diocesan Association newsletter, and her hair had been trimmed and dyed to rid it of the last traces of peroxide blonde. MacDougall was waiting in the front room to take Lydia to the court by omnibus, which they caught at the top of Lambeth Road. Lydia had a full view of the Houses of Parliament as they crossed Waterloo Bridge.[32] They travelled along the Strand, past the offices of the National Vigilance Association, past the offices of the *Daily Mail* and the New Zealand Press Association on Fleet Street, until at Ludgate Hill they turned to see the intimidating edifice of the Old Bailey.

It was a brand-new and imposing building, built in 1902 on the site where the infamous Newgate Prison once stood. It had only officially opened in 1907, but by the time of Carvelli's trial its courtrooms had heard almost 3,000 cases. As they walked through the courthouse's grand entryway, Eilidh MacDougall glanced up, as she always did, to read the inscription above it – 'Defend the Children of the Poor & Punish the Wrongdoer' – etched into the Portland stone. Much later, reflecting on more than twenty years of trials like Antonio Carvelli's, she confessed that 'As I sit in court listening to the summing up in these cases I sometimes wonder why they engraved those big stone letters outside that building.'[33] She did not share this doubt with Lydia Harvey, who stood beneath the open eyes of Lady Justice, waiting to tell one last time her story of abuse to a room filled with strange men.

The architects and legal professionals who had designed the new building had failed to provide a space for girls and women like Harvey, who had come to court to testify against their abusers. This oversight incensed Miss MacDougall. Earlier that summer, while Lydia stayed at Lambeth Road awaiting her trial, MacDougall was in court with fifteen-year-old Dolly, nine months pregnant and there to testify against her uncle, who had raped her. They waited for hours amid the abrasive and graphic conversation and in excruciating heat, and her uncle was later found not guilty.[34] MacDougall cited the case in her address to rescue workers in Lincoln that same year, where she advocated for set trial days, expedited trials, separate waiting rooms and *in camera* hearings, where testimony was given in private rooms and relayed afterwards to judge and jury. She noted bitterly that all the while Dolly waited in great discomfort and fear, 'the prisoner who has ruined the child for life is kept quietly clear of all contamination'.[35] The following year a separate room was finally provided for child witnesses, and the trials were scheduled on set days.

The room came too late for Lydia Harvey, who waited with Miss MacDougall on an uncomfortable bench in the court's busy hall. Perhaps she kept her hands folded tightly in her lap, or perhaps she grasped hold of Miss MacDougall's. It is very likely Antonio Carvelli and Alessandro di Nicotera were led straight by her on their way to the courtroom. As he walked past, Carvelli uttered his final threat to his young victim: he would 'do for her' if he ever saw her again.

In the end the trial at the Old Bailey was a short one.

Lydia Harvey never left the bench on which she sat waiting, and did not hear the reflections of the presiding judge before handing down the sentence. 'Although some of the foreign women whom the prisoners had induced to come to this country had probably been leading loose lives before,' he mused to the court, 'there was certainly one case in which it was not so.' He sentenced Carvelli and di Nicotera to six months in prison – but without hard labour.[36] MacDougall sat beside Lydia as she watched the man who had trafficked and abused her led out of the courtroom, off to serve the lightest sentence he could possibly have received for the least serious of his offences. It is difficult to say whether she felt anger at the injustice of it or profound relief at not having to take the stand again. Later that week *The Common Cause*, the official newspaper of Emmeline Pankhurst's Women's Social and Political Union, pointed out that Carvelli's sentence was far lighter than that which was routinely given out for petty theft.[37]

The idea of trafficking as a distinct offence was so engrained in legal and cultural thinking that it seems not to have occurred to the prosecution that there were a number of other charges they could have preferred upon Carvelli and di Nicotera: rape, forcible confinement, uttering threats. For these, perhaps, the burden of proof was even higher. How could a woman be raped if she had consented to let the man into her room, if she had already agreed to sell sex? How could the confinement charge proceed, if it happened in international waters? And why would the judge accept the word of one silly girl who claimed to have been threatened?

'I am very angry,' Miss MacDougall wrote a few years later, after she had witnessed another string of five acquittals. She watched men being found not guilty on the grounds that the child they assaulted had not immediately reported it; but, MacDougall countered, 'it is seldom mentioned ... that the child had been threatened with many horrors if she did tell'. Others were acquitted on the grounds that only the uncorroborated evidence of a child aged eight and over would be accepted in the courts, leaving an abuser free to 'commit any offence he likes upon a child under seven'. This injustice took its toll, even on the self-controlled MacDougall: 'It is awful to be in court and hear the magistrate say, "I believe what this little girl says, but I am powerless to do anything; you can go."'[38] MacDougall experienced this feeling frequently: prosecutions for sexual assault increased dramatically at the same time as other crime was falling, but the conviction rate was lower than for any other set of offences.[39]

After the Central Criminal Court trial, Carvelli and di Nicotera were taken immediately to Brixton Prison and this, as far as the judiciary was concerned, ended its interest in the case. The three French girls were sent back to the convent, and William Coote began to arrange for their repatriation to France. Lydia Harvey was sent back to 198 Lambeth Road in the care of Miss MacDougall, while DI Anderson tried to make arrangements to get her home.

'There is a young girl from New Zealand who has been here for more than three months,' MacDougall wrote in her first annual report of 1910.[40] Lydia worked on the jigsaws until she could do them with her eyes closed, she crocheted and sewed; she played quiet games of backgammon and pick-up-sticks and draughts. She took her meals with Miss Jackman, the kindly old house matron, and helped her with the cleaning. On Sundays she was invited to Miss MacDougall's flat across the road to play the piano with other young women, who laughed and worked and talked together as though everything was normal. Miss MacDougall called them her 'old girls', and they seemed to love the older woman dearly.

It must have been difficult for Lydia to put the thought of Carvelli's threat from her head during this long period of waiting. After all, she knew better even than the police how many of his former associates still lurked around the streets and cafés of North Soho. She could not quite reckon the size of London. How far was Lambeth Road from Piccadilly Circus? Not far enough.

At last Miss MacDougall came to the Home with the news that DI Anderson had finally secured Lydia's passage back to New Zealand from the Home Office repatriation fund, although the home secretary, in a particularly miserly mood, refused to authorise a journey any further than Wellington. If Lydia wished to see her mother in Oamaru, she would have to find the extra £4 on her own. But the plan was for her to stay in Wellington: MacDougall had corresponded with the YWCA in that city, which had found her work as a hospital-ward maid once she arrived. Miss Mac-Dougall and Miss Jackman bade Lydia a warm and tearful farewell when Anderson came to collect her the following week, assuring them both that he would see Lydia directly into the care of the ship's matron. A month or so later Miss MacDougall received the first of several letters from Lydia, which were, in MacDougall's words, 'a constant expression of her gratitude'.[41]

The letters she received from Lydia Harvey have not survived amid the scant papers of the Metropolitan Police Home for Women and Girls, so we only have MacDougall's own account of Harvey's gratitude to go on. There is reason to be circumspect. MacDougall was, after all, writing for a particular audience: the organisations, individuals and government departments that had funded the Home and clearly wanted to hear stories of redemption and thankfulness. But it could also be that much of Lydia's gratitude was genuine. Miss MacDougall had likely shown her rights that she didn't know she had: the right to say no, the right to anonymity in court and in the newspaper, and the right to move on. She had landed in a home that was a far cry from the cold and crowded rescue homes run by many other organisations, or the desperately needed but chaotic overnight shelters run by others. It was small – for a time she was the only resident. There was no enforced labour, and few arbitrary rules. The girls who had lived through sexual assault and abuse, explained MacDougall, 'often find it hard to bear the restraint of Homes, or even service, and they need untiring patience and constant encouragement'. In an era when some homes were still run like penitentiaries, with enforced silence, coerced domestic and laundry work, dormitory-style sleeping and routine invasions of privacy (including opening the girls' post), the Police Home would have been a significant contrast and a crucial lifeline for young victims of sexual crime. 'The quiet gained by the smallness of the Home has been everything to many a poor young girl facing the ordeal of giving, in Court, the detailed evidence of some vile sexual offence,' MacDougall wrote in the Home's sixth annual report.[42] Or, as police commissioner Edward Henry put it, 'the number of girls lodged there is comparatively small ... but when needed the Home is needed badly'.[43]

Yet those who needed it badly were, usually, not in the

same position as Lydia. By 1918 the Home housed thirty girls and young women, and more than half of them were victims not of international trafficking but of familial or intimate sexual abuse. It was not out of keeping with the wider trends. In the ten years that the Home was most active, the National Society for the Prevention of Cruelty to Children alone prosecuted more than 3,000 cases of child sexual abuse, of which a significant proportion was familial or intimate abuse. By the time the Home closed in the 1930s, almost all of its residents were there because they had experienced abuse and assault in their own homes, schools, families and neighbourhoods. Most newspaper readers were barely aware of the crimes themselves, or of their sheer numbers. This was in part because the Punishment of Incest Act 1908 included a provision that made it unlawful for the press to report such prosecutions.[44]

Compared to the panic over sex trafficking, the public seemed relatively unaware or unconcerned with the abuse that was going on in their own streets and institutions, even though it was happening in numbers many times greater than cases of women being kidnapped and imprisoned and forced into prostitution. They were also less willing to believe it was happening in the first place: MacDougall reported many juries who acquitted because the man on trial did not 'seem like an abuser'. This was a very old and long-lived phenomenon, today known as the 'monster myth': the idea that sexual assault was only real or credible when committed by a man who was easily identifiable as a monster. This required him to be some combination of mentally deranged, physically violent, predatory, a serial offender and, most of all, a stranger to the victim. These monstrous characteristics were even easier to apply to men who were not white, or who were migrant, poor or mentally or physically disabled. That the fathers, grandfathers, uncles and brothers of respect-able working- and middle-class families, or the teachers and priests at schools and other children's institutions, could be capable of sexual abuse was, for many people, quite literally beyond speaking and beyond reckoning.[45]

The silence and the disbelief over abuse in homes and neighbourhoods by family and friends lay in dramatic con-trast to the loud and omnipresent stories of 'white slavery', in which foreign men took women to far-off cities to be abused by strangers. Trafficking literally externalised the idea of sexual abuse, exporting it not only from the home but also from the nation. 'The story of the child prostitute was simply the most acceptable articulation of the problem [of child sexual abuse],' the historian Louise Jackson argues. 'It was clear who was "good" and who was "evil" and it did not open up the moral and emotional can of worms that a narrative of incest would have involved.'[46] The narrative of trafficking was premised on the idea that the home was safe, and that leaving it rendered young women vulnerable to exploitation and abuse. But Eilidh MacDougall knew that leaving one's home, or the home of one's employer, was often exactly what a young woman had to do to protect herself.

The 'fresh start' that MacDougall repeatedly claimed to offer girls in her annual reports was also a repudiation of the idea, so common in the sensational stories of 'white slavery', that a girl, once abused, assaulted or coerced into the sex industry, had been irrevocably ruined. She repeatedly explained that her work as a statement-taker, in the courts and at the Home, was driven by the belief that victims of sexual abuse and assault should not be further traumatised or punished by the system or by society, but instead should be recognised as performing a great public duty in accusing and testifying against their abusers, often at great personal and emotional expense. 'One girl of seventeen started in service,' she relayed in a report about the Home, for police commissioner Edward Henry in 1917. 'She is bravely struggling to save, always buoyed up with the hope that "one day I am going to make a home for them again", meaning two younger sisters and two small brothers. There are many heroes among these innocent victims.'[47] Miss MacDougall surely would have recognised the courage it took for Nellie Mathie to enter a beauty contest and stand and receive a prize onstage in front of an entire town who knew all the details of what had happened to her as a child. MacDougall, quite possibly like Nellie Mathie herself, wanted to highlight young women's immense ability to survive and overcome their experiences. Perhaps she sometimes wondered what became of the New Zealand girl she had in her temporary charge, hoping that Lydia was able to find a happy life free from the trauma, or at least the stigma, of sexual abuse.

Long after Lydia Harvey had left, MacDougall insisted on keeping the Home open to the 'old girls' whenever they wished to visit, especially on Sundays, which was a domestic servant's day off. Most young women workers in London took this day to visit their families if they were near enough, but the former residents of the Home had often cut all ties with their previous lives and the abusers within them. MacDougall's tea parties gave them a place to go and a support network of young women who had suffered as they had. 'One of the values of the Home is that it acts as a safety net for family-less girls,' MacDougall explained in the twenty-second annual report of the Home in 1932, 'which will best help them to make their way in the world, and without which the ordinary mischances of their working life – an illness, or the loss of a situation – can so easily assume the proportions of a disaster.'[48] This would be the last annual report she would ever write.

'White slavery' had been a moral panic and cause célèbre in the late nineteenth and early twentieth centuries, but by the interwar years it had begun to fade from public view. The role that Eilidh MacDougall played within the Metropolitan Police was also being called into question. During the First World War, because of concerns about young women, called 'amateur prostitutes', selling sex to soldiers, a legion of female volunteers were recruited to work alongside the regular police force. After the war, a core group of these volunteers fought for professional status, and the Women Police branch of the London Metropolitan Police was officially founded in 1918.[49] MacDougall, despite being invited by the police commissioner himself, refused to join the new Women Police, arguing that she was a social worker, not a police officer.[50] Soon, many of her duties were being handed over to the ambitious Woman Police Officer Lilian Wyles, who became the first woman to work in the CID. As part of her work, Wyles was tasked with taking the statements of victims of sexual assault and trafficking, north of the Thames. MacDougall retained control over the south.

There was no love lost between the two women. Wyles, the daughter of a brewer who had fought hard for his family's social mobility, resented the ease with which MacDougall gained professional recognition through her wealth and titled family and friends.[51] MacDougall, on the other hand, was profoundly disturbed by the way Wyles allowed her allegiance to the police to take precedence over her duty to victims of sexual assault. Wyles took pride in being a good detective who caught young women in lies. 'Taken as a whole there are not a large number of cases of genuine rape, though there are many spurious and doubtful complaints alleging that offence,' Wyles wrote in her autobiography.[52] It is difficult not to wonder what might have happened to Lydia Harvey had it been Lilian Wyles taking her statement and not Eilidh MacDougall.

MacDougall was in many ways fighting a losing battle. By the 1920s the kind of work she and her colleagues were doing was taking on a decidedly old-fashioned air, and the women who did it were ageing. Across the West, social workers were beginning to carve out a separate, more scientific and more professional identity from that of the philanthropic workers who once dominated these kinds of social services.

Eilidh MacDougall was not the only early social worker who found herself pushed out of her job by the 1930s. In 1931 National Vigilance Association worker Rosalie Lighton Robinson gave up her fifteen-year-plus residency in Argentina and her work on the Buenos Aires docks, citing a combination of exhaustion and cynicism. 'There is really nothing to keep me here now, conditions have changed so much since I came here, and are still changing, there is no longer the same necessity for our work, young women are so independent and well able to look after themselves,' she wrote, recalling, one might imagine, the many women who had spurned her offers of assistance over the years. By the

1930s she saw worldly flappers alighting from the sleek new steamships, not innocent 'white slaves'.

'So far as the white slave traffic goes,' Lighton Robinson added, 'as I think you know we have never been able to accomplish anything.' Immigration officers and police constables increasingly stood between her and anyone she may have wanted to help, surely adding to her sense of defeat: 'What there is to do the Authorities do themselves, they do not want help from a Private Association.'[53] Her last trip to what she described as 'the cold, bleak dockside of Buenos Aires at 7 a.m.' was on 11 March 1931, when she boarded the SS *Duilio* bound for Genoa. She spent her last years in retirement in Florence.[54] The full record of her twenty years of work with the NVA in Argentina is scattered, missing or lost.

By the interwar years the widespread belief in the 'white slave' had given way to the idea that the sex trade was staffed by foreign, greedy and depraved prostitutes – women who could not be saved. And without the narrative of trafficking to sustain public interest, the Home no longer attracted the donations from philanthropists and the attention from government that it once had. Frederick Bullock had died in 1913 ('and with him went the Home's greatest supporter in the Police Force', MacDougall wrote in that year's annual report).[55] Edward Henry, the police commissioner who had also supported the Home, retired in 1918 and died in 1930.[56] Miss Mary Leaf, the Home's main benefactor, died in 1919. By the 1930s MacDougall's own health was also failing.

She was also increasingly seen as an annoyance in a new world of rational welfare. The professionalisation of social work had, in many ways ironically, left women like Eilidh MacDougall out of its new vision of standardised, centralised care.[57] The state, which played an increasingly prominent role in social services, was simply not prepared to engage in the kind of long-term aftercare that was, for MacDougall, crucial to the former residents' well-being. What she saw as 'inspiration', the authorities increasingly came to view as 'sentimental interest'. Ultimately they succeeded in forcing Miss MacDougall out of the door when she reached the mandatory age for retirement. After a meeting in which she felt 'she was being ignored and badly treated', they informed her that her post as statement-taker would be terminated after Christmas 1932.[58] The Home was closed in 1933.

After its closure, Lilian Wyles wrote to the police commissioner to tell him that 'The new plan is to send girls to whatever home suits, and to try to distribute them so that all the homes can benefit and there is no jealousy among the superintendents.'[59] State funding to house the witnesses, noted Dorothy Peto, should be limited to the time it took them to testify.[60] Women like Lydia Harvey would no longer be automatically provided with a safe-house in which to stay while awaiting repatriation after their trial. The removal of this long-term, consistent support meant that MacDougall's worries came true for many young vulnerable women: a minor crisis, such as the loss of a job, assumed 'the proportions of a disaster', as they slipped through the enormous holes in the social safety net.

The only people who seemed to remember Eilidh Mac-Dougall after her retirement were the women police officers who took over her work. Dorothy Peto wrote warmly of MacDougall's significant contributions to police work, to the criminal-justice system and to social work, but admitted that very little had been said about this woman's now-invisible career.[61] In Lilian Wyles's view, nothing was said about Miss MacDougall's career because she never sought to advertise her 'revolutionary' work. 'Content in the knowledge that her work, and all that it stood for, was known to those who mattered most, she was satisfied to pursue her way without trumpets heralding her achievements.'[62] But this was surely insincere, coming as it did from a woman who had been instrumental in pushing MacDougall out of the door. It is far more likely that MacDougall's career was 'invisible' because most people did not wish to see the work she did, because that would mean also bearing witness to the crimes and their victims. If it was recognition she was after, she would have done far better as an anti-trafficking campaigner.

In the end, she did not go entirely unmentioned. Miss Eilidh MacDougall was awarded an OBE in the New Year Honours 1933 for her service to the Metropolitan Police. It must have seemed to her fairly empty praise, coming as it did the same year that the Home shut its doors and statement-taking was handed fully over to the Women Police.[63] She must have found some succour in the constant contact she continued to have with the Home's former residents. Even after she retired, Miss MacDougall received upwards of 200 Christmas cards every year from, as she would have put it, her 'old girls'.[64] But there are many layers of silence in an archive, and there is no way to account for the countless other girls and young women who slipped away from the loving but demanding gaze of Eilidh MacDougall, and who may never have given her a second thought.

The building where Lydia Harvey had lived for her last months in London, and which had housed the Metropolitan

Police Home for Women and Girls for more than two decades, was demolished one night in 1945 by a German V-2 rocket.[65] By March 1954, Miss MacDougall was eighty-two years old and, according to her sister Winnifred, 'in very frail health and suffering from loss of memory'. She had by that point been living in a nursing home for several years, after her sister had found her 'incapable of managing her affairs'. The intractable MacDougall must have been infuriated at her own decline, so much so that her sister went through the Chancery Court to have her declared her ward.

It is difficult to say how much Eilidh MacDougall remembered at the end of her life, as her dementia worsened. Did she sometimes catch herself in an imagined conversation with one of her 'old girls', sitting in the town house in Lambeth on a Sunday? Or did they all begin to blur together, a kind of composite portrait of thousands of girls, their hazy features bearing the marks of abuse and pain, and the signs of hope and heroism? She died less than a month later, in April 1954. But, surely, many people never forgot her. Lydia Harvey, and the thousands of other girls and young women whose words she had recorded in midnight police stations, whose hands she had held in crowded police-court waiting rooms, whom she had embraced, comforted, sought justice for, found jobs and homes – they likely thought fondly of Miss MacDougall for the rest of their lives.

The Court of Protection made Winnifred her receiver and, left with a small pile of her sister's old papers, Winnifred began to make enquiries about where she might send them. Miss Robinson, an official with the Southwark Diocesan Association, gratefully received them.[66] When the Diocesan Association's social-work branch itself closed, they sent all their papers to the London Metropolitan Archives, among which are the traces that remain of Eilidh's decades-long social work: some annual reports, minutes from meetings, some correspondence and a few entry books, their bindings crumbling. The rest is gone: the Christmas cards, the case-books, the letters from Lydia Harvey.

The bulk of the writing Eilidh MacDougall has left behind are not her words, but the words she coaxed from the hundreds (if not thousands) of women and girls whose statements she recorded in her handwriting. The statements that survive are now scattered through the archives of the criminal-justice system, tucked into police files, criminal-court files and the records of the Department of Public Prosecutions. Collectively they bear testament to MacDougall's lifetime of work, and the suffering and bravery of the victims she interviewed. But they should also remind us how many statements were never taken, how often testimony was disregarded and disbelieved, and, amid all the clamour to stop the 'infamous traffic', how very rarely real justice was served.

Chapter Five

THE DANCING MASTER

Antonio Carvelli, wearing his striped prison uniform, stood to receive his sentence in the packed courtroom. The judge, in his long white wig, had a great deal to say, including – to Carvelli's great relief – that he regretted he was unable to prefer a sentence of hard labour on either of the prisoners because the charges for procuring had been dropped. As it stood, the six months that Carvelli and di Nicotera were given was bad enough for the two men, but it could have been much worse had they been tried on all of the charges: they had been looking at more than two years of stone-breaking in an English gaol. They would, of course, be deported as well. 'Both of you have very bad characters,' the judge intoned. 'You are both foreigners, and it cannot be tolerated that foreigners of bad character should come over to England, and pursue their criminal courses here.' Carvelli would have to find another place to carry out his work.

After the short trial ended, he and di Nicotera were led by the bailiff to the Black Maria, as the English coppers called the police van, and taken not to Brixton Prison, where they had spent the three months waiting for the trial, but to Wormwood Scrubs. Di Nicotera, whose experience of prison was more extensive than Carvelli's own, assured him that Wormwood Scrubs was far from the worst place to be, and much better than Brixton, where prisoners were crowded into older, airless cells.[1] Carvelli cannot have relished the thought of spending another six months behind its thick stone walls, but must also have been resigned to the plea bargain he had made, even as he fumed against the young witness who had put him there. He would 'do for her', if he ever saw her again.

Carvelli arrived in prison at a time when real efforts were being made to improve conditions, and Wormwood Scrubs was regarded as one of the most forward-thinking, well-lit and well-managed English gaols. But conditions remained relatively dire. Upon arrival, Carvelli's hair was cropped, and he was handed another tattered and ill-fitting striped uniform. He was led down a long corridor to the solitary-confinement blocks, where he spent his first twenty-eight days, sleeping without a mattress on the cold stone floor. According to the prison reformer and activist Stephen Hobhouse, writing during his own incarceration as a conscientious objector during the First World War, prison was still a place where 'Self-respect is systematically destroyed ... the sanitary arrangements are degrading and filthy, and the dress is hideous, slovenly, and humiliating.'[2]

Amid this destruction (or attempted destruction) of his self-respect, did Antonio Carvelli regret what he had done? And, either way, why should we care? Men like Carvelli occupied a very particular place in the public imagination: they were both despicable and fascinating. In other words, people loved to hate them. Most often pimps and traffickers were depicted in caricature: they were well dressed, effeminate and racialised, and were believed to exert a total power over the women they controlled. They were imagined as a subculture: inhabiting certain kinds of urban geographies, and speaking the accented argot of the underworld. They were the ideal monsters, avatars of a foreign and externalised sexual violence that was – as women like Eilidh MacDougall knew all too well – in reality usually far more local, ordinary and familiar.

As MacDougall herself would argue again and again, pretending that men who abused women were a class apart, unconnected to normal society, culture and economies, did little for their victims or for the cause of justice. Juries, expecting the exaggerated imagery of the storybook pimp, often did not recognise the perpetrators they saw in the dock. If we want to understand trafficking, we must understand Antonio Carvelli as a complicated man who was very much a product of the ordinary world in which he lived, even if his story was rather extraordinary.

Like the young woman he trafficked, Carvelli left very little of his thoughts and feelings behind. He wrote letters to his father from prison, sent in plain white envelopes so that Luigi could hide the shame of his son's crimes from his neighbours and friends. These letters are long gone, burned perhaps in Luigi's grate to make sure the truth was never discovered, so we cannot know what they contained. Apologies for having misled his father, excuses for his crimes, professions of innocence and misunderstanding? He wrote also to his wife Marie, who had fled London before his unfortunate arrest and was by now re-established in New Zealand. While these letters too are long since destroyed or lost, we can assume some of their contents: professions of love, expressions of frustration and anger, entreaties to keep working hard, requests to set money aside for him upon his return.[3]

From the fact that no records of his time in prison survive, we can presume that Carvelli gave the guards and the governor no cause to remark upon him. Perhaps he took the opportunity to engage in activities that the prison rationalists who ran Wormwood Scrubs felt might contribute to his reform: making things in the workshops, taking educational classes, engaging in outdoor recreation, seeking out the spiritual support of the chaplains. Then, in February 1911, just after his thirty-second birthday, Carvelli received his dark tweed suit, his brown overcoat and the black bowler hat he'd been wearing that day back in July 1910 when the coppers nabbed him, and walked out into the daylight. He wasn't exactly free, however, and the two police officers who accompanied him saw him straight onto a train to Dover, and then onto a ship bound for the port of Genoa. But Carvelli had bid that city goodbye more than ten years before, and he had no intention of going back.

Antonio Carvelli had grown up in Turin, listening to the sound of his father's French horn and the clatter of trains. His family's apartment at 9 Via Saluzzo, with its huge windows overlooking a narrow street, was a stone's throw from Porta Nuova, Turin's newest and largest railway station, where passengers from all over Piedmont, laden with travel chests and dragging wide-eyed children, embarked for the bustling port of Genoa, to the steamships that waited to take them around the world. The restless young Antonio drifted off to sleep dreaming of joining them one day.

He grew up in an age when people – and none more so

than Italians – were migrating around the world as they never had before. He was born in Turin in the winter of 1879, while the Piedmontese countryside, in the middle of an agricultural depression, emptied and the city grew apace. His parents were two of the tens of thousands of new migrants to the city. His father, Luigi Carvelli, had moved first to Verona from the small town of Petilia Policastro in the southern province of Calabria to work as a musician in the 1870s, in the early years of Italian unification, when many southern-ers sought better fortunes in the north and encountered widespread prejudice. His mother, Anna Maria Courrier, had travelled south to Verona from where she had been born in Chambéry, France, the ancient capital of the Savoy kingdom: one of thousands of borderland migrants in the age of European nation-building. The pair had met in that city, where Luigi was working in the growing entertainment industry, and it could be that Anna Maria was working in music or theatre as well. The couple's marriage was enforced, or at least expedited, by the fact that Anna Maria became pregnant. They wed in Verona in the summer of 1878, and Antonio was born just six months later in Turin, where Luigi had taken up a post of *maestro di musica*.[4] Here the boy was raised as a Franco-Italian, speaking both the languages of his mother and his father perfectly, and able to move effortlessly between the two cultures.

By the early 1890s the family was enjoying the modest fruits of Luigi's musical success: he had played first horn in the premiere of Verdi's *Falstaff* at La Scala and was a pub-lished composer. They had settled in the respectable, if not affluent, streets on the eastern border of Turin's San Salvario quarter. This neighbourhood bore all the signs of late nineteenth-century economic and industrial expansion. According to the beloved Torinese writer Edmondo De Amicis, this newer quarter was filled with 'large houses blackened and veiled by great clouds of smoke from the largest station of the railway', with the 'cobblestone clatter of colossal horses, the noise of wagons loaded with goods staggering between the omnibus, trams, and carts'. The place was marked by 'the metallic din of life: rude, rushed, and restless'.[5] Everything and everyone was moving.

But for the time being Antonio Carvelli's world was a small one. In the mornings he would leave his apartment and walk among a swarm of rowdy children, past the horses and the wagons and omnibuses to his nearby municipal school, part of the very first class of the first nationwide school system.[6] This system was an important element of Italy's unification project, designed to instil a sense of brotherhood, patriotism and morality in the young nation's youth. In his municipal school as well as at home Carvelli obtained, by all indications, a very good formal and cultural education. He finished his schooling at the age of eighteen speaking four languages: his father's Italian and his mother's French, as well as German and English. He could read and write Latin and ancient Greek. He was numerate, able to do accounting sums with ease. He read the novels of the romantic revolutionaries Giuseppe Garibaldi and Alessandro Manzoni, as well as De Amicis, who together had helped to forge a new national identity. Thanks to his father, Antonio could play several instruments and sing opera to a professional standard. He had gained the skills necessary to get by in polite society. He was, by these measures, a model product of Italy's post-unification project. An ideal modern boy.

Yet perhaps Antonio also had a less celebrated side to his education. At home in the evenings, as the trains came and went, he may have gorged himself on the stories of the famous Emilio Salgari, the pioneering and bestselling adventure novelist who spun tales that fed Italians' fascination with the world's frontiers: the Wild West, the African jungle, the Indian and Pacific Oceans. The young Carvelli may have blackened the glass of his oil lamp reading the popular serial about the Malaysian pirate Sandokan, which appeared in his local newspaper in the 1880s; and he may eagerly have bought Salgari's first three novels that were published in 1892, after Salgari himself had moved to Turin and Antonio Carvelli had turned thirteen.[7] It is easy to picture the teenager daydreaming of Caribbean and Malaysian seas, Middle Eastern deserts, steaming jungles and icy mountains: worlds filled with pirates, bandits and women held captive by evil men.

But no matter what the young Antonio grew up reading, we can be confident that he preferred to see himself as his own story's protagonist. So what happened? Why did this model modern boy become a pimp and a trafficker?

It was a question that few people sought to answer in the early twentieth century. In a world obsessed with discovering why women became prostitutes, little ink was spilled on why men got involved in the sex industry. Those who did ponder the question concluded that a man's descent into pimping was similar to that of other criminals: a childhood marked by poverty, a spiral of youthful delinquency, a stint in prison and, while behind bars, an initiation into the underworld of sex and crime.[8] A transnational investigation in 1927 determined that pimps and traffickers were primarily criminal businessmen, master exploiters of others, concerned only with profits, which, in the early twentieth-century sex industry, were substantial. Others argued that pimps were different from other criminals. They were sexually deviant, weak and effeminate, obsessed with their mothers and had mental, moral and physical defects.[9] They were hardly men at all.

None of these impressionistic accounts can tell us much about the schoolboy Antonio Carvelli, who would grow up to be a man who pimped, trafficked and abused women. There is no trace remaining of his relationship with his mother or siblings, or any explanation for why his parents lived apart for more than half their marriage; though for most estranged Italian couples during this period, this was as close to divorce as they could get.[10] The financial state of his family is similarly obscured: despite appearances, they may well have struggled. Later in life Luigi Carvelli would be forced to leave Italy and go to England in search of work, and would earn very little indeed as first horn in the Brighton Municipal Orchestra. After all, cultural capital was far from a guarantee of wealth: just ask Emilio Salgari, the beloved grandfather of Italian pop culture, who committed suicide in penury after his publisher took almost all the profits from his books. He was found in a park in 1910, just a few streets away from the Carvellis' old family apartment.

Of Antonio's teenage life, only scant clues remain. The sole trace of him in the Turin archives is one ironic sheet of paper: a certificate of good conduct that was issued in March 1897, with a small handwritten note from a local police captain attached to it, stained with the rust from the 100-year-old pin. The note asked that the good-conduct certificate be drawn up at the request of Antonio's father, Luigi, in order that his eighteen-year-old son might enlist in the army.[11] While the certificate contains only the smallest amount of detail, it provides a brief glimpse of a relationship between the boy and his father. Luigi, a man with enough social standing to call in a favour from the local police, was eager that his son should make something of himself. By procuring the note, Luigi was framing the story that might be told about his son: Carvelli would represent the pinnacle of late nineteenth-century Italian manhood, an army volunteer with a certificate of good conduct who had not waited for the draft toss, or *estrazione*, that would determine whether he was placed in the regular army or the provincial reserves at the age of twenty, but instead sought enlistment in one of the most demanding regiments as soon as he had finished formal education. On the other hand, the note tells another story: of a son who was unwilling to take charge of his own career, and of a father who was perhaps concerned about the friends that his boy was making in San Salvario and wanted to get him away from them. Despite his good education, Antonio had perhaps failed to transform into a respectable man, and indolence, effeminacy or absence of sexual morals – traits that deeply concerned both his father and the architects of the new Italian nation – had begun to manifest themselves in the young Carvelli.[12]

In any case, the military promised regeneration. Shortly after the certificate of good conduct was issued, Carvelli joined the 6th Artillery Regiment, part of the famous Alpini – the regiments known for bravely enduring the hardships of their mountain posts. He also remained in the regiment for longer than he had to, training at the grandly designed military artillery academy in the heart of central Turin. This military life could have mapped out a clear path towards adult respectability and honour.[13]

This was also very probably where his first initiation into the world of commercial sex took place. Around Carvelli's garrison in Turin lay the highest concentration of registered brothels in the city, and in the town's winding alleys and small piazzas women sold sex illegally on the streets. Turin was a big, busy, growing city. In addition to the large garrison, Fiat's new automobile factory led to an explosion in its population, an expansion of its working-class neighbourhoods and a growth in its underworld. For a young man in uniform, there was always drink to be had and sex to buy – and this was widely regarded by soldiers and their superior officers as a necessary component of military life.[14]

Like Carvelli, Italy's first regulated prostitution regime was born in Turin, when mid-century medical men and military leaders began to reckon with the extent of gonorrhoea and syphilis in both the army and the civilian population. In 1855 Piedmont introduced a regulated system that would register prostitutes, monitor brothels and inspect women for venereal disease, modelled on regulations that were already in place in France and Belgium. These regulations, like many others, spread from Piedmont into the rest of the new Italian nation after unification, and became the Cavour Regulation of 1861, which required women to register and be inspected for VD, and also set brothel prices and locations.[15] By the time Carvelli was born, these regulated systems of prostitution were the status quo in Italy, in much of Europe and in European imperial territories, where states collected no small amount of revenue from brothel registration fees and fines.

Antonio Carvelli, the young army officer, could not have been blind to this reality. It determined the brothels he went to and the price he paid for sex; it helped to shape the commercial sex market that surrounded his garrison and weaved its way into each of Turin's *quartieri*. Prostitution for this young man was normal, visible and legalised. He had surely seen examples of third parties – including pimps, brothel-keepers and, most importantly, the state itself – making money from organising the labour of women who sold sex, long before he did so himself. When Carvelli became a pimp (that is, when he attempted to control and make money from independent women who sold sex) he was following in the footsteps of many Western and imperial states.[16]

The military did not just normalise prostitution. It could also help to engender the emotional and social disruption that could push men towards the sex industry.[17] Life in the army or navy frequently left men physically disabled and diseased, emotionally scarred and – particularly if their actions or inactions earned them a dishonourable discharge – without any money or pension. It is not surprising that unlucky or unsuccessful soldiers were often found among the ranks of pimps.

But pimping was not the cause of the promising young Antonio's initial downfall. His first brush with the law would be in 1900, at the age of twenty-one, when he was charged by the *questore*, or police superintendent, of Turin with theft. Carvelli's original criminal file is missing from the Archivio di Stato in Turin, and no other details are given. The original arrest warrant – which does not offer a description of the crime – was sent by the *questore* of Turin to London's CID in 1910, and now resides in the National Archives file: part of the great traffic in paper that signalled the dawn of international policing. The only real clue as to the nature of his theft lies in the sentence he received: two years and eight months' hard labour – a very harsh sentence for a first-time offender.

This sentence could suggest Carvelli had committed a substantial theft, but it is just as likely that he was one of the many young men who were made examples of by the Italian criminal-justice system as the nation grew more concerned about crime rates, national degeneracy and economic instability at the turn of the century. Carvelli was arrested as the total number of prosecutions for people under twenty-one peaked in Italy (at 44,172 in 1898), and while the discipline of criminology was being born in the very city where he had committed his first crime.[18]

How would Antonio Carvelli have been classified by his fellow Torinese, and a founding father of criminal anthropology, Cesare Lombroso? At the time of Carvelli's arrest, Lombroso was a famous professor of forensic medicine and public psychiatry at the University of Turin. In the Anatomical Institute where he worked he kept a collection of hundreds of skulls, skeletons and the masks and portraits of so-called degenerates, which he used to 'prove' his theory of criminal atavism: that the propensity to crime was an inherent trait. Carvelli bore few of Lombroso's arbitrary and racist stigmata of born criminality: his face was fairly symmetrical and his jaw not overly protruding; there were no signs he was epileptic; and his brows were not bushy enough to mark him out as a typical murderer or rapist. There was little that would make Lombroso conclude that Carvelli had been 'doomed from birth to a career of crime', and perhaps he would have fallen into the category of men that Lombroso labelled 'criminaloids', who were 'candidates for good and evil according to circumstances'. There was, however, one small physiological sign that nature, and not nurture, had been the cause of his downfall. According to Lombroso's daughter, the professor had discovered that dichromatism of the iris was a common trait in criminals.[19]

The man with the memorable eyes did not stay in Turin long enough to serve his sentence or even attend his trial, let alone come under Professor Lombroso's scrutiny. He was tried for theft on 10 August 1900, but he had left Turin in February – almost six months earlier.[20] His trial, held *in absentia*, must have been for a crime that had only been discovered after he was long gone.

Carvelli got out of Italy the same way millions of his countrymen did: by scrounging, borrowing, stealing or saving for a third-class ticket on a steamship out of Genoa. Indeed, the theft for which he was later charged may well have been what funded his departure. At last he was among the throng in Porta Nuova station, boarding a boat-train and off to see a new world. The steamship he booked himself on, the SS *Karlsruhe* of the Norddeutscher Lloyd Line, was bound for Sydney, Australia and ports in between. After stowing his meagre belongings in his wooden steerage bunk, Carvelli stood against the deck rails and watched as the ship pulled away from the bustling port, its yellow, pink and red buildings growing smaller and smaller in the winter sun. It would be the last time he would see Italy for more than a decade.

The ship steamed through the Messina Strait and across the southern Mediterranean, through the Suez Canal to Colombo, and then on to Fremantle in Western Australia, where the majority of Carvelli's fellow Italians disembarked to meet the employment agents from mining and forestry firms there. The ship continued along Australia's south coast to Adelaide, Melbourne and finally Sydney. When Antonio made his way down the gangplank and onto the bustling Circular Quay, he must have felt every bit like one of Salgari's adventurers. He had reached the other side of the world – *il continento misterioso* – where no one knew him, and where the possibilities were endless. He even told the ship's registrar that he was two years younger than he really was.

He was joined in his departure by a staggering four million other Italians who left Italy in the seven years between 1898 and 1905. Carvelli's Antipodean voyage, while not so popular as those routes to the United States, Argentina and Brazil, was made by hundreds of thousands of Italian men in that same decade alone. These men – and they were almost all men – often left behind wives and children and, having struck out on their own or contracted with an employment agent, frequently called a *padrone*, they could mostly be found doing hard manual labour in various industries. Italians from both the north and the south spread out all over the world, but especially in the United States and South America. These men were motivated to leave Italy by an agricultural crisis that left millions without work or a living wage; by unrest and crime in the countryside, a plague of phylloxera that had destroyed the wine industry, poor public health and transportation and a general desire to improve their lives. They cleared forests and laid tracks for the railway; they worked in gold, silver, copper and coal mines. In bigger cities they worked in manufacturing, and in the restaurant and food-packing industries. In South America and in Queensland, they worked on the sugar plantations; in Western Australia they mined the gold and cut the timber that the mines consumed so voraciously.[21]

Many of these Italian migrants were in a state that approached, or was, indentured servitude; earning so little and owing so much to their *padrone* for the voyage and the contract fees, and to their employers for room and board, that the only way they could manage any savings and remittances was to work themselves practically to death.[22] But they also found ways to survive, and resist, and persist: building up local communities, amassing savings and making investments, reuniting their families and even (often imperfectly) fulfilling the dream of return.[23] Fourteen million Italians left their homeland between 1880 and 1914, making their emigration the largest one, so far at least, in world history.[24] It also sparked a wave of anti-Italian sentiment in host countries, especially the United States and Australia, which viewed Italians (especially southern Italians) as criminal, backward and the wrong kind of white. Indeed, had Carvelli come to Australia only one year later, his entry would have been significantly more difficult, because of the newly inaugurated 'white Australia' policy, enacted after federation in 1901, which aimed to keep Australia 'white' – that is, English-speaking and British – by putting up bars to entry for non-English speakers and non-white migrants, especially those from East Asia.[25]

It was not in Australia's mines or forests or sugar plantations that Carvelli found work. All that education and training he had received led him into another kind of mobile labour, in quite possibly the fastest-growing sector in the world: the global entertainment industry. This era witnessed an unprecedented explosion in the market for popular entertainment around the world.[26] The young Antonio Carvelli was able to make good in this new international business, and contracted as a chorus singer with the Italian Opera Company, which in 1901 had just begun the first of its many successful tours in Australia. The company's first performance was Verdi's *Aida*, but in the grainy archival photographs it is impossible to say which man in the heavy 'Egyptian' make-up and robes is Carvelli. This tour took him from Sydney to Melbourne and Adelaide, telling the story of an enslaved woman who tries to escape her captors, but who ultimately follows the man she loves to her death.[27]

Being part of the chorus in a touring opera company paid poorly – no more than a pound or two a week – and when the tour ended and the Italian Opera Company moved on, Carvelli stayed in Sydney. He may have tried an honest living at first, looking for work in the theatre or in language tuition; and perhaps work was found. But it was not work that could afford him the things he really wanted in life, and so Carvelli turned once more, as he had in Turin, to theft.

His modus operandi played to his strengths and made the most of his ability to pass as every inch the gentlemen. The Australians called it 'hotel barbering', and it could be described as partway between burglary and a confidence trick. The first step was to pay for a room at a well-to-do boarding house or hotel and use a false name. The second was to charm the staff and fellow lodgers, convincing them they were speaking to a gentleman of good breeding, in town to make an investment or oversee a business, or perhaps to perform in a theatrical production. The third was to wait in the common room or lobby until a marked guest left the premises and then slip upstairs to the vacated room. Hotel and boarding-house room doors were far from secure and could be prised open with little noise or effort. Fourth, pilfer the room for valuables; and fifth, slip out completely undetected: just another guest off to see the city for the day. Back in London, Metropolitan Police Chief Cecil Bishop had specialised in catching hotel thieves in the early twentieth century, and explained in his memoir that they were 'men apart and very different from their colleagues who specialise, for instance, in robbing flats ... Generally speaking they are well-educated and well-dressed men. They can pass as the guest in a foyer of the most expensive hotel. Above all they have self-confidence since most of their coups are brought off by sheer cheek and effrontery.'[28]

There is no telling how many successful stints as a 'hotel barber' Carvelli enjoyed before he was caught. Then, around the beginning of March 1901, he burgled a violin belonging to a professor of music. He knew a valuable instrument when he saw one, and was able to pawn it for £25 – the equivalent of almost half a year's work in the opera. The police were never able to tie the theft to him, but the professor's expensive trousers and his silk scarves, found on Carvelli's legs and neck, would prove his downfall. They earned him one month's hard labour in a Sydney gaol.[29] This incident also created the first recorded photograph of him, a mugshot, taken on 20 March 1901, when he was twenty-three years old.

In this photograph Carvelli appears young, with just the shadow of a moustache on his upper lip. His dark tweed suit fits him badly on the shoulders, giving the impression that he is not yet fully grown. A plain button-up cardigan and a rumpled narrow collar complete the look of a young working man who has not yet cashed in on the fortune of the stolen

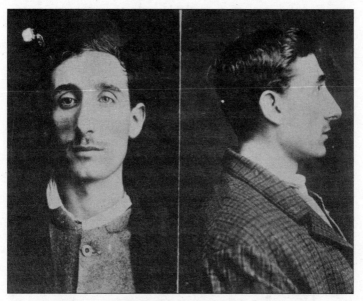

13: Antonio Carvelli's first mugshot, taken after his first arrest
for theft in Australia in March of 1901 at the age of twenty-
three. His different-coloured eyes are clearly visible, as is the
beginning of what would become an impressive moustache.

violin. In profile, we can see a Roman nose and large ears,
and hair oiled back from his forehead. Front-facing, he stares
unabashed into the camera, his expression unreadable. His
most distinctive feature is clearly visible even in the black-
and-white image: one eye is dark and the other far lighter.

On the form that accompanied this mugshot the police
seemed to think Carvelli was born five years earlier than he
really was, called him 'Alfredo' and listed his occupation,
somewhat mysteriously, as 'architect'. These kinds of mis-
takes on supposedly official registers – on birth, marriage
and death certificates, as well as crime records – were very

common, especially when they concerned those who actively sought to obscure their real identities. Carvelli was thousands of miles from anyone who knew him: he could be any age and take any name he liked.

He was only out of prison for a week when he was charged again, in May 1901, with theft. This earned him another month in a prison cell. While still inside, it seems new charges came up against Carvelli and he was sentenced to an additional ten months' hard labour. Five more charges in three separate trials followed in 1902 and 1903, this time for crimes committed in Adelaide and Port Adelaide: unlawful possession and four counts of stealing. His love of fine clothes frequently proved his downfall: he was caught wearing a pair of expensive boots that he had stolen. He served almost two and a half years for these crimes.[30] There are no records of what Carvelli may have learned and whom he may have met during his various stints behind bars, but it is very likely that the dining halls, cells and exercise yards of the gaols of Sydney and Adelaide were key sites where his early criminal-business networks began to form. For many men, prison made for an excellent education in bookmaking, fraud, confidence tricks and pimping.[31]

Then, in 1904, he passed his prison uniform over to the guard for what he hoped was the last time. He had his sights set on Australia's 'wild west', where the growing towns of Perth, Fremantle and Kalgoorlie stood as gateways to the expanding goldfields.[32] He stepped on the boat in Adelaide as the notorious thief Antonio Carvelli, but alighted in Fremantle as Aldo Cellis: translator, teacher and frontier entrepreneur.

*

Carvelli seemed genuinely to want a fresh start, and his hunger for social status was soon on full display. Signor Aldo Cellis, who claimed to hold a degree in belles-lettres from the University of Turin, advertised his language school in the Moir Buildings in busy downtown Perth in the local newspapers.[33] Soon he had found work as a translator for the French consul who, it was said, thought very highly of him, and he also taught classes in Latin and Greek at the Christian Brothers College. He sang opera for the mayor of Subiaco, a suburb of Perth, to the guests' great delight.[34] He also established himself as a shipping and indent agent, importing goods from Italy and Colombo, so that the residents of Perth and Fremantle could dine on salami and olive oil and wear cheap Ceylon cotton.

Over the course of three years it seems Carvelli experimented with every respectable identity that he had pretended to have while robbing hotel rooms. He cultivated, outwardly at least, a mature kind of Italian masculinity.[35] He had graduated from the plain shirt and tweed coat that he wore when he first arrived in Australia, and now sported a wide collar, a silk cravat and a suit jacket tailored at the shoulder. The scraggly moustache of his youth had grown into a thick, carefully oiled and sculpted adornment. He was also, it seems, a star on the local *bocce* pitch. In September 1907 Aldo Cellis won a narrow victory against Victor Morocco in a 'much-discussed' game of Italian bowls, after Morocco lost his lead in the final round and got 'in the *zuppa*': these were Carvelli's words, immortalised by an exuberant local games reporter. Both sides enjoyed claret and *frittata* after the match.

But Carvelli, even as the upstanding citizen and bon vivant Signor Cellis, could not resist the opportunity to make money through fraud. His degree from the University of Turin, which he used to obtain his language students and his teaching job at the Jesuit College, was completely fabricated.[36] Soon the French consul began to discover irregularities in the office's finances. People began to say that 'Signor Cellis' was making frequent trips into the goldfields, staying in a town called Leonora in the company of 'certain women'.

Leonora was an Eastern Goldfields supply centre, more than 500 miles north-east of Perth and almost 150 miles north of Kalgoorlie, connected to these towns by a newly opened railway line. Leonora was linked by a short stretch of road and an electric tramline to Gwalia, where the Sons of Gwalia mine had been taken over by the industrialist and later American president Herbert Hoover in 1897 – a paragon example of globalising industrial capital in this era. He reduced wages, extended working hours and eliminated bonuses for more difficult work.[37]

Seeking to lower wages still further, decrease union influence and protect himself in the event of a strike, Hoover had been recruiting Italian men to work one of the largest and deepest goldmines in Australia for a decade by the time Carvelli arrived in the area. These men stood as a very good example of the different kind of exploited labour that so concerned trade unions and socialists at the time. They worked for wages far below what unionised Anglo workers would accept, in conditions that were gruelling and dangerous. They toiled in the excruciating heat of the Northern Goldfields, where temperatures regularly climbed to forty degrees Celsius. Red dust caked the sweat of their arms and faces. It was, in the words of one miner, 'like being dressed in cement'.[38] Workers were lowered deep underground by a

14: Tower Street, Leonora around 1909, shortly before Antonio Carvelli and Vanda Williams arrived. Otterburn Street runs parallel to this thoroughfare.

clattering steam-powered lift system, risking serious injury and breathing harmful, stifling air that was blown from the surface to the shafts by giant fans. Because Gwalia residents were refused business permits, on their day off the miners often travelled from the loud industrial mineworks of Gwalia on the electric tram to nearby Leonora, a tidy if barren town, whose main street offered shopping, drink, food and entertainment; and whose side-streets offered more. This large, all-male workforce helped to create a healthy market in both licit and illicit alcohol and commercial sex.[39]

Carvelli, like the 'certain women' he kept company with, had come to Leonora to mine these miners. He used the profits from his licit endeavours to front money to women so that they could rent and furnish their houses. He bought them little brass plates to hang on their doors that said 'dressmaker' and 'seamstress'. He even supplied them with the sewing machines they could use as flimsy evidence when they were charged with keeping a brothel in the town's make-shift court. He kept them company. He collected a cut of their earnings.

It was the profits – the incredible profits – that could be made as a third party in the frontier sex industry that had drawn him in, and it was his middle-class artiste charm, his sheer cheek and effrontery, that made him so good at it. By 1908 he was associated with at least three women who sold sex in Leonora and had formed an especially close bond with one woman in particular, who had come to Leonora with him. She called herself Miss Vanda Williams. From Vanda and the others, Carvelli collected up to £20 – around £2,000 in the present day – every week.

Even after the expenses of rent and supplies for the brothels he ran, it was money for all the clothes, jewellery and first-class steamship tickets he could ever want. He could buy his own silk scarves, his own fine leather boots, his own violin, should he want to. He could get the newest and best-made suits, and was soon known back in Perth and on the Fremantle docks as an ostentatious dandy. It was said that he dyed his moustache to match these suits, even when his suit was green.[40] It is a far-fetched description, but not out of keeping with the image of Carvelli as a performer, a risk-taker and an aspirational social chameleon. In any case, his love of finery needed financing, and the £20 a month that he cleared in Leonora was probably largely spent on clothes.[41] For the time being, no one seemed to question where the money was coming from.

The profits he was turning put to shame what he could earn from teaching Latin or translating French. And they completely dwarfed what the Italian men, covered in cement dust down in the goldmine, would make in the same era: less than £2 a week, for long hours and back-breaking labour that – thanks in no small part to a lack of safety gear and a constant pressure to work more quickly – was five times more fatally dangerous than any other industry. Workers could look forward to their families getting £200 if they were killed or incapacitated.[42] Carvelli could make the same in ten months, for doing barely anything at all. Like the pimps interviewed by undercover investigators from the League of Nations a decade later, Carvelli very likely believed that 'there were plenty of women who wanted to fuck for a living' and it was a good business to invest in. No one, after all, got rich with their morals intact.

Carvelli was a charming man, a trickster, adept at convincing hotel guests he was respectable, easily gaining the trust of the French consul in Perth, even as he had his hand in the cash box. Perhaps he has even convinced us, seeing him 100 years on, as well. Perhaps we are inclined to feel some admiration for this gold-rush vice-entrepreneur, the sort of man who plays the attractive anti-hero in many a frontier narrative, a picaresque 'wild west' kingpin. Amid his string of aliases and constant self-reinvention, it is difficult to say what kind of man Antonio Carvelli had really become.

It was not long before the police in Leonora believed they had the measure of him. One morning in late October 1908 Antonio Carvelli was asleep in one of Leonora's distinctive corrugated-iron houses, in the bed of Miss Vanda Williams. The pair were woken by the sound of a policeman's fist

15: Antonio Carvelli's mugshot from his first arrest on charges of pimping, taken in Leonora, Western Australia in 1908 at the age of twenty-nine. His iconic moustache is now on full display, and his tailored suit is evidence that he was far wealthier than he was seven years earlier.

rattling the door, and Sergeant O'Donovan strode into the room without waiting for a reply. He arrested Carvelli in his underclothes, to the sound of Vanda Williams's protests, and searched the room for evidence. In Carvelli's coat the policeman found a ledger, written in code, that he assumed was used to communicate with prostitutes and keep the books on the brothels he ran.

Sergeant O'Donovan was more than used to turning a blind eye to the less-than-salubrious goings-on in Leonora and, like many police officers on the frontier and elsewhere, he felt uncomfortable hounding women who sold sex. Signor Aldo Cellis, on the other hand, made a much more palatable target.[43] He was a dandy with a tinted moustache, a fine suit and jewellery, and seemed never to have done a day of real labour in his life, preferring to take money from 'unfortunate' women, who in turn took it from hard-working men. Not only that, but he was also a fellow countryman of the Gwalia Italians, who were seen as union breakers and blacklegs by self-imagined 'white' Western Australians. It was probably with no small amount of enjoyment that Sergeant O'Donovan took Carvelli's fingerprints and mugshot, and hauled him before the town's honorary judges a few days later.[44]

Aldo Cellis was charged with 'living on the earnings of prostitution', a newly passed state law designed to give police more powers to prosecute what they called 'bludgers', what the English called 'ponces' and what we would today call pimps. This law required evidence that the man in question earned money from women who sold sex, which often consisted of exposing his wealth and comparing it to what a man of his class would expect to earn through legitimate labour, or showing that he was making money while unemployed. Here the pimp's stereotypical but common mode of dressing doubly condemned him: it suggested that he was weak and effeminate, but it was also used as evidence of the money he was making from his life of vice. How else could working-class boys afford fine suits; how else could poor immigrants cover their fingers in gold? The law – and the proof that it required – seemed to suggest that such men's real crime was living above their stations. The exploitation and violence that some of them engaged in, on the other hand, was immaterial to their prosecution.

When he appeared before the honorary judges of Leonora, Carvelli denied it all, playing the role of an incredulous and innocent businessman. Defended at his trial by a local solicitor, he catalogued the many legitimate trades and occupations with which he was involved, and produced evidence of these, along with proof of his Australian investments. That was how he afforded his fine suits, he explained; that was where the money came from for the jewellery that adorned his neck, fingers and tie. What is more, he claimed, he was not living on Vanda Williams's earnings, but rather had rescued her twelve months ago 'from the life that she was living', having previously known her 'in a very respectable position' in Fremantle, where he had 'contemplated' marrying her, gifting her with a gold bangle as the symbol of his affection. He 'defied the prosecution to prove that he had ever lived on the proceeds of prostitution'.[45] He managed to confound the local honorary judges enough to have his case referred to a resident magistrate.

As defiant as he was in court, Carvelli knew that he was now the one 'in the *zuppa*'. Whether he was found guilty or not, his hard-won, if fraudulent, place in the respectable circles of Western Australia had just gone up in smoke. Newspapers across that state, and even in Melbourne and Sydney, carried the story of 'a well-dressed Frenchman' involved in 'an interesting case at Leonora'.[46] It would not be long before the French consul discovered his inventive bookkeeping. The mayor of Subiaco would never have him round to sing again. Carvelli paid his £40 bail and appeared in court one more time, trying to get the case thrown out, demanding the return of shipping documents – crucial for customs clearance – that had been confiscated.[47] He managed to obtain them, and presumably got his hands on the import goods that had been stuck in the customs house back in Fremantle. His third trial, in front of the resident magistrate, was conducted in his absence. By the end of October 1908, Carvelli – in his Aldo Cellis incarnation – had fled Western Australia.

He turned up like a bad penny a few months later, in Wellington, New Zealand. This new persona enjoyed views of Wellington harbour from the Arcadia Hotel's rooftop garden, and soon gained a reputation as a merry fellow to have a drink with, in the bars of Lambton Quay.[48] It was here, perhaps, that he first met the man who would become his business partner and friend for many years: a dark-eyed, beautiful man who was almost ten years his junior and who, like Carvelli, also spoke both Italian and French. In Wellington they called him Alex Berard.

His real name was Alessandro di Nicotera and he was born in Piacenza, but had left the city by the time he was sixteen. After a misadventure in New York, where he was hospitalised for some unrecorded illness and then deported, he wound up in London, where shortly afterwards he was caught stealing from a fellow Italian in a café in Clerkenwell and sentenced to six weeks' hard labour. From there, he travelled to Bruges and worked in odd jobs, until he was caught stealing from another man at a public bath-house, imprisoned and then escorted to Belgium's border.[49]

He returned to Italy at the age of eighteen to worse luck: he was conscripted to the 91st Infantry Regiment, stationed in Civitavecchia, a seaside town just outside Rome. It wasn't long before the authorities found his abandoned uniform near the port. In the pocket they found a prison journal, presumably from his time in Belgium, whose back pages were filled with recipes for explosives. Branded a deserter and an

16: Alessandro di Nicotera, pictured in a mugshot from around 1908. Young and sharply dressed, it is possible to see how he was able to charm his associates, despite his reputation for violence.

anarchicho, di Nicotera was sentenced to two years in military prison *in absentia*.[50] This certainly helps to explain why he chose to flee to the other side of the world.

Di Nicotera was well established in New Zealand by the time Carvelli arrived, but the pair became fast friends. They went to the horse-races and drank together in the bars. They gained a reputation as bookmakers, as men who were good at playing the odds.[51] He introduced the older man to Wellington's Club Garibaldi, which brought together the area's small but thriving Italian community. The pair played *bocce* and gossiped with the fishermen and market gardeners, who had chosen 'brotherhood, education, work' as the club's motto. The Wellington police later reported that the pair were never seen outside each other's company, but whether this was to prove their status as conspiratorial criminals or to intimate that they enjoyed a deeper illicit relationship, shall for ever remain hidden between the lines.[52]

The men of the Club Garibaldi were not the only friends Carvelli and di Nicotera were making in Wellington in 1909. Di Nicotera cultivated a relationship with a woman called Annie Sawyer, who, according to later reports, 'pretended to be his wife'. Carvelli, meanwhile, met Camelia Rae, also known as 'Tit'. He was also seen in the company of a woman called Marie Vernon, who bore a striking resemblance to Vanda Williams, the woman from whose bed he had been hauled by Sergeant O'Donovan several months before. It seems that when Carvelli fled Leonora, Vanda followed.

Whatever their murky romantic and commercial entanglements, Carvelli and his associates were probably in New Zealand for a very clear reason: in 1908 a case ruling had formally decriminalised one-woman brothels in the country. Following the English case law of Singleton v. Ellison, which in 1897 had defined a brothel as a place used by more than one woman for the purposes of prostitution, the New Zealand court found that any premises where only one woman sold sex could not be considered a brothel. This meant that, for a brief period, if women sold sex behind respectable shop fronts and alone in houses, they could avoid harassment from the Wellington police. More than used to adapting to legal changes, women who sold sex began to run sweet shops and tobacconists as a widely tolerated cover for 'one-woman brothels', as they were known, in both Wellington and Auckland.[53]

It was an ideal opportunity. Carvelli began to speak to estate agents and furniture dealers, and secured numbers

14 and 24 College Street as one-woman brothels. Di Nicotera did the same with premises on Dixon and Gray Streets,
where he installed Annie Sawyer, who presented herself as
his wife. Camelia Rae moved into number 14, and Marie
Vernon took up residence at 24 College Street. The women
earned enough to hand over £20 each per week to the men
who 'protected' them.

Money seemed to do little but make Carvelli and di Nicotera want more. Rumours had reached them of men who
knew men who had gone with their women to Buenos Aires,
who told tales at the bar of easy gold for the taking. True to
the popular saying, they came back 'rich as an Argentine'.
By late 1909, about a year into their New Zealand venture,
Carvelli and Marie Vernon, alongside di Nicotera and Annie
Sawyer, began to hatch a plan. Taking a page straight out of
one of the growing number of sensational books on 'white
slavery', they offered money to lodging-house tenants to keep
an eye out for young women who had recently come alone to
the city. They were looking for what was known as 'seconds'
or 'kids' – younger women who would work for pimps who
already had partnered with a slightly older woman. 'You
can pick them off the streets,' other pimps reported. 'If they
fuck for charity and you offer them a trip, they'll come.'[54] Di
Nicotera found a girl named Florrie, who agreed to travel
with him and Annie to South America.

This young woman has left barely a trace behind. We
know that she boarded the ship with di Nicotera and Sawyer,
because of an incident that transpired on board. In a heated
argument, or in reaction to her perceived insolence, di Nicotera struck her in the face in full view of fellow passengers.
The blow was so hard that it sent the girl sprawling on the

deck of the ship. Witnesses went to the captain, demanding that Florrie be disembarked in Montevideo and sent back home. After this, the trail fades. Did Florrie fall back, or go back, into the hands of di Nicotera in Montevideo and, if so, could she be the girl 'Marguerite Carl' who accompanied Marie Vernon back to New Zealand on the RMS *Tainui*? Did Florrie manage to secure passage home from the steamship company, or the British consul, whose records were lost? Or did she disappear? In any case, no action was taken against the man who had hit her, who seems to have been allowed to simply stroll off the ship.

Carvelli, meanwhile, found his 'kid' one evening in January 1910, when he arrived at 24 College Street to find Marie in conversation with a mousy-haired girl who said her name was Lydia Harvey. The vetting process began. Marie did most of the talking, but Carvelli wanted to emphasise caution. He added to Marie's warnings to be careful, and told Lydia to make sure the police didn't see her meeting them. What he didn't say was that people around town had begun to suspect who he really was. A rumour about him had already reached the Club Garibaldi, and he and di Nicotera were asked not to return.[55] As already-suspect immigrants, the mostly southern Italians of Club Garibaldi clung tightly to their respectability. Whatever their moral position on prostitution and on the role of the *mezanno*, or middle man, they could not afford to be associated with the likes of these men.

Vernon and Carvelli booked tickets to travel on the same ship as di Nicotera, Sawyer and the girl Florrie, departing in late January 1910. They were there to witness the violence that di Nicotera exacted, but their reaction – or lack thereof – went unrecorded. In any case, they knew better than to travel with their underage 'kid'. They asked Camelia Rae to book Lydia Harvey another passage, leaving a couple of weeks later – unwilling, it seems, to take the same risk as di Nicotera did in travelling with his 'lightweight baggage', as underage girls bound for brothels in Buenos Aires were known. The house at 24 College Street was closed up, the furniture was sold off and customers who called were sent up the road to 'Tit' at number 14.

There was one last thing left to do before their trans-Pacific adventure began. On 27 January 1910, Carvelli and Vernon took the tram from central Wellington just a few miles down the road, to the pleasant suburb of Island Bay. In the hot summer sun they walked to St Hilda's Anglican Church room, where the vicar married them.[56] Carvelli wore his finest suit and his widest collar, with his pearl tie-pin and gold watch chain. He smoothed his hair with pomade and sculpted his moustache with wax.[57] Afterwards they walked along the esplanade to see the beach and the hills and islands around the town. They boarded the steamship a few days later: part honeymoon, part business venture. The newly-weds arrived in Buenos Aires together in late February 1910.

The port where they arrived was pulsing with goods and people, and their hopes and dreams; it was a place where, after passing through the customs house, a man could be anyone. There were neighbourhoods near the old port that looked as though they had been plucked from Genoa and set down on the other side of the world.[58] As they made their way deeper into the expansive metropolis, Carvelli recognised a cityscape in a fever of constant transformation, not unlike the Turin of his boyhood, where cranes outnumbered church spires by a dozen to one.[59] It was a place where a charming, respectable-looking man could buy himself social status, and where he could thrive in the half-light.[60]

He began to sniff around, to meet acquaintances of acquaintances in bars and cafés, and in registered brothels. The informal information network had to be navigated carefully. Carvelli spoke to mostly French small-time pimps and – if he was lucky – won himself some invitations to speak with the more established brothel-keepers and landlords. The message was that Buenos Aires was a land of opportunity for commercial sex, but one where you had to play your cards right. Established pimps and brothel-keepers resented any new man moving in on their girls; there was rivalry between the immigrant Jewish and French men and local men, who each had an interest in a different element of the city's sex trade. Worse still, the police were under more and more pressure to crack down on illegal activity, which was perhaps beginning to encroach on their willingness to take bribes. A man could wash out of the city quickly.[61] 'Don't invest in a house until you are sure that you will stay' was the common advice. The Teatro Casino on Calle Maipu, Carvelli was told, was the place for *franchuscas* (the name for Western European women who solicited in Buenos Aires, whether they were French or not) who were not registered with the police. It was crowded with girls, his informers warned, but there were plenty of men as well. All the johns want to be sucked here, they said. 'When a girl gets a reputation there as a good cock sucker,' the pimps told the undercover investigator in Argentina a few years later, 'her fortune is made.'[62]

Having done the requisite research, bought the expected

drinks and shaken the necessary hands, Carvelli found a *pensión* (the Argentinian term for furnished rooms) for himself and Marie, and told her about the Teatro Casino and the prices she could charge for oral sex. They would have to be careful, he'd been warned, not to let anyone know the girl's real age. With that, he boarded a river steamer and travelled up the mouth of the Rio de Plata to Montevideo, in time to greet his 'lightweight baggage' when she alighted from the SS *Ruahine* in early March 1910.

They returned the next day, and Marie greeted them on the docks. After a day or two of shopping – which saw Marie drag home a strange little black-eyed parrot – Carvelli sent the women off to the Casino together, trusting that Marie would show Lydia how to get a man. But she didn't get a man that night, or the one after that. The following night he showed her how it was done.

Carvelli probably gave little thought indeed to Lydia's feelings when he forced her to have sex with him. In his world – indeed, in the world at large – such things were completely normal. The concept of rape was largely limited to sex with violence, and many men (and indeed women) believed that so long as a woman did not put up a sustained physical fight, then whatever occurred did not constitute rape. If this was something the average man believed – and, for that matter, what a woman police officer like Lilian Wyles believed – then Antonio Carvelli certainly believed it, too. Afterwards he put on his suit and jewellery and dined out on Lydia and Marie's earnings, among the electric lights and bars and fountains.

But Lydia, however cowed and coerced she was, maintained her own ideas about what was and was not sexually acceptable, much to Carvelli and Marie's frustration. She refused to perform oral sex on clients and, when the couple demonstrated it to her, said she would never do it. She only allowed Carvelli to have sex with her in what she called 'the proper way', rather than 'the French way'. Whether this name for oral sex came from a fantasy of French sexuality, or from a reality among French sex workers, is difficult to say. What is certain is that the act permeated the commercial sex culture of Buenos Aires and that, as far as many women were concerned, it offered a way to see more clients in a day, for more money per client (being taboo meant they could charge more than they would for vaginal sex).

These concerns did not sway Lydia's opinion. To her, oral sex was depraved and disgusting, and she made her feelings clear. Carvelli appeared to have accepted her stance on the matter in the end, and despite his other coercion and abuse, he let the matter of the 'French way' drop. She was what pimps called a 'clean girl' and there was nothing much that could be done about it.[63]

To Carvelli, this was probably the first sign that his Argentinian business venture was not shaping up to become what he had been told it could be. To make matters far worse, the police raided their *pensión* a few days later and he found himself in yet another country's police station, paying yet another treasury his bail money. He returned to the rented rooms, barely able to contain his temper. He told the women to pack their things and took them to a registered brothel, telling Lydia to lie about her age and say she was twenty-one – the age at which women were permitted to register as prostitutes in the municipality. Marie protested at her abandonment in such a place; Carvelli promised it would only be for as long as it took him to book a steamer out of the country. Di Nicotera and his woman had already left and were waiting for them in London. But when he returned to his hotel room, Carvelli discovered that some of his things had been stolen – and was probably too furious to appreciate the irony.

He returned to the brothel after two days. Marie was sullen and angry with him, telling him that the women in the place were full of disease. Lydia told him she was feeling unwell. He found a doctor and dragged her there, and he was told that she had the clap and scabies. Medicines and creams for her set him back more money. A few days later he booked a passage on the SS *Asturias* for London, surely glad to see the back of the city where he had not, in any way, grown 'rich as an Argentine'.

They boarded the ship and found their second-class cabin. The parrot squawked and hopped about in its cage. Before they left Buenos Aires it seemed that every day the newspapers carried a new story about 'white slavery', and the ship's passengers were on high alert for anything that resembled it. Carvelli was clearly aware how easily he could become a target for their suspicions, if seen with two young women in tow from Buenos Aires, even if they were technically headed in the opposite direction of the 'traffic in women' that everyone was so concerned about. Increasingly paranoid, Carvelli insisted that Marie and Lydia stay in the cabin for the whole voyage. Both women were miserable and, trapped in a windowless cabin for two weeks, were predictably seasick. Carvelli, for his part, soothed his frazzled nerves over drinks and cigarettes in the second-class passenger lounge.

Despite his fears of travelling at the height of the 'white

slave' panic, in early April 1910 they arrived in Southampton, unaccosted by the authorities or by fellow passengers. The health inspector boarded, checked the eyes and lungs of the third-class passengers and let them all alight. From there, the travellers, their bags and the bird took the boat-train to London and a taxi to the Piedmont Hotel in Soho, one of the many Italian- and French-run businesses in London's most cosmopolitan area. By day, it was like many other continental neighbourhoods, with sandwich shops and cafés, and children on their way to school; but by night it came alive with entertainment seekers, diners, drinkers, gangsters and, of course, working girls.[64]

London had never been home to any system of regulated prostitution, and brothels and street solicitation were technically proscribed, but often tolerated. But thanks to pressure from anti-vice campaigners, both indoor and outdoor commercial sex had increasingly become the target of uneven police crackdowns and moral crusades since the 1880s. This caused an immense clandestine commercial sex industry to grow up in Britain's capital. Women who sold sex in London found ways to evade criminal measures, but this resilience came at a cost. Women solicited on the street by walking continuously: keeping up their end of the bargain with police officers meant always 'moving on'. They took clients back to one-room flats, which technically did not constitute brothels, and operated out of coffee houses, restaurants, hotels and massage parlours. Working in an atmosphere of increasing criminalisation meant that women needed pimps more than ever: to pose as husbands in order to get flats, to watch for police officers as they solicited on the street, to pay bail and fines in the police stations and police courts, and to protect them from clients who thought no one could hear them scream in isolated flats.

Carvelli left his wife and Lydia Harvey in the hotel room and headed out into the busy Soho streets, with a list of addresses of bars and cafés in his pocket. He reconnected with his old friend di Nicotera, and the pair spent the next few days and nights buying men drinks, shaking hands, kissing cheeks and learning the names of the pimps who were known as 'boys' in London's West End. They met some men who really were just boys, like Charles Peneau, the nineteen-year-old from France with protective parents.[65] They also met men like Max Kassell, a seasoned leader in the business. Kassell advised Carvelli to get himself a gun – things were getting more territorial these days, he explained. Bookies and pimps, club owners and racetrack gangs, they all had a razor, a knife or a pistol hidden somewhere on their person. Many years later, Max Kassell would be shot by another pimp and left to die slowly in the bathtub of his Soho flat, before his body was dumped in a ditch in St Albans. The papers would have a field day.[66]

But for now these well-dressed 'boys' embodied the louche and cosmopolitan reputation of Soho. They strolled up and down Charing Cross Road and Shaftesbury Avenue, chastising the women who were working for them if they saw them socialising rather than soliciting. They ducked into pawnshops to buy furs, trinkets and purses for themselves and the women who accompanied them; they enjoyed drinks at the Admiral Duncan public house in Old Compton Street and in Café Henry near Fitzroy Square. They wandered in and out of the Alhambra and the Empire music halls, and dined on oysters and champagne at the Hotel d'Europe into the wee hours of the night.

Carvelli, new to the scene, depended on these other men to give him the lie of the land. They told him about the best places to send his women; about which cops might take a bribe; about bringing in new recruits; and about what to do with the young prude from New Zealand that he needed to get off his hands. They must have given him a hard time about that one. Pimps didn't think too highly of 'proper white slavers' who went for the inexperienced girls. 'There's plenty of charity cunts,' one pimp explained to the under-cover investigator for the League of Nations. 'But I wouldn't take any chances.' Most men advised their colleagues to keep their hands off the 'greenies': 'too much fucking bother'.[67]

The 'boys' nonetheless told Carvelli where to find the VD hospital, and he took Lydia there in a taxi in mid-April. In the hospital entrance on Harrow Road he saw Lydia into the hands of the nurses, telling them that she was his child's nursemaid who had got herself into trouble. He insisted that she not do any work while there: he had promised her, after all, that she would not go back into service. He kissed her on the cheek, like he did that first day they met back in Welling-ton, and bade her farewell: there was, after all, more money to be made.

He arranged a flat for himself and Marie on a street off Tottenham Court Road, an area that was then known as North Soho.[68] He showed his wife the best route to walk and how to avoid arrest. In London this meant constantly moving, so that the cops on their beats could not observe them as easily. If the coppers saw a girl once, the 'boys' had told him, they wrote it down. If they saw her twice, they cautioned her and told her to 'move on'. If they saw her a third time, it was back to Great Marlborough Street Police

Station, her name in the charge book, a night in the police cells and, if she was a foreigner, deportation.

Carvelli communicated these risks to Marie. He bought her a new purse at the pawnshop, in which to put her clients' money, and kissed her fondly. She styled her hair and put on her silk stockings and headed out into the West End night. She came back with decent earnings, and they ate their suppers late beneath the lights of Piccadilly.

Lydia Harvey remained a liability. In May, Carvelli visited her again at the hospital, renewing his threats. 'If the police get a hold of you they will tell your mother about what you have been doing,' he told the girl. 'They will put you in a home and make you work for other people.' He sent Marie to check on Lydia each Wednesday afternoon for the full month.[69]

But Marie was also becoming increasingly difficult to manage. She told him that she hated London. She had to keep walking and walking or the coppers harassed her, and her feet were blistered and aching.[70] It was cold and rainy and the sun never seemed to shine. Carvelli was, he admitted, inclined to agree. But they could not return to New Zealand after all this travelling without something to show for it, and there was all that money they had lost in the failed Buenos Aires venture to think about. And so it was decided that Marie would go back to Wellington, taking one of the 'kids' along as well: if Florrie had not been successfully saved by her vigilant fellow passengers, this might have been her. Carvelli would stay on for a few more weeks. He would go back to Paris, where he was sure to find some old contacts right where he had left them: drinking Pernod at the terrace bars of Montmartre and Pigalle.[71] He would find some more girls and get them on the game, and then he and Marie would be reunited in the happier and sunnier Antipodes, their wealth restored.

Carvelli sent Marie to the hospital to fetch Lydia and she brought the girl back to the flat and gave her a cast-off dress that had not joined the rest of the clothes in her travel case. Marie assured the girl that her husband would 'see her settled'. Telling Lydia to wait in the flat and not go out, Carvelli and Marie travelled together from Liverpool Street Station to the Royal Albert Docks. He saw her onto the ship and to her berth, where the valet installed Marie's possessions and set the parrot's cage down gently. A tearful farewell, many kisses and then Carvelli left the RMS *Tainui* before it sounded its evening departure horn.

Returning to the flat in Wells Street that night, Carvelli told Lydia that, despite what Marie had said, he had no intention of handing her even tuppence. It was common for the 'boys' of Soho to exchange women, and he planned to be rid of her as soon as he could. At first he tried to convince her to work for di Nicotera, but the girl refused, telling him that one of the other girls said he beat his wife Annie for not bringing in enough money. Carvelli could not deny this – di Nicotera had always been a hothead – and there was no convincing her. He finally found an older pimp in Soho who wanted a new girl and, after some money changed hands, wiped his own hands clean of her.[72]

With business matters seen to, it was time to take care of some affairs of the heart. In early June 1910, Carvelli took the train south from Victoria Station. Alighting at Brighton's central railway station, he walked a short distance to Devonshire Place, which afforded fine views of the harbour and the lines of tidy Regency-style houses. He found the address and knocked on the door, which was answered by a housekeeper. An Italian voice asked who it was as he emerged from another room, to find himself standing before his long-lost son. Tears were surely shed, hands held and embraces exchanged; but a decade of distance must have hung heavily between them.

Luigi Carvelli, who had not heard from his son for almost ten years, was living just a short walk from the Royal Pavilion, where he performed in the Brighton Municipal Orchestra.[73] He had also established himself as a minor composer, publishing several serenatas, marches and waltzes. We shall never know Luigi's precise feelings about his eldest child, who had gone off when he was barely a man to the other side of the world. Antonio's early letters had spoken of work in the opera, of promising business opportunities, of the life he was building for himself. But then the letters had stopped, and for almost ten years Luigi hadn't heard from him. Yet there were signs that Antonio was never far from his father's heart: two years before his prodigal son's unexpected visit, the orchestra had played a special performance of Luigi's composition, the 'Serenata Napolitana', on 13 February, Antonio's birthday.[74]

Antonio told him his news, or at least the version he wanted his father to hear. He had married an Australian woman from a good family, and had taken a job at the consulate as a French translator after a stint on the stage. Antonio was perhaps also taken aback to discover the close relationship that had grown up between his father and his twelve-year-old cousin Pietro, the son of Luigi's brother Giuseppe, who was living with him in Brighton and was also a student of music. Seeing the way in which Pietro, who had been a baby when Antonio fled Italy, had become like a son to Luigi may have encouraged a jealous Antonio to elaborate on his adventures. He had recently moved to New Zealand, he told the little family, where he was working as the valet for a millionaire. He had come to visit London and to see his beloved papa and was soon off to Paris on business. Why do you go by the name Aldo Cellis? asked his father. For business reasons, his son replied.

It was a short – possibly painfully short – visit, and it seems Luigi remained completely unaware of the actual business that awaited Antonio in Paris when he bade him farewell. From nearby Newhaven, Carvelli took the ferry to Cherbourg and the train on to France's capital, speaking his mother's native tongue comfortably. At a hotel in rue de Rodier he found his constant companion, di Nicotera, and the pair set off to find new recruits in the pleasant Parisian late spring.

It was, as usual, easy. They wined and dined three working-class French girls, all of whom were new arrivals in the capital and had spent the past few years bouncing around between domestic-service posts. They encouraged them to leave the basements and garrets where they slept and come to their nice hotel rooms to stay the night. They charmed the girls, had sex with them and bought them lovely clothes. They invited them to London as lovers, promising them good and well-paid work. A few weeks after arriving in Paris, Carvelli and di Nicotera steamed back across the Channel with seventeen-year-old Mireille Lapara, nineteen-year-old Marguerite Bescançon and twenty-one-year-old Victoria Bricot in tow. They once again avoided any scrutiny by immigration officials by travelling second-class: the 1905 Aliens

Act only provided for immigration inspection of third-class passengers.

Carvelli seemed blissfully unaware of the men who followed his every movement the moment he set foot back in London. Naïve or simply cocky, he continued to carouse and dine and on 23 June met di Nicotera at Terroni's Restaurant in Old Compton Street, where the pair enjoyed a very long traditional Italian lunch. Afterwards they strolled towards the corner of Wardour Street, full of wine and grappa, perhaps discussing plans to leave London and return to the Antipodes.[75] Before they knew what was up, two English men in trenchcoats were beside them.

Carvelli heard the dreaded words through a haze: 'We are police officers and I am arresting you on warrant for procuring, or attempting to procure, three French women whose names are unknown to become common prostitutes.' He was only able to splutter, 'What for?' in reply.

'I don't know any women – where are they?' he heard di Nicotera say beside him, gesticulating angrily at the empty space around them.

Carvelli knew that the loaded revolver they were about to find in his jacket would do nothing to help his case. After its discovery, he and Alessandro were marched down Wardour Street to Great Marlborough Street Police Station. They wrote his name as Aldo Cellis in the charge book, pressed his fingers onto an inkpad and rolled them onto the squares of the fingerprint card. Perhaps he wondered how long it would take before the police connected these prints to the ones that lived in some filing cabinet in Australia. The two men were then brought to the dark police cells at the back of the station – the same ones in which Marguerite Leroy, the young woman whose case had first tipped off the police, was held months earlier.

Carvelli asked for a solicitor, a Mr Newton, whom he had been told was the man to call in this sort of situation. Mr Newton, when he arrived, explained the charge: 'Procuring, or attempting to procure, women or girls to become common prostitutes.' The key, the solicitor most likely said, was to prove that the girls were already of 'immoral character' or prostitutes before they came with you. Carvelli and di Nicotera insisted that of course they were. Mr Newton was businesslike and explained that, given the character of the female witnesses, he was hopeful the charges could be overturned. To Mr Newton's evident frustration, Carvelli had challenged the copper who arrested him to 'prove it' in court, believing that he had covered his tracks. Then, at the next police-court trial on 10 July, he was greeted with a profound shock. Sitting on the bench beside the three French girls, looking thin and pale, was none other than Lydia Harvey. Carvelli had thought himself rid of her, and he had not seen fit to mention her to his solicitor. The omission surely did not endear him to Mr Newton, whose job had just become a great deal more difficult.

One by one, the girls were called to give damning evidence against him. Lydia made for an especially effective witness: she sounded every bit the sweet colonial girl, pale and fragile, and told the crowded courtroom she had been seventeen years old when Aldo Cellis had sent her into a Buenos Aires brothel. There was nothing Mr Newton could do. Mr Denman decided there was enough evidence to proceed and sent the case to trial at the Central Criminal Court.

Carvelli spent the summer in Brixton Prison awaiting

trial and writing frantic letters to Marie in New Zealand. He was damned, Mr Newton explained, by the testimony of the star witness, whose story sounded just like every tale of trafficking the jury would ever have heard.

Sure enough, Carvelli's story soon joined the long list of 'white slavery' tales peddled by the local and national press. *Reynolds's Newspaper* sent a sketch artist to the 10 July trial, and Carvelli's aquiline profile was there in the paper, emphasising his Italian features in cheap caricature. He was an 'alien in the dock', the police-court report columns explained, charged with the most despicable of all crimes.

Mr Newton advised the two men that, given the new testimony from this New Zealand girl, they could not risk a trial for four charges of procurement, which could carry with them consecutive maximum sentences of two years in prison with hard labour – a potential eight years in all. After weeks of persuasion, Carvelli and di Nicotera reluctantly agreed. They sent Newton looking for a deal, and one was secured. On 13 September 1910, at the Central Criminal Court, Carvelli stood and pleaded guilty to the charge of conspiring to procure Mireille Lapara and Marguerite Bescancon, and the other charges were dropped. He was given six months in prison without hard labour, and would be deported as an 'unwanted alien' after the sentence was served.[76] It was better than it might have been, but he longed to see the girl whose testimony had damned him paying for it. He would 'do for her', he assured her as he was led from the court. He would kill her, if he ever saw her again.

Prison gave Carvelli plenty of time to make plans. Anticipating deportation to Italy, he made alternate arrangements to slip away before he reached those shores. This was imperative: the warrant for his arrest, issued for the theft in Turin back in 1901, was still very much in effect. Di Nicotera, for his part, was facing two years in military prison, and probably worse for desertion and being a suspected anarchist. The ease with which the pair were able to evade the fates that awaited them in Italy is testament more to international policing's infancy than to the criminals' cleverness. Once on board the ship, they rebooked their journey, alighting at Calais or Cherbourg, whichever port they first called at, and taking the boat-train to Paris. The ship continued on to Genoa without them.

The men, now far from the watchful eyes of DI Anderson and his plain-clothes police constables, were free to come and go as they pleased; and their activities, unrecorded, are invisible to the historian. It seems they remained in Paris for several weeks, no doubt reconnecting with whatever network of pimps and bookies they knew there and securing whatever funds remained to them. The coppers in London had seized or frozen many of their assets, but upon their release from prison, Carvelli was able to access the funds. One significant cache of money waited for him at the Paris branch of the London & River Plate Bank, to which he had transferred the money he had deposited in Buenos Aires.[77] These earnings, which really belonged to Lydia Harvey, were enough to pay for his steamship ticket on the SS *Scharnhorst*, bound for Fremantle and Sydney in April 1911. He travelled under his mother's misspelled maiden name, 'Courier', and this small change enabled him to slip under the noses of the Australian police, despite the fact that DI Anderson had written to them, warning that the man was coming. Perhaps some money changed hands somewhere along the way.

The Australian press, which had somehow caught wind of the warnings Scotland Yard had sent to their police forces, had a field day. For the Australian pundits, Antonio Carvelli became yet another example of how Britain thought it within its rights to steer its riff-raff towards its former colonies. 'The authorities in England did not care what became of him,' wrote the Perth *Sunday Times*, 'so long as they got him out of England.'[78] 'The brazen effrontery of coming out here when he knew there was a warrant for his arrest in existence can almost be admired,' wrote the paper's reporter.[79] Brazen seems to have been the right word. Carvelli had evidently regained his style, and some of his assets, since leaving prison: he made the voyage in first-class and was frequently seen in the saloon, as well as in the cabin of two young Italian women who were bound for Fremantle as domestic servants.

Despite the noise in the press, the police in Australia seemed disinclined to search very hard for one former 'white slaver'. Local police in Leonora were told that since all the witnesses – the French girls, as well as Sergeant O'Donovan – had moved on, there was no point in pursuing the charge of pimping. Carvelli, free from the eyes of the law, lived for a while in Sydney and then returned to New Zealand.

This time he went to Auckland, and called himself Anton Courrier. He was an unassuming shopkeeper, running a small import business that sold oriental goods and European delicacies: silver picture frames, batiked silks, Chinese fans and Indian lanterns were displayed in the windows, and olive oil, salami, cheeses and dried fruits were stocked on the tidy shelves. He obtained these items as a commercial traveller and indent agent – a business that traded in a different kind

17: A shop in Auckland, New Zealand around 1915, owned by Antonio Carvelli, known now as Anton Courrier, which sold 'oriental goods' and 'European delicacies'. His import–export business was genuine, but likely also a place where he laundered the money he made in organised prostitution.

of traffic. He bought goods such as silverware, cotton and silk, and craftwork made by enslaved, indentured or other highly exploited labour, and sold it at a steep mark-up in more affluent markets.[80]

This import business supplemented, but did not replace, Carvelli's work as a pimp; nor did it end his associations with Alessandro di Nicotera. Police believed that di Nicotera, now going by the name of Alec Denis, had established himself as a 'leader of a gang' of pimps whose interests spanned the Tasman Sea, and both he and Carvelli were spotted regularly travelling back and forth between Auckland, Sydney and Melbourne. Carvelli, it was said, collected 'large sums of money from his shop'. It is unlikely this income came entirely from salami and bronzeware. He used the shop to launder the money he had made from brothels: a convenient front that could be used to disprove any potential charge of brothel-keeping or living on the earnings of prostitution.[81]

Business was booming, but on a regular visit to Sydney in 1914 his luck ran out again. Carvelli was arrested by one DI Gleeson, who charged him with a breach of the Immigration Restriction Act. Carvelli was convicted for being 'a prohibited immigrant'. He avoided three months' hard labour by entering into a bond of £150, but was immediately deported. October 1914 was not a particularly auspicious time to be an Italian migrant.[82] Though Carvelli escaped internment in Australia because his country was not yet at war with theirs, the commencement of hostilities between Britain and her allies and Germany and her allies (of which Italy, for the time being, was assumed to soon be one) meant that Carvelli had little hope of getting clemency from Australian immigration officials or the police.

After his deportation he travelled via Hawaii and San Francisco and then disappeared amid the confusion, as the world plunged into the largest and most widespread war it had ever seen. He would later tell the authorities that he had served as a solider in Italy during the First World War and had been decorated as a war hero.[83] But Italy's records of servicemen do not bear up these claims. The war, it seems, had been unkind to the Carvellis of Calabria, Antonio's father's family. Five of his cousins died: two in combat and three from disease, which, judging by their dates of death, might have been malaria, cholera and Spanish flu.[84] There is no sign that Antonio served at all.

Carvelli spent some time in Italy during the First World

War, but by 1917 was rumoured to be back in Australia.[85] Marie continued to run a brothel in Auckland, providing succour to the young soldiers of the king before they were shipped off to the Dardanelles, or after they had returned as older and more damaged heroes.[86] For men like Carvelli, and for the women they were associated with, business had never been better. They probably finished the war many thousands of pounds richer than they were when it began.

It was this wealth, perhaps, that enabled Antonio Carvelli to undertake what would be his most dramatic act of self-reinvention. Steering clear of the streets of Sydney where he was known to the police, he made his way to Hobart, Tasmania, where he became Monsieur Anthony Coty, a man who claimed to be an accredited dance instructor, band leader and renowned master of the tango. In 1923 he presided over the grand opening of Hobart's hottest dancing club, the Continental Hotel Deluxe. Sporting his most impressive moustache to date, he began to teach the bright young things of Hobart how to tango and foxtrot during dance nights at the club, and offered private lessons in well-to-do homes. His business partner was also his dance partner, and these days she went by the name Miss Kathleen Williams.

It was certainly a way to put all his skills to work: he sang, danced and played instruments; he dressed in tuxedos and behaved ostentatiously; he charmed women by offering them a glittering new world of dresses, music, excitement and entertainment. He was even able to tap into his South American misadventure, importing Argentina's most famous and deliciously 'forbidden' dance craze to Tasmania.

The tango was born in the brothels of Buenos Aires,

but by the early 1920s 'Tangomania' was a global craze: a symbol of the bright, new and more sexually relaxed post-war world, in which young women's roles as consumers of popular culture, glamour and leisure were being drastically redefined.[87] The tango, according to the Argentinian essay-ist Ezequiel Martínez Estrada, had 'clandestinely infiltrated a world that denied it access. It reached the cities under dis-guise and triumphantly entered into parlours and homes.'[88] In this, Carvelli was the tango in human form. Using this dance itself as a vehicle, he had once again infiltrated respectable society. A thousand miles away from London, the parents of Hobart had no idea that their daughters' dance instructor was a convicted sex trafficker.

Yet the very mobility that had helped hide Carvelli's true identity was about to expose him. After all, you never knew who would turn up in the town that you happened to be in; who you would run into in the streets of Wellington, the docks of Hong Kong, the cafés of Soho or, in Carvelli's case, the dance halls of Hobart. He was about eighteen months into his new commercial venture when an old acquaintance from Western Australia happened to call into the Conti-nental Hotel Deluxe. The man got a shock: he was sure that before him stood 'Signor Cellis', despite 'Monsieur Coty's' protests: he could never forget the man's mismatched eyes. This acquaintance knew that Aldo Cellis had skipped out on a charge of living on immoral earnings in Leonora, Western Australia.

Once he knew that he had been discovered by the Kal-goorlie acquaintance, Carvelli attempted to slip away before the local police caught wind of who he really was. He packed his bags in a panic, while the sounds of jazz drifted up from the club below. He raced to the booking office and bought a ticket on the next steamer out of Launceston, the SS *Nairana*, travelling overnight to Melbourne, arriving on 27 February 1925. He left Hobart by train that night.

Upon arrival at the mainland, the *Nairana* made her way up the mouth of the Yarra past the docklands of Melbourne, and Carvelli disembarked just after nine in the morning. Perhaps as he made his way down Australia Wharf towards the bustling city he thought he would successfully disappear into the crowd. But the Hobart police had telegrammed ahead to their colleagues in Melbourne, and DI Gleeson had been informed. The officer knew the man and his many names well, and had kept a photograph of Carvelli in his possession since he had arrested him for being a 'prohibited immigrant' when he worked in Sydney in 1914. Gleeson made his way to the docklands and waited.

Thanks to the photograph, it wasn't long before Gleeson picked his quarry out of the crowd. Carvelli was asked his name, which he said was Anthony Coty, although he hastened to add that was a stage name. Gleeson, surely pleased with himself for catching up with an old nemesis yet again, arrested Carvelli for a second time as a 'prohibited immigrant'.[89] The next day Carvelli was up before the magistrate at the City Court, who sentenced him to six months in prison, commuted to deportation from Australia and a fine. His wife arrived by his side shortly afterwards, having left Hobart as soon as she heard about his arrest, and she paid his bail. They would plead his case, she assured Carvelli. They had friends in high places. They would convince the authorities that he was a changed man. During this time he visited the Home Department regularly, begging his case, telling the officials

18: 'Hobart's Pet with the Odd Eyes', screamed the headline in
Smith's Weekly News in March of 1925, after it was discovered
that Anthony Coty, the dance master and manager of the city's
Continental Hotel Deluxe, was not who he said he was.

that her husband had reformed himself, that all his business
dealings were now thoroughly above board.[90]

Whether or not this was true would matter little, because
it seemed Carvelli wasn't the only man who knew the value
of a pound. The old mate of Carvelli from his Fremantle
days sold his story to two of Australia's most widely read
tabloid newspapers, *Smith's Weekly* and *Truth*, and by
7 March, while Carvelli waited for his meeting with the
Home Department in Melbourne where he would plead his
case, the story broke.

'Hobart's Pet with the Odd Eyes,' shouted *Smith's Weekly*.
The article delighted as much in exposing the cosmopolitan
follies of one of Australia's hinterland cities as it did in the
scandal of the 'polished scoundrel' who had been a 'white
slaver'. 'That portion of Hobart Society which pursues the
pleasures of the dance has been sitting in shocked silence
wondering how ever it came to make such a fool of itself
… but let it not be thought that Hobart Society is a novice
of making a fool of itself,' went the article. Conscious of its

readership, who fancied themselves patriotic, hard-working, independent men, *Smith's Weekly* pilloried the dances Coty was famous for, as a critique of the superficial nouveau riche. 'No fashionable party was complete unless he was there to demonstrate his favourite tango,' the paper sneered. He would often be seen 'shaking as merry a toe as ever charmed a flapper'.[91]

Truth went easier on the well-to-do flappers of backwater Hobart and fixated more readily on Mr Coty's foreignness, playing to a widespread anti-immigrant sentiment. Declaring him a 'white slaver' in its headline, the byline explained that the dancing master Coty was really an 'Italian of many aliases' who was 'Teaching Flappers to "Jazz"'. He was slim, graceful and 'very proud of his upper lip adornment ... which he waxed with meticulous care'.[92] He was also a fifth columnist, a potential Fascist. *Truth* noted that the 'actor-soldier' showed no anxiety to leave 'Mussolini Land' after the war. His caricatured face, mysteriously missing its moustache, was blazoned across a half-page in every town and city where *Truth* enjoyed its wide circulation. All of Australia now knew Carvelli as 'the man with one brown eye and the other grey, white-slaver, linguist, actor, teacher of dancing, thief, and general reprobate'.[93]

Carvelli was ruined and devastated, helpless fodder for the new interwar tabloids, which, combining William Stead's investigative journalism with new technologies for printing photographs, sought out sensations, scandals and controversies to boost sales. The rest of the papers followed suit, reporting on Carvelli's past crimes, speculating on his current ones and relishing his misfortune at being caught. The Home Department official in charge of his file was

19: A caricature of Antonio Carvelli that appeared in *Truth* (Melbourne) in March of 1925. His Italian facial features are stereotyped to emphasise his foreignness, and his tuxedo marks him as a typical character from the dance halls of the interwar era.

inclined to grant him clemency, but Carvelli himself was so disturbed by the vitriol of the 'gutter press' that he agreed it was best for him to leave.

Carvelli, ever the conman, played his roles to the last: the dancing master of Hobart, the businessman and artiste regretting the folly of his youth, the self-proclaimed war hero, the desperate victim of sensationalised reporting, the loving husband fearful for his own and his wife's fate under Fascism. But the stories he spun did not prevent his past from catching up with him. He was deported back to Mussolini's Italy in March 1925. The papers delighted in his imminent departure: 'Vale, Carvelli; your country calls you,' *Truth* chimed, while *Smith's Weekly* advised that, should he ever want to sneak back into Australia again, 'he had better change his eyes.'[94]

CHAPTER SIX

THE WOMAN UNKNOWN

She was not sad to see the back of London. The day she was due to depart she dressed herself at the very height of fashion: a corset, a slim petticoat, a white blouse and a dark walking skirt of Panama chiffon, and over that a form-fitting jacket to guard against the north's abominable summertime chill. She tied a white silk scarf around her neck in a loose bow. She arranged her dark hair in billowing curls and pinned them around her head. Upon them she placed her latest acquisition, a magnificent turban hat that was all the rage in Paris that year. She fixed it to her head with an enormous hat-pin, sharp as a weapon. Then, before she left the Soho flat for good, she slipped a heavy golden bangle around her slender wrist.

She boarded the ship with baggage in tow – a large travel chest, a suitcase and her pretty parrot in its cage, which a beleaguered-looking valet carried gingerly. And behind her came Marguerite Carl, whom she towered above, wearing a hat that had seen too many seasons. The tall woman was boarding the RMS *Tainui*, bound for Colombo, Fremantle, Melbourne and Wellington, in the name of Miss Williams, but this was no more her real name than Marie Vernon or Vanda had been. She changed her name almost as often as she changed her clothing, and just as easily.

Veronique Sarah White would always remain, to a certain extent, as she was described in the official charge read out against her accomplice and husband Antonio Carvelli back in July 1910: a woman unknown. The police in London never learned her real name, and she escaped from that city before they could question her or press charges. Again and again she managed to slip away from the gaze of the authorities, defy the law and work in the twilight. She did not leave behind any letters, diaries, memoirs or explanations; only traces of a long and unexpected life. Yet these traces reveal a great deal about a mobile, ambitious and often troubling woman as she worked in the global sex industry and moved through the tumultuous early twentieth-century world.

Veronique was born in Carlton, Melbourne, in 1883 and her unremembered toddler years were spent in Bowen Street, Richmond, where her parents had moved after spending the early years of their marriage in the gold-rush town of Bendigo.[1] Veronique's mother, Sarah Daley, had emigrated to Australia from England as a child; and her father, Frederick White, had been born in Sydney.[2] Thanks to her father's booming draper's business, the Whites joined a wave of middle-class families cashing in on Melbourne's property boom. Her father bought a house on an easily obtained mortgage at 15 Invermay Grove, in the leafy suburban town of Hawthorn. Veronique, along with her parents, four sisters and brother, moved into the four-bedroomed home in 1887. It was a villa in miniature, with a lovely veranda, a little white fence, pretty iron lacework and a garden for the six children – Frances, Ethel, Keppel, Blanche, Beatrice and Veronique – to play in.

Her parents managed to protect her and her siblings from

the worst, when recession hit and 'Marvellous Melbourne' came crashing down. Housing prices plummeted, banks collapsed and small-business owners struggled. In the twelve years between 1889 and 1901, Hawthorn's 61 per cent home ownership fell to 34 per cent, and the Whites contributed to this statistic.[3] Thirteen-year-old Veronique probably hated having to leave the beloved family home in Invermay Grove in 1895, when her father had to sell at a loss and become a renter once more. But unlike some, the Whites did not seem to suffer total economic ruin during the Depression years. The next two houses on Leslie Street and Henry Street were just as well appointed, and larger, than the one they had owned; but the family probably never forgot the potential fragility of home. Perhaps it bred in the teenage Veronique the desire to find a more recession-proof form of wealth.

Veronique grew from a girl to a young woman on the sleepy green streets of Hawthorn, 'Melbourne's middle-class heartland', which, like so many growing suburbs, was a microcosm of modern life at the turn of the twentieth century. Gas lit the main thoroughfares. Sewerage was improved, though it would be another decade or more before all of Hawthorn's effluent ran down the hill to Spotswood pumping station.[4] The railway arrived just as the Whites did, allowing workers and day-trippers easy access to Melbourne's dense urban centre. Electric trams vied with horse-drawn carriages; new coffee houses and clothes shops stood alongside small factories and brickworks. Double-decker Daimler buses brought people to a growing town centre. The town hall hosted vaudeville, and Chinese laundries, hotels, grocers and banks lined the streets. Thanks to a very active and successful Women's Christian Temperance Union, Hawthorn had 'more churches than public houses'.[5] It was a safe, clean, tidy and respectable place for a girl to grow up.

The worldwide dramatic rise in the consumer market for clothing was what funded these early years of Veronique's life. As a draper, Frederick White imported and sold cloth to tailors, factories and individual households. It was a family business. Veronique learned dressmaking; and her sister Frances helped to run the draper's shop. Ethel worked for a time as a milliner, probably behind her father's shop front. Keppel, the only boy, became a commercial traveller, most likely in the cloth and clothing business. This was the era when prêt-à-porter clothing exploded into middle-class suburban households, and it filled the catalogues that working girls like Lydia Harvey thumbed through on their dinner breaks. This cotton, silk and woollen cloth and clothing was produced more cheaply than ever before with the help, in part, of new machinery. But it was also made possible by a global network of exploited labour: in cotton fields in India and the United States; in silk farms in China and Japan; in industrialised weaving and spinning factories around the world; and in small sweatshops and larger factories in cities like Paris, where Mireille Lapara had toiled. It would be another twenty years before synthetic fibres began to create a global market for fully disposable fashion, but the labour and environmental exploitation that continues to underwrite the industry to this day was in place long before.

Clothing and cloth also helped buy Veronique an education. She, like most children, attended new state primary schools, but girls like Veronique were also sent on to small private secondary schools, where they would learn the skills essential to female middle-class life: dancing, singing, elocution, literature and various other social graces and worldly knowledge that would make them good wives and mothers. Veronique learned French, which would come in handy later in life, passing her third-division Alliance Française examination with honours in 1893.[6] Most of her schoolmates aimed to make good marriages to clerks, bankers and businessmen, and had no intention of earning a living for themselves.[7] Still, change was in the air. At charged meetings in the local coffee house in Hawthorn, women demanded the vote, access to universities and professions and a right to public space.[8] But Veronique, when confronted with the plans of her schoolmates, the hopes of her family business and the aims of the suffrage campaigners, chose a different path altogether.

In 1901, when she was eighteen, the family left Hawthorn and moved closer to the city, renting a house at 36 George Street, South Fitzroy. The house had servant bells, pretty iron lacework, a small but well-appointed garden, an elegant fireplace and a high-ceilinged sitting room that looked out on a quiet street, where Methodist schoolgirls passed on their way to classes.[9] In 1900 Fitzroy retained vestiges of its history as a well-to-do suburb, but the 1890s Depression had taken its toll and the area was gaining a reputation as a vice-district and slum, where prostitutes and pickpockets drank in 'sly grog' shops, and where children whose parents couldn't afford to wash them played in the streets and alleys. The boarding houses and hotels that lined Victoria Parade, just round the corner, were increasingly filled with itinerant, poor, disreputable people.[10]

Veronique's own parents, who had always made sure she washed, had mapped out the streets upon which she was not

Auburn Road, Hawthorn.

20: Auburn Road in the town of Hawthorn in 1905, around the
time the White family left to move to Fitzroy, Melbourne.

to set foot, and guarded their family against the encroaching
unrespectability. It was a typical way in which middle-class
families protected their daughters, but it was a surveillance
that middle-class girls were increasingly rejecting. Despite
parental warnings, Veronique was drawn to the bars and
boarding houses and the bustle of downtown Melbourne.
Perhaps there were arguments; perhaps she told lies. But in
any case, up the narrow, steep staircase, in the new room she
shared with her sisters, Veronique was making plans to leave
her safe, mediocre and middle-class life behind. By 1903 she
was no longer listed with the rest of her family on the Fitzroy
electoral register.[11]

Why did young women leave home at the turn of the
century, and what happened to them when they did? This
was a question at the heart of the panic around sex trafficking that began to sweep the Western world at the same time

as Veronique bade 36 George Street farewell.[12] But popular as these 'white slavery' stories were, they were not without their critics. The English feminist and Women's Freedom League founder Teresa Billington-Greig was incensed by the way that campaigners used false stories of entrapment that portrayed women as 'impotent and imbecilic weaklings' to bolster their claims for repressive legislation. She pointed out that far more men and boys than women and girls left home and were never accounted for, and – as a young woman who left a poor and unhappy home herself to work at the age of seventeen – she railed against the idea that the only reason a daughter might go missing was because she was coerced into the sex industry.[13]

Part of Billington-Greig's point was that while people were deeply fearful for the daughters who left home, they were simultaneously enamoured with the heroic tales of young men who did the same thing. These young men made names for themselves on the streets of the world's cities and made their fortunes on frontiers. Foreign places and gold-rich hinterlands were, for them, spaces of opportunity and adventure. So-called respectable women only arrived later, to civilise the frontier as domestic servants and wives.[14]

And yet it seems that adventure was precisely what Veronique White was undertaking. 'Every afternoon, away in far Australia, there comes over us all at half past two in the afternoon a feeling, an intolerable ennui, a sense of emptiness and discontent,' wrote the Sydney-born poet Louise Mack in London in 1902, 'a longing for something large and full that cannot be exhausted.' Mack spoke of her dream of going to England.[15] Veronique may have had a different dream and saw the 'wild west' as a place to make that dream come true:

to become the woman who wore fine clothes, not the woman who made them.[16]

But the reasons for leaving home and for having dreams can be manifold: a mix of factors that push and pull a person. For starters, all the census returns, electoral registers and postal directories in the world cannot reveal the secrets that someone keeps. The home Veronique left may have been a place of safety and love or a place of misery and harm, or something in between. She may have encountered sexual abuse from a family member or a neighbour, at a youth club or a French lesson, in a church or at school, which made her want to put the whole continent between her and her home town. History echoes with the unwritten and often purposely hidden record of children who were beaten, sexually assaulted or emotionally manipulated: just ask Eilidh MacDougall. Simply by being a child, Veronique had a very good chance of experiencing this silent story.[17] If she did, she certainly repeated the story later in life, when she helped to traffic Lydia Harvey and other young women.

Tall and well dressed, nineteen-year-old Veronique walked down the gangplank in Fremantle sometime in 1902 or 1903, onto a dock that was crowded with gold-seekers and other adventurers striking out on the eastern railway, and with shipping agents waiting for the mail steamers. She waited at the railway station that sat at the mouth of the inner harbour, for the train that took her the short distance across the Swan River and up to Perth. Here she was probably met by an employment agent who saw her settled and took her to the McNess Royal Arcade, where she was to start work.[18] Veronique joined a worldwide army of women who migrated for work in the clothing and textile trades, a cohort second only in size to domestic servants. These women pursued better pay and better conditions in this vast and complex global industry. Some worked in sweatshops for a pittance; others, like Miss White, had their own very small businesses or consignments in department stores and shops, which often earned them a decent livelihood. All the same, moral reformers like William Coote fretted over the moral welfare of shop girls and dressmakers like Veronique, who were exposed to the temptations of the luxury goods and global commodities they were selling, but did not make enough to afford such things themselves.[19]

The Royal Arcade was opened only five years earlier, and the ornate building with its pastel peach-and-white plasterwork proclaimed that it was the equal of any other establishment in the newly born Australian Federation. As Perth's first shopping mall, it was a key marker of the city's coming of age, its transition from gold boomtown to the established capital of Western Australia. With sixty-four vendors, it had everything the growing town required, including the latest luxury goods from Europe, Britain and the empires they controlled.[20] Outside, the town hall's clock tower loomed above bustling Hay Street, with its iron balustrades, its electric trams, its bicycles, carriages and camels – a handy animal for use in Western Australia's hot and arid climate.

Veronique spoke into the historical record only a handful of times in her life, and at no point did she mention how she came to know the man who would become her lover, pimp and future husband. We are left to imagine the story of their meeting in Perth around 1906, under the vaulted ceiling of McNess's arcade, or in a nearby tea room or restaurant, or along the dusty, busy street. Veronique was around twenty-two and Antonio was twenty-seven. The tall and elegant young woman caught his eye. The slender, stylish man caught hers: he wore a suit the like of which she'd never seen, and his enormous moustache was tinted, waxed and curled. He told her that he taught Italian and French in the Moir Buildings around the corner from the arcade. His eyes were enthralling. He was charming, well spoken; Italian, or maybe French. He asked her to join him for a drink. Veronique delighted in practising her French. He told her she was a lovely girl; he told her he could get her a better job. As their relationship grew closer, he delighted her with an expensive and symbolic gift: a Nellie Stewart bangle.

Veronique, like almost every other young Australian girl, doubtless grew up adoring 'Australia's rose', the actress and light-opera singer who was one of the country's first real celebrities. And everyone knew that Nellie Stewart's lover and patron, the theatrical entrepreneur George Musgrove, had designed her a solid, twenty-two-carat gold bangle, which she wore on her upper forearm in every picture and every performance for the rest of her life. It was a symbol of their love, and replicas soon became one of the chief ways in which young Australian women signalled a romantic attachment. A 'Nellie Stewart bangle' was a sign that you had a man who intended to keep you well. The original bangle was worth thousands of pounds, and most of its imitators were only a fraction of that price, but Veronique's suitor Carvelli had done well. The bangle he gave her was solid eighteen-carat gold, heavy and thick, with a hinge to keep it tight upon her arm.[21]

After his love and commitment to her were declared, the couple moved on to discuss business. Had she ever been to the Northern Goldfields? Now that was truly the 'wild west'. Up there, they had the biggest goldmine in Australia, and hundreds and hundreds of men in need of women to keep them company. 'We'll make a fortune, darling.'

The journey itself is easy to reconstruct, because in 1907 there was only one way for any sane person to get to Leonora, a supply town in the Northern Goldfields: one long, lonely stretch of railway. Earlier, miners and supplies had travelled by foot, horse, bicycle, coach or camel but, as of 1897, the Goldfields Railway had linked Leonora to Kalgoorlie.[22] Veronique watched for hours as the red-earthed, wild-flowered bush stretched out in every direction from the train window, vast and alien. Every now and then the train would clatter into a tiny station, which looked like little more than an abandoned shack with a tiny cluster of houses in the distance, the smoke rising from their chimneys, with a blue haze of hills behind them. Even the small Victorian station in Hawthorn was grand by comparison.

Even though she would continue to report her occupation in Leonora as a dressmaker, it seems incredibly unlikely that Veronique would have made a two-day journey into the outback, via Kalgoorlie, to answer the tiny town's demand for seamstresses. It is certain that she had come to Leonora to sell sex.

Long before the panic over 'white slavery' imagined women being literally kidnapped into prostitution, scholars and moralists the world over tried to understand what might make a woman *choose* to sell sex. The books, pamphlets, articles and treatises on why young women became prostitutes could have filled a small library. Women 'fell' into sin; or became 'unfortunates'. Girls who turned to selling sex came from 'bad' and 'broken' homes. The young women them-selves had 'bad characters'. Some were 'led astray' by false promises of marriage, and others were misled, entrapped and raped and 'never regained their purity of character'. A pitiable minority were 'feeble-minded' or 'morally insane'. Most of all, many of these future prostitutes had a sinful 'love of finery'. They were, in one moral reformer's words, 'ignorant self-willed girl[s] with only one idea of life, namely to have a good time'.[23] They wanted to wear nice dresses and buy pretty ribbons and lace and gloves. They were 'lazy' and did not want to work; to sew, or do laundry, or scrub steps. They acted above their station. They wanted a life of comfort and luxury.[24] These women were not 'white slaves' in need of protection from criminals, but were of 'known immoral character' and deserved to be criminalised themselves.

Of course many young women – being human – wanted nice things, but comparatively few sold sex to get them, even when their lives were lived in penury. A decision to sell sex, or a vulnerability to being coerced into selling sex, was the product of hundreds of different factors and life experiences that played out differently in the heart, mind and pocketbook of every woman who wound up in the sex industry. For many it was simply a way to make ends meet, to abolish that worry in the pit of one's stomach about where the next month's rent was coming from. It even enabled them to afford some of life's little luxuries: a trip to the cinema, a meal out, a nice dress or a fashionable hat.[25] What early twentieth-century moralisers like William Coote cited as frivolous reasons to fall into sin, many working-class women saw as the things that made life worth living.

As for the unwanted, non-pleasurable sex, that was on

the cards for many young women anyway, and there were numerous reasons why a young woman would consider sex to be transactional rather than sacred. We have plenty of evidence from historians of this period that young women remained profoundly ignorant about sex, and about their own sexual rights and pleasures; and a huge number of them viewed sexual intercourse as something they would be forced or compelled to do by a lover or husband, rather than something they would seek out willingly themselves. For uncounted hundreds of thousands, sexual abuse constituted their first sexual encounter. In a period when an unwanted pregnancy could not be safely terminated, and when there was very little social support for single working mothers, the consequences of both wanted and unwanted sex could be severe and could leave women desperate and bitter.[26] 'If a girl is to be seduced it is better she should be seduced by a gentleman, and get something for it, than let herself be seduced by a boy or a young fellow who gives her nothing for it,' said Miss X, a brothel-keeper interviewed by William Stead in his 'Maiden Tribute of Modern Babylon' exposé.[27] This is strikingly similar to Veronique's own words as she began to convince Lydia Harvey to come to Buenos Aires and 'see gentlemen': 'It is silly to do it for free, when you can make good money,' she told her.[28] Had she said this before? Had she been told it herself?

Veronique grew up in a world where good girls did not ask or hear about sex, let alone have it. Even grown women were not supposed to have sex out of wedlock and, when they did, they were not expected to enjoy it. By the early twentieth century there were some efforts to educate young women in order that they would live clean, disease-free lives, and there was a growing idea that a happy marriage was also a sexually pleasurable one; but for the most part, sex was thought of by girls as something frightening, exciting and mysterious, and by many married women as a duty.[29] All the same, there were legions of women who had different and more liberal attitudes to sex, who did not deign to record them for future historians. Veronique was likely one of them.

Despite the pages that moral reformers and social investigators dedicated to dissecting why women sold sex, very few words were spared for the selling itself, and the profits that could be made by it. Every shred of evidence we have suggests that these profits could be substantial, especially when compared to what women could earn in a licit job, with the skills and training available to them in this era. Most women selling sex in the same period as Veronique charged 30 shillings for a 'short time' – about ten to fifteen minutes, during which they would engage the client in vaginal sex or manual stimulation. In some places, most famously Buenos Aires, women performed oral sex on clients, for which they charged the same or more. To put this in perspective, 30 shillings was what a skilled tradesman made for one or two days of labour. If a woman in London, charging 30 shillings, solicited four men a night for five nights, she would make £30 a week: about fifteen times more than the police officer who might arrest her, at least twice as much as the barristers whom she would see in court, and about thirty times more than the average domestic servant. To be sure, many women who sold sex charged less than this – 5 shillings (often for manual stimulation rather than penetrative sex), 10 shillings in poor neighbourhoods – but even with this reduced charge and the inflated costs of rent and protection money that many women had to pay, they would be making a decent living compared to what they would earn for many more hours of work in any other trade.

Between tales of riches to be made in the sex industry and sensational stories of 'white slavery', there lay very real stories of grooming, abuse and entrapment. Young women who came alone to places like the 'wild west' were far away from their social networks and very vulnerable, often sexually ignorant and usually poor. This made them prey, as a series of shocking exposés in the Kalgoorlie *Sun* put it, to 'the men who fatten on misfortunes: the vice-syndicates, and agents, and the church-going landlords, these are the culprits'.[30] They were also prey to the increasingly intolerant legal code that could see them arrested, fined and imprisoned for selling sex, and accused of running brothels if they worked with other women. More and more women turned to pimps to protect them and help manage their businesses. 'Whilst she sticks to the "gang" she may at least find shelter, food, garments and companionship,' the *Sun*'s reporter noted, 'but gaol and starvation stare her in the face if she attempted to leave it.'[31]

Veronique was one of thousands of women who weighed up these risks and rewards and made journeys to mining frontiers in this era.[32] Only mining could create a demand for bought sex that equalled the demand in times of war. It began with the California gold rush of the 1850s, when men all over the world flocked to the North American west to pan the rivers for nuggets of gold, but soon 'rushes' spanned the globe, from South and East Africa, to the Klondike, Otago and the Australian west. As the twentieth century dawned, the gold rushes gave way to more organised resource extraction. Instead of panning rivers, heavily financed multi-national companies used the latest machinery to dig pits and shafts to extract gold, diamonds, ore and other valuable metals. Wealth conglomerated and labour exploitation operated on an even greater scale. Indigenous land claims were overwritten, and foreign workers were imported to undercut unionised labour. This was change on a massive scale, one of the most important stories in modern global history.[33]

It was also the story of tiny Leonora, which sat in the middle of what is now called the Northern Goldfields and, according to the local newspaper, the *Miner's Friend*, 'possessed reefs and lodes of enormous value'.[34] These goldfields were the latest in Australia's series of unfolding mining frontiers, and they were hungry for labour. Hundreds of men came along the short electric tramline that linked Leonora with the Gwalia mine site over the course of the week, desperate for anything that got their heads out of the dark, dangerous, forty-degree mine shafts.[35]

Veronique found Leonora more promising than its tiny railway station suggested. The small town of little more than 200 people had created a pocket of civilisation, seemingly overnight. Leonora's main street was lined with grocers, restaurants, hotels, stationers, clothiers and jewellers as well as the more predictable ironmongers, explosive agents and outfitters.[36] It buzzed with the excitement of the frontier, an end-of-the-line kind of place with a strong sense of community and a need to invent its own entertainment. To this end, Veronique – almost certainly with the money that her Italian suitor had fronted her – took a small house made from wood and corrugated iron in Otterburn Street. She placed an old sewing machine on a table in the front room and hung a little brass plaque on the door. 'Miss Vanda Williams, Dress-maker', it read.

Both were fabrications, but in stating her occupation as dressmaker, she was not simply celebrating her skills and past employment. This was a common tactic used in Western Australia mining towns, where brothels were technically illegal, but where police only needed the slightest excuse to look the other way. Because everyone in the town knew the euphemism, Veronique's little plaque served an ironic dual purpose: it legally obscured her one-woman brothel, while at the same time advertising it as one. Despite the popular image that we may have of crowded 'wild west' brothels and saloons, the majority of commercial sex on mining frontiers, by the late nineteenth and early twentieth centuries at least, took the form of women working in individual premises: huts, shacks and houses that they occupied alone or, if the law allowed it, with one or two other women.

For a time Veronique White, now known as Vanda Williams, was one of them. The days were as hot as hell in her little house, and her usually immaculate hair clung to the sweat on her forehead. The nights were cold, and she looked forward to the evenings when Carvelli would come up from his job at the French consul in Perth to warm her bed. Her clients were British men and Gwalia Italians, who placed their coins on the table. She would offer them drinks, get them to wash in the basin, maybe show them some dirty pictures, and then within a few minutes it was done. They left, and she slipped their money into a box on the shelf.

The men she saw were exhausted, overworked and the scars and bruises on their bodies documented their labour history. 'Women, being so few, are looked upon in these parts as goddesses,' noted the genteel lady traveller May Vivienne, who visited Leonora at the turn of the century, 'and are treated with reverence, and I was made quite an object of adoration.'[37] Perhaps Veronique could count on worship from a few of her more sentimental clients, but for the most part the work would have been of the more corporeal variety. Afterwards, as they buttoned up and she chivvied them towards the door, they told her tales: the near-miss rockfalls; the fingers lost in machinery; the girl back in Italy; the dreams of a better life. She probably appreciated her clean, polite regulars; she laughed at most of them when they were gone, pitied many of them and hated some of them too: their fists on the door when they knew she was closed; the sour smell of liquor on their breath; the way some got rowdy and aggressive when they drank.[38]

The women Veronique worked alongside all had stories, too. Leonora was an isolated and rough place. Earlier that year one woman's house had been deliberately set on fire with kerosene by an angry rejected customer; later, two 'Gwalia Italians' were arrested for verbally and physically assaulting women in a brothel.[39] Another woman named Emma Smith had had £230 stolen from her by a client, which is evidence at once of her vulnerability to such crimes, however carefully she hid her coin box, but also testament to the amount of money that could be made by women selling sex in in the town.[40] The women who sold sex in Leonora made regular deposits with Mr Hosking, the local manager of the National Bank of Australia, or with their pimps and protectors, so the funds Emma Smith had probably amounted to no more than a month's earnings.[41] This was an incredible twenty times more than a man would make in a month for more than

200 hours of hard labour in a sweltering, dangerous pit in the ground. This was more than a man's family would get, if he died down there. The case also allows us a glimpse of the place of such women within the municipal polity: Emma Smith did not hesitate to take the perpetrator to court.

On 30 March 1908 it was Veronique's turn to appear in front of the honorary magistrates. Vanda Williams, 'of respectable appearance', was brought to the little court, charged with permitting a premises to be used for an immoral purpose. It may have been the first time she encountered the criminal-justice system, but her brief and rehearsed testimony suggests there were earlier appearances in other courts, or perhaps coaching from her pimp and lover.

'I am a dressmaker by trade,' she glibly told the bench. 'I'm prepared to do work as it comes along, but I suppose there is a look about the place which brought one or two men there.' She swore before the bench that she hadn't had more than a half-dozen visitors, and that she neither drank nor smoked.

'I suppose you plead guilty,' the magistrate asked wearily.

'Yes,' Veronique-cum-Vanda replied. Sergeant Houlahan, the prosecuting officer, told the court about the little brass plaque and the sewing machine, saying that he had told her to leave the town, but she hadn't.

'I will go by tomorrow night's train,' she answered then, asking for enough time to sell her furniture.

This seemed to satisfy the policeman, who didn't press the charge further. Veronique was fined 5 shillings, plus 3s 6d costs. Everyone knew she wasn't going anywhere.[42]

Veronique spent the winter in Leonora, and over July and August 1908 the weather became cooler and more bearable.

Sometimes Carvelli would come up to see her, collect her money and make sure she had everything she needed. He helped two other French women as well, Bertha Duval and Marie LeFay, but didn't spend the night with them. Veronique paid £2 a week to the agent who rented her the house, and gave Carvelli much of the rest to keep safe for her.

What else did she do with the hundreds of pounds she was making? Certainly she bought fine dresses and hats and lace, and gloves and jewellery. And perhaps Carvelli was not the only person to whom she was sending cash. Back in Melbourne, the White family was seeing its lot improve significantly. Their slip down the social ladder, which forced them to sell up in middle-class Hawthorn and rent a house in increasingly unfashionable Fitzroy, was dramatically reversed in 1908 when Frederick White bought a four-bedroomed house at 28 Jolimont Terrace, in one of the poshest postcodes in East Melbourne. Two of Veronique's sisters and her brother Keppel lived there with their parents, helping their father run his business. From the windows of 'Trafford' – the beloved family name that Frederick bestowed upon the new home – the Whites could see the green of Melbourne's famous cricket ground.[43] Perhaps it was a new boom in the patriarch's drapery sales that brought about this permanent upswing in the family's fortunes; or perhaps it was remittances from their second-youngest daughter, whose letters reported her good luck in the goldfields in vague but happy tones.[44]

Despite promising Sergeant Houlahan that she would leave on the next night's train, back in March, Veronique was still to be found in Leonora in October as the days began to grow hotter once again. Carvelli came to see her towards the end of the month, bringing her the latest news from civilisation. She showed him the money she had made. Then one morning, as they lay asleep in the back room of her little house on Otterburn Street, there was a clattering at her door and in strode Sergeant O'Donovan, another of the town's limited supply of policemen. Before Veronique had quite come to her senses, the sergeant was hauling her lover out of bed and he stood, diminished, in his underwear, asking what it was all about. She protested and tried to get between them. The policeman searched Carvelli's clothes and found his pocketbook, where everything was written down: the money for the houses, Marie's money, Bertha's money, Veronique's money. They arrested him for living on the earnings of prostitution.[45]

A few days later, while Carvelli was waiting for his second trial and trying to get his hands on some customs forms the police had confiscated, Sergeant O'Donovan arrested Veronique, alongside Bertha Duval and Marie LeFay, on charges of soliciting. They were each fined £1 – which they promptly paid. Carvelli went back to court, secured the return of his documents and was given a new trial date for the charge of living on the earnings of prostitution. This time 'Vanda Williams' – with Antonio Carvelli by her side – really did leave on the next night's train.

Carvelli had a plan. He had heard from friends that New Zealand had just made brothels legal – so long as only one woman worked there. There would be no more fines, like there were in Leonora. He had made some contacts and figured he could get them a place. They stayed in Kalgoorlie long enough to book a steamer to Wellington, then in November 1908 continued by train to Fremantle and their next adventure, with hundreds of pounds, perhaps close to

£1,000, in the bank. That same month, on 18 November 1908, the women from the coffee house in Veronique's home town of Hawthorn finally achieved their dream, when the state of Victoria gave women the right to vote in state elections. But of the two – the vote and the money – Veronique surely thought the money more important.

Wellington, when at last they arrived, greeted them with a cool wind and a wide turquoise harbour, and made a refreshing change from the red dust of the outback. They had their cases delivered to the Arcadia Private Hotel, and the next day Carvelli went out in search of his contacts. Veronique explored the city, its shops, its waterfront, its cafés. Carvelli, whom she called by the pet name of Aldo, brought her many lovely gifts: another gold bangle, this one set with pearl and sapphire, worth more than £10 (£1,000 today), and an eighteen-carat gold watch, which, when she turned it over in her hands, read 'From Aldo to Veronique' in delicate engraving. All of this was bought and paid for from her earnings, and the earnings of other women, but it was, we can suppose, the thought that counted.[46]

Wellington was the kind of place she might like to stay. Within a few days Carvelli had acquired a house on College Street for her, and saw her settled in. He introduced her to other women whom she would be working with nearby, and to a man called Alessandro di Nicotera, who was dark, handsome and sinister and went by the name Alex Berard. She got on well with the others – a French woman called Camelia Rae, but whom they all called 'Tit', and some other girls who had places on College Street and the streets nearby. They had dozens of pseudonyms and addresses between them, which they changed frequently.

Veronique got down to work. Men who lived in Karori or Lower Hutt, but worked in the offices, shops and banks of Te Aro, came to see her in their lunch hours; and as daytime business gave way to night-time pleasures on nearby Cuba Street and Vivian Street, she got busier. She felt secure. Working alone meant avoiding arrest for brothel-keeping and, while it would have been safer to have 'Tit' in the house with her, she was thankfully only two doors up the road, and Carvelli was always keeping an eye out for trouble. Wellington was a small city, but of course felt like a bustling metropolis compared to Leonora, and it was beautiful. With Carvelli and Tit, Veronique improved her French as they wined and dined late into the evenings and plotted new business ventures. She called herself Marie Vernon now, and told clients she was French – they seemed to like that. Occasionally a police officer knocked on her door and gave her 'the chat', as they called it. Look here, Marie, Detective Lewis would explain, if you keep things quiet we won't bother you. Yes, she agreed. She was glad they understood each other.[47]

The work could be difficult, and was not without its risks. Not all policemen were as understanding as Detective Lewis, and some threatened her, asked for bribes, maybe even demanded sex as a form of protection money. Some clients got rowdy, while others tried to steal from her. One succeeded, and she was forced to place a notice in the *New Zealand Police Gazette* in September 1909 after her Nellie Stewart bangle, the watch and other jewellery were stolen from 24 College Street, together worth more than £20.[48] She must have been devastated, particularly at the loss of the watch and the bangle, those symbols of Aldo's dedication and love.

In the bed in the little house in Wellington, she and Carvelli must have discussed the stories they had heard from the men and women who had gone to Buenos Aires, who went to '*fare America*', as Carvelli and his fellow Italians put it. The money they reported making put her Leonora earnings to shame. She wanted to travel and see the world, Veronique said; Carvelli said he could arrange it. But wouldn't it make sense to find a girl to bring with them? Their earnings would then double. Men would pay through the nose for young girls. He'd find a kid for them, get some friends of his to keep an eye out – they'd make a fortune. Did she agree? Did she suggest it in the first place? Did she argue against it? Did she say nothing? No one will ever know. In any case, it fell to Veronique to do most of the recruiting. Carvelli had sent out feelers, offering a German man who was in town £5 if he found her a girl. The plan worked and, when the time came, Veronique played her role perfectly.

'It will be no different to what you've already done with your sweetheart,' she reassured the girl, and smiled. 'It is silly to do it for free, when you can make good money.'

Carvelli booked first-class tickets for himself and Veronique to Buenos Aires, in celebration of the fortunes that awaited them there. The girl would travel third-class a few weeks later. Amid these plans, Carvelli seemed determined to prove his love and devotion, and asked for Veronique's hand in marriage.

She agreed, presumably with delight. On 27 January 1910 she donned a fine lacy blouse and cinched her waist into a corset, with the buttery feeling of silk stockings against her legs and her feet in brand-new boots. She wore a heart-shaped glass pendant that Carvelli had given her, and it sat as red as

Supposed name
WILLIAMS.

{ Aldo Antoninus Cellis @
{ Alfred Shanks @
{ Gustav Coptini etc.

21: Antonio Carvelli and Veronique White studio photograph, quite likely taken around the time of their wedding in January, 1910. Veronique sports several pieces of distinctive and expensive jewellery, including a 'Nellie Stewart' bangle, a very popular romantic gift in this period.

a ruby against the white blouse. She had the hairdresser call at College Street, to style her thick dark hair into a *coiffeur français*, which billowed in shiny pinned curls from the sides of her head and swooped across her brow. She hung drop earrings in her earlobes. She greeted her soon-to-be husband, who looked a perfect gentleman with his wide starched colour, silk tie, gold watch-chain and pearl tie-pin, and they had their picture taken at a studio. It was a simple portrait. She leaned on a chair in front of a plain background, perhaps to hide the fact that she almost matched him in height. He stood beside her in his dark suit, one hand slipped into his pocket. They both looked into the camera, with traces of happy smiles on their lips. On her arm she proudly wore a thick gold bangle, a replacement from her new husband perhaps or, by some miracle, the stolen one now recovered. They made a handsome couple.[49]

They travelled by tram to the little town of Island Bay, just beyond Wellington. By this point they had had many names between them, but they married in the church room as no one but themselves: Veronique Sarah White and Antonio Aldo Carvelli, she a spinster and the daughter of Frederick Soutten White and Sarah Jane Daley, he a merchant and the son of Luigi Carvelli and Anna Maria Courrier. But their commitment to the truth only went so far: both took three years off their age.[50] They said their vows in an Anglican ceremony that neither of them – not being Anglican – were familiar with, but it didn't matter much. It was a beautiful, warm sunny day, the very height of summer; though the wind threatened to wreck her hair. Veronique wrote to tell her parents, who proudly announced the marriage in the *Melbourne Argus*, though from the fact that this family notice appeared four months after the marriage took place, we might surmise that she had not kept them regularly updated about her romantic life.[51]

A few days later they boarded the SS *Corinthic* at Wellington's Queen's Wharf. She was a new, enormous ocean liner. Alongside her two sister ships, she was built in Belfast in 1902 after the White Star Line was taken over by J. P. Morgan's International Mercantile Marine Company, another part of the story – which spanned the deep mines and the open oceans – of corporatisation and multinationalisation in this era. With 112 first-class passenger berths, the SS *Corinthic* boasted all the modern conveniences of this new generation of steamship, as well as the capacity to ship fresh and frozen produce between the world's increasingly interconnected markets. First-class passengers like Veronique would enjoy chef-prepared meals, designer furniture, beautiful Art Deco glasswork and a sweeping central staircase that led to the grand, chandeliered dining room, staffed by waiters from continental Europe.[52] Beneath them hummed the two eight-cylinder, quadruple-expansion steam-powered engines, fed by firemen recruited from around East Africa and the Middle East, which propelled the ship across the Pacific at fourteen knots an hour.

Veronique surely loved life aboard this ostentatious floating city: being waited on; having her bed made to perfection each morning; enjoying entertainments in the salon; watching the spray of the waves and the churning foam from a sunny deckchair. This kind of life was the carrot that traffickers and other exploitative employment agents dangled in front of desperate young women whose only experiences were the drudgery of service and a mundane life in a deprived area – this kind of voyage, even in the third-class cabin that Lydia travelled in, was a world apart from anything they had ever known.[53] In first-class, where Veronique lounged, it was the veritable lap of luxury.

The ocean liners were the avatars of a brave new modern era, and when the SS *Corinthic* set sail with Carvelli and Veronique on board in 1910, it would still be another two years before the world was reminded of modernity's fragility, when the biggest and grandest ocean liner ever built struck an iceberg and was swallowed by the cold North Atlantic. William Stead, the author of the 'Maiden Tribute of Modern Babylon', was pulled beneath the waves alongside another 1,500 souls lost on the RMS *Titanic*. Two years after that, the world came to truly understand the cost of this modernity. Torpedoes tore through the hulls of the steamships – now filled with artillery, guns and nervous troops – that only the year before were filled with dancing couples, Argentinian steak served on Egyptian cotton tablecloths, and the travelling chests of the affluent classes.

But as Veronique crossed the Pacific in 1910, this war was a universe away. They arrived in Montevideo in late February and took the river boat to Buenos Aires, as grand and strange a place as Veronique had ever seen. In 1910 Buenos Aires, celebrating its centennial as a city, was thriving. It pulsed with energy and possibility. Along the rue de la Paix and calle Florida, mannequins donned evening dresses, tea gowns and lingerie made of soft, light, clinging and semi-transparent materials like chiffon, lawn, muslin, faille and thin silks, like crêpe de Chine. It was a city into which one could disappear, masquerade as anyone one liked, reinvent oneself. It was the kind of place that would chastise anyone trying to live a mediocre life.[54]

They rented a small *pension*, and Carvelli left Veronique in these two adjoining rooms while he travelled back to Montevideo to collect Lydia. Veronique may have fretted, worrying that there would be trouble with the police, or that he would linger too long and leave her here, all alone, in this chaotic city, which offered equal measures of fortune and destitution.[55] But they arrived two short days later, just as he said, and she greeted them on the docks in a merry mood. She wanted to have their picture taken, she said, and they found one of the men who made their living from capturing the excitement and bewilderment of the hundreds of people who newly arrived off steamships every day. The flashpaper lit up in a curl of smoke as the three of them stood beside each other. Antonio said he'd collect the picture at the man's studio in a couple of days.[56]

Veronique took Lydia out shopping the next afternoon, buying her some dresses and other nice items, and telling her how to solicit men. Tilt your head to the side and smile; wait for them to approach you. They wandered in and out of shops, and when she came to the pet shop she couldn't resist the small blue-green parrot in the lovely white cage. The man who owned the shop told her it was a Quaker parrot and she could teach it to talk, that it would live for twenty years and that many people who came to Buenos Aires couldn't resist taking one home.[57] She gazed at its round little face and its pink beak and bought it then and there. The two women walked home carrying the bird. Veronique stood back and looked at the girl's hair. 'It's too mousy,' she said, and arranged for a woman to come to the *pensión* and dye it blonde.[58] That evening, as the parrot chattered, she watched as Carvelli went into Lydia's room and closed the door. We cannot say how she felt, but we can be certain that she knew precisely what was happening.

Veronique tried her best to get the girl used to the life she was living – tried to train her like a bird in a cage. But she could not, it seems, resist the urge to use Lydia. Having Lydia around meant that the old and disgusting clients could be put on to her. Afterwards she pocketed the girl's earnings and handed them to Carvelli. Whatever justifications she deployed in her heart and mind are lost for ever.

No one was exaggerating when they told them that all the men liked to be sucked in Buenos Aires, which made Lydia's refusal to do so an irritating problem, and they were not doing as well as they had hoped. However Veronique felt about her role in Lydia's abuse, it was taking up a lot of energy. Then there was a further misfortune. Their *pensión* was raided by the police for being an unregistered brothel. Carvelli was taken away and had to fork out a fortune in bail money. Then he took both Veronique and Lydia to a registered brothel and deposited them there, like unwanted pets.

It was a nasty place. There were too many women, and some of them were full of the pox. The pink curtain in the door was tattered. Men came back and forth through it, getting their cocks sucked. It was like an abattoir. Lydia began to complain that she felt unwell, and refused to take any clients. 'You owe Aldo money for the passage,' Veronique told her sharply, taking her own fears out on the girl. 'And he paid five pounds to the man who brought you to College Street.'

The doctor came in the morning, and they all lined up in the front room to have his cold hands inspect their vaginas. One of the women had syphilitic sores, and the doctor opened his case and injected medicine into her veins, right in the middle of the room.[59] Veronique was horrified. In her line of business, venereal disease was a constant threat that women tried to mitigate and take in their stride; but that did little to stop the ever-present worry. They had all seen what syphilis could do, and had heard about the horrors of unchecked gonorrhoea and chlamydia, and the nastiness of genital warts. The doctor's visit reminded Veronique of the risks she was taking, particularly in this foreign country filled with foreign men, where they could lock you up if you had it. When Carvelli returned she railed against him, telling him he had to get them away. This was no place for a woman like her. He soothed her and told her he'd be back the next day, that he was booking tickets to London and they were all leaving.

True to his word, her husband fetched them the next morning. His mood was dark. He had had his things burgled and had lost money, clothes and jewellery. He cursed the city. They went to a new *pensión* where they prepared to leave, but the girl grew even more ill. She had a raised red rash and was itching all over. Veronique could not help but wonder if it would hit her as well.

They boarded the SS *Asturias* the next day, and nothing was the same as it had been on the SS *Corinthic*. There was no sunning in deckchairs, no steak dinners, no dancing. The parrot was probably Veronique's only solace, and teaching him to speak and letting his tiny, sharp talons wrap around her finger helped to pass the days at sea. At last they arrived at Southampton, then at Waterloo Station, and took a taxi to the Piedmont Hotel, a middle-of-the-road sort of place in an area known as North Soho.

There were no brothels in London, and in order to get clients Veronique had to walk and walk for hours on end. Carvelli warned her that the police were always watching, and that she had to keep moving or they would arrest her. He followed her and watched out for them. Her feet were aching each evening when she turned out her purse, back at the flat.

On Wednesdays he made her go to visit the girl up in Paddington, where she lay, pale and small, in a hospital ward filled with other young women like them. Lydia told Veronique that the staff had begun to ask questions, enquiring who the man who brought her was, and who she was. 'Tell them I am your sister,' Veronique whispered to the girl in her bed. 'Tell them you are here to be cured and not questioned.' That had a nice ring to it.

The streets of London, it turned out, were not exactly paved with gold. And they were cold! Veronique was used to Melbourne, to the scorching heat of Leonora, to the swelter of Buenos Aires in the spring. This city was no more than fifteen degrees in May! The girls on the street told her it was an unusually chilly spring, but she hardly believed them.[60] They had been born in this cold, sunless place and didn't know any better. One evening Veronique had had enough and told Carvelli that she hated London. She wanted to go back to New Zealand. He acquiesced, and booked her a ticket on the next ship bound for Auckland, with the girl Marguerite Carl. He would stay behind, he explained, and see if he couldn't find some other, more experienced girls to join him in the Antipodes.

Before she left, he pressed Veronique to go and fetch Lydia from the hospital and, much as she disliked the idea of returning to the girl's bedside, she agreed. Lydia sneered at the plain brown dress she had brought, but dressed quietly and left with Veronique, under the suspicious gaze of the ward maids. She told the girl that she was leaving London a few days later. 'Do you not intend to leave me any money?' Lydia asked her.

'Aldo will see you settled,' Veronique told her. She surely had her doubts that he would. In any case, Lydia Harvey was no longer her problem. Veronique had no intention of ever seeing her again.

On 27 May 1910 she and Carvelli, alongside di Nicotera and his new girl, travelled to Liverpool Street and then southwards to the Royal Albert Docks, where the RMS *Tainui* waited to take them to New Zealand, travelling through the Suez Canal and across the Indian Ocean, calling at Colombo, Kalgoorlie, Sydney and finally Wellington. She told the clerk that her name was Miss Williams and that she was a dressmaker. The other girl gave her name as Marguerite Carl. Veronique fretted over her parrot as they boarded the ship, trying to make sure that the valet took extra care as he carried its cage.

This fleeting moment was captured by DI Anderson, who stood, undercover and unnoticed, with a Brownie camera pointed at the gangplank. But Veronique would be on the other side of the world before this evidence was used in the case against her husband, when he was charged with conspiring with 'a woman unknown' to procure girls for the purposes of prostitution. As Veronique was caught between the categories of victim and criminal, the police both in England and New Zealand seemed uninterested in finding her and charging her with procurement. Anderson's surveillance photograph, alongside her brown dress, was all that she left behind her in London. Veronique had performed her own disappearing act.

Back in Wellington, Veronique reconnected with old friends and business networks. Tit, who had kept the one-woman brothel just down the road from her on College Street, greeted her warmly and helped Veronique find a similar place that she could run. She must have rejoiced in the fact that she no longer had to walk up and down Charing Cross Road and Shaftesbury Avenue, day in and day out. She set her little parrot by the front window. She called herself Miss Williams again now, leaving Marie Vernon's misadventure behind her. Her business resumed, the money started coming in and she wrote a letter to Carvelli telling him all the news. Then, a few weeks later, his reply arrived. At first she would have been happy to see her name in his messy handwriting, until she noticed that it was postmarked 'Brixton Prison'.

What she didn't learn from her husband, she read about in a few brief paragraphs that appeared in the *Evening Post* on 22 July, which spoke of a woman named 'Marie' who had helped one Aldo Cellis traffic a girl, Doris Williams, from New Zealand to London via Buenos Aires. It told Veronique everything she needed to know: she could not stay in Wellington. It was only a matter of time before the police put it all together, if they hadn't already; before they connected Marie Vernon to Miss Williams, and came knocking on her new brothel door. Maybe they would even press charges against her, connected to her husband's case. So she did what so many others in the business did, and moved on.

She and Tit booked a coastal steamer for Auckland

– bound together, it seems, by the trouble Carvelli had landed them in. They found accommodation, set up their one-woman brothels and bided their time. Then, a few months later, Veronique enjoyed a happy reunion with her husband, who had managed to evade the police and return to New Zealand. He probably looked diminished from his time in prison, but was delighted to learn of all the money she had put away in the months he'd been behind bars. He had a surprise for her as well, though possibly a significantly less delightful one: he had brought with him a girl he had met in Paris, who went by the name of Violette Baron, and she was going to work with them in Auckland. Veronique's reaction can only be presumed.

In order to mitigate the risk of being charged with running a brothel, they did what many other women had taken to doing, and opened shops that acted as fronts for the real business that happened in the small back bedrooms. Tit ran a tobacconist under the name of Camelia Rae, which had one or two packs of cigarettes behind a makeshift counter. Veronique, now Marie Vernon again, ran a soda shop in Grey Street, with a few piss-warm drinks in glass bottles on a shelf. Annie Sawyer, back on the game now that her husband Alex di Nicotera had returned from prison, ran a sweet shop, which comprised little more than a sad-looking bunch of lollies in a jar. Violette Baron, the new girl sent to New Zealand by Carvelli, ran another shop in Hobson Street. There were a dozen of them in all, working with Carvelli, di Nicotera and two other men.[61]

Veronique's husband also opened a shop – a real shop – in Auckland, at 85 Shortland Street. *A. Courrier*, read the sign, *Importer and Indentor*.[62] The shop necessitated constant travel: from 1911 Carvelli was a man who spent practically half his life on steamships. He steamed regularly back and forth to Italy and France – confident, it seems, that he would not be recognised as a wanted man in his home country. Veronique got his postcards from Milan, Rome and Paris, as well as Colombo, Singapore, Hong Kong and Australia. He kept an office in Brisbane as well as the shop in Auckland. If she visited him or sometimes travelled with him, there is no record of it in the newspaper passenger lists – perhaps because she was using one of her many pseudonyms. When police in Auckland prosecuted one of Carvelli's business associates, it was discovered that she regularly sent hundreds of pounds to Carvelli in Australia.[63]

Whatever money Veronique was making increased many-fold in late 1914. Alongside the rest of the country, she rushed to read events as they unfolded in the newspaper. Guy Scholefield, the New Zealand Press Association's London correspondent, was no longer covering trafficking trials and imperial politics, but was instead reporting on the outbreak of war. It would not be long before he began compiling lists of New Zealanders' deaths.[64] Before they became the tragic subject of Scholefield's newspaper articles, these young men poured in from the countryside to Auckland and Wellington, where they would be enlisted, trained and shipped out to the Southern, Western and North African fronts on the steamships that had only weeks before carried civilian passengers and the finest New Zealand dairy products. Here was the Dominion's newest export: young, male bodies in fighting form, with smiles on their faces and rifles across their backs.[65] The cities buzzed with the excitement of fresh-faced farmers' sons and schoolboys who were about to go off to fight the good fight for the Empire. Veronique could barely keep up with the work.

The huge amounts of money she was earning could not make up for the distressing news she received just a few weeks after war was declared: Carvelli wrote in haste from his office in Brisbane. He had been discovered on his way back from Singapore by a police officer, DI Gleeson, who recognised him as Aldo Cellis – 'long been wanted in connection to the white slave trade'. His letter spoke of the ridiculous test in Dutch that he had been given to determine his right to remain in Australia, which he had, of course, failed. He was to be deported at the end of the month, back to Italy. Veronique does not seem to have gone with him, because he departed Sydney, en route to San Francisco, 'looking sad', according to the gleeful telegram sent by DI Gleeson to the Australian Home Department.

There was little for Veronique to do but wait it out, as her husband attempted to make his way back to the Antipodes through the chaos of the First World War. She tried to keep her brothel quiet and discreet, as debates raged in wartime New Zealand over the legal loophole that allowed her to operate a 'one-woman brothel', and over the rise in venereal disease brought about by war.[66] Women like her, the newspapers declared, were responsible for diminishing the war effort, by seducing and then infecting the fresh-faced 'soldiers of the king' with the 'deadly scourge' of syphilis.[67] The police, with whom Veronique had once been on such good terms, were under more and more pressure from their superiors to do something about the 'avaricious money-making harlots ... who contaminate the nation from one end to the other'. Superintendent Ellison called Veronique and her friends 'female vampires' who 'fatten and become wealthy while they disseminate disease'.[68] The papers went so far as to liken the women to the bloody Huns: 'the fight has to be against the social plague as well as against the Prussian plague', intoned the *Evening Post*.[69]

Veronique had always known that her particular line of work was widely condemned, of course, but the fury of this language was new. Never in her life had she encountered so much invective from the public and the papers. Soldiers who frequented the back room of her Grey Street shop told her that men were being asked by army officials where the brothels they visited were located.[70] Finally, in 1916, the loophole that allowed one-woman brothels to operate legally was closed, and all brothels – regardless of the number of women inside them – were criminalised. No doubt encouraged by furious army officials, the police moved quickly. Gone was their laissez-faire attitude, and instead came a systematic crackdown: the shops were raided, their suspect inventory inspected, their back bedrooms unmasked. By 1917 the police reported that one-woman brothels were 'a thing of the past'.[71] Alongside dozens of other women, in May 1917 Veronique found herself arrested and charged.

As was her usual practice, Veronique attended court in style, 'dressed in the latest fashion and wearing a fur coat', as the police-court reporter noted. She must have been pleased at the headline: 'Young Woman Charged', it read, reporting her age (as she herself had done) as twenty-seven, while in truth she was thirty-four. She spoke with practised confidence. She claimed that after the cops had 'made things too warm for her' back in 1912, she had left New Zealand, going first to Australia and, after war broke out, to France, where she had volunteered for the Red Cross. She had invested heavily in the Bourse in Paris, and had lost everything. Her defence attorney explained that she had returned to run a one-woman brothel, unaware that the war regulations had made them illegal. The magistrate was unconvinced by this globe-trotting, far-fetched tale and sentenced her to three months in prison.[72] I have been unable to either substantiate or disprove these claims.

It was the first time Veronique had ever been behind bars. There are no records of her time in prison, and this absence speaks volumes, because it means she was not in the extremely small minority of women whose behaviour warranted a disciplinary record. Like the vast majority of female prisoners, she kept her head down and complied: she washed and slept when she was told to, wore and ate what she was told to, sewed and laundered what she was told to. She probably did whatever it took to serve her sentence quietly, swallowing the confinement and the loneliness and the drudgery, in order to avoid any further charges and be able to leave prison on the day her sentence was up. If she was really lucky, she could get points for good behaviour and leave before her time was served.[73]

Yet however well she played her cards, prison took its toll. Veronique's prison photograph, taken at some point when she was behind bars, reveals a weary, poorly slept woman with dishevelled hair, who had no access to the styling upon which she usually relied to face the world. A thread escapes from the neckline of her tattered, ill-fitting prison uniform. She had spent years being harassed by the cops, worrying about her husband, and was now serving time in an

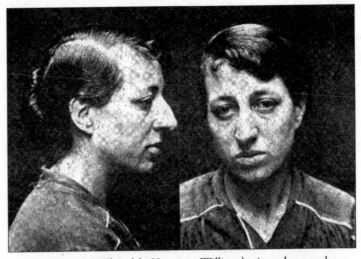

22: Veronique White (aka Veronique Williams) prison photograph, taken after her conviction for brothel-keeping in 1917. Older, wearier and without access to make-up or accessories, she is much changed from her wedding portrait seven years earlier, though she has clearly attempted to style her hair with finger curls and pins.

uncomfortable cell: no wonder her face had begun to show the signs of age. Even a friend might have had to look twice to see that the woman in the wedding photograph and the woman pictured in prison were one and the same.

At last, in August 1917, the day of her release arrived, and her fur coat and fashionable dress were handed back to her. Veronique donned them like armour and walked out into the sunshine. We can imagine that she vowed to never put on a prison uniform again; and, as far as I can tell, she didn't. However she passed the last year of the war, she did so in a way that did not attract the attention of the police. From late 1918 she travelled regularly between Auckland and Sydney, and eventually settled in the latter. Because women lost their birth citizenship if they married a foreign national, she was forced to register as an Alien Italian in Sydney in 1921.[74] It must have been a bitter pill to swallow: having to register as a suspect alien in the country where she was born and grew up, and which all her family called home. There was no official sign of the man who had made her Italian, though Carvelli was probably living in Sydney as well, having returned the year before from wherever he had spent the war, hoping no one would recognise him. So far, no one had.

It was peacetime at last, and crowds poured into the street in 1918 at the celebration of the Armistice. It was time for a new beginning. This time the couple would move away from the commercial sex and commercial travels of their younger years and return to the stuff of Carvelli's earliest training: entertainment. The immediate post-war era embraced and then commodified the hedonism of the war days: dancing, drinking and screwing away the memory of mass death that still clung to everything. In London, revellers baulked at the new licensing regulations that remained after the war ended, by joining 'night clubs' that operated on the razor edge of legality. They danced to jazz, they took cocaine. In Paris a new bohemianism was the order of the day, and the drink, drugs and sex flowed freely from Montmartre to Montparnasse. Flappers appeared in tiny towns and bustling metropolises – young women who abandoned the pre-war corseted blouses and ankle-length skirts and danced, drank and smoked all through the night. Meanwhile in Rome, a decorated general by the name of Mussolini was capturing the hearts and minds of Italy's betrayed generation with a new kind of aesthetic – railing against the louche and weak cultures of the clubs and cabarets, but still dressing for a new world order.

Hobart, Tasmania, was by no means immune to these sweeping cultural changes. While it was widely regarded by Australian cosmopolitans as a backwater, the city was still ready when the Roaring Twenties came to town. It is unclear what drew the Carvellis to Hobart. It was, perhaps, the sort of place that suited them: where modernity was arriving unevenly, where possibilities for new business were ripe and no police officers were likely to know them. Hobart had had a difficult war, which decimated its male workforce and dampened its shipping industry, but by the early 1920s it was recovering, with new factories and mining ventures opening nearby and new infrastructure enabling the city's expansion. In the stately city centre, double-decker electric trams made their way down pleasant avenues, and shops, restaurants and theatres opened their doors – despite persistent post-war shortages – to a growing population, which included a large number of southern European émigrés. Perhaps this is what had landed it on Antonio Carvelli's map.[75] They arrived as summer began in 1924. This was where Carvelli became Monsieur Anthony Coty, and Veronique became Miss Kathleen Williams.

They began their new life in the city as dancing instructors, and soon her charming husband had worked his magic on one of Hobart's most wealthy socialites, who agreed to invest in remodelling the Continental Hotel Deluxe to become 'a most up-to-date cabaret'. Monsieur Coty would manage the place, and the Hobart *News*'s 'Women's Interest' columnist swooned. 'Nothing has been spared by the

23: The Continental Hotel Deluxe, opened by Antonio Carvelli
and Veronique White and bankrolled by a wealthy socialite in
Hobart, Tasmania in 1923. It offered 'dancing every evening', and
Carvelli, before he was disgraced, ran a dance studio upstairs.

management to have here what is in season in the cabarets of
London and Paris,' the columnist explained. Monsieur Coty
was backed 'by considerable experience in Paris and other
Continental cities'. Experience was one word for it.[76]

Veronique and Antonio spent weeks outfitting the new
cabaret, with the seemingly unlimited bank account of Mrs
Duncan at their disposal. They chose lush red carpets for
the hall and stairway, and negotiated with an electrician to
install recessed lights, covered in Art Deco stained glass, in
the gallery that overlooked the ballroom. They sought out
the best musicians that Australia had to offer for the orchestra. They fitted card tables with little shaded electric lamps,
and suspended globe lights wrapped in red oriental paper

from the ceilings. They ordered glass tabletops from the mainland for the supper room. Above the door in the hall they placed a curious, ironic sign that Antonio had surely got as part of his trade in 'oriental goods': three monkeys that bid patrons not to see, hear or speak evil.[77]

On 19 January 1925 crowds flocked downtown to attend the grand opening of the Continental Hotel Deluxe. The viceregal party was in attendance, and Lady Ashbolt, it was reported, wore a cream crêpe de Chine dress.[78] Veronique, now forty-two years old, but still pretending to be younger, got ready in the dressing room. She made up her face, its fine lines thrown into relief by the electric dressing-room lights, and patted her finger-waves into place along her brow. Over silk stockings and a garter belt she pulled a pretty black georgette dress. Its dropped waistline sat along her hips, and the wide neck emphasised her collarbones. Gone were the corsets that were standard back in the now-distant 1910s, and the dress hung on her frame loosely. Feathers brushed her legs as she put on her dancing shoes and checked her appearance in the dressing room's wall of mirrors.[79] As she took her husband's arm and strode onto the dance floor, the band struck up the tango. Their bodies moved together, their legs in perfect time. The delighted crowd applauded as they bowed.

The grand opening was a resounding success, and Veronique and her husband celebrated the newspaper reports that declared the Continental Hotel Deluxe 'as stylish as any in London or Paris'; 'lavish' and 'sumptuous', while also being perfectly respectable. The 'Women's Interest' columnist rapturised over all the wonderful 'frocks' on display, and felt that the monkeys over the door reminded patrons that it was 'a place where you can take your wife and daughter if you desire them to have a perfect evening's enjoyment'.[80]

The couple made the most of life in remote Hobart. Then, one night, it all fell apart. Hobart, it seems, was not nearly remote enough. A man from Western Australia turned up at the Continental, recognising Anthony Coty as Aldo Cellis and calling him a 'white slaver'. Veronique watched as panic set in, helped him pack his things, looked on as he shaved his moustache. She had never seen him without it, and surely reeled at the new face that stared out at her. The new life, the new business: it had all come crashing down. Mrs Duncan, watching in horror as her multi-thousand-pound investment was ridiculed in the tabloid press, must have cursed the day she met them.

Things went from bad to worse when Antonio wrote to say he'd been arrested on the Melbourne docks. Veronique rushed to his side, calling in the help of her wealthy and well-to-do family. As luck would have it, her sister Ethel had married a high-ranking civil servant, Arthur James Pitcher, and both came to their aid. Mrs Pitcher and Veronique called at the Home Department daily, citing their respectability and social standing, offering bail and fine money, making desperate entreaties against Antonio's deportation.

And then the tabloids found him, exposing his past crimes and speculating on others. 'White slaver,' they called him, and intimated that he was an enemy of the state, saying that he belonged in 'Mussolini land'. There was no hope for him any longer. The Home Department denied their request, and all parties agreed it was best for him to leave.

Veronique left Australia with him in March 1925, probably still reeling from the shock of their sudden fall. They settled in Palermo, and tried to make the most of it. They even made friendships with the local elite, and were given the opportunity to use a prominent army general's address for their post. But still it was far from home. Veronique was in Italy and not at 'Trafford', the Jolimont Terrace house of the White family, when her mother died there in early December 1925. She probably wept bitterly when the news reached her, and never quite got over having been denied the chance to say goodbye. The small obituary listed 'Veronique (Mrs A. Carvelli)' as one of the 'loving daughters': a perfunctory line that likely hid a well of mixed emotion.

In October 1926 Veronique helped Carvelli craft another letter to the Home Department from their temporary home in Sicily: 'Against a fault of youth there is a life long of honest intelligent work in my favour,' he wrote, pointing out that he had 'been over twenty years in the colonies and am married to an Australian so that my sentiments are Australian and find it very hard to leave [*sic*] away from it.' He positioned himself as an upright citizen and a financial asset to the country, and made reference to his very respectable brother and sister-in-law: 'I have many relations in high positions in the Colonies and myself possess a few thousand pounds ready to invest in your sunny land.' He was willing to undertake a substantial bond against his good behaviour, if permitted to re-enter. His Italian flair for drama was in evidence as he closed the missive. 'Please pardon me the liberty I am taking,' he wrote. 'With my anticipate thanks assuring you of my deep sentiments of gratitude, believe me, Dear Sir, Yours Faithfully, Antonio Carvelli.'

But the letter that arrived care of General Cornaro on 23 November 1926 was a bitter disappointment to them both. While the Home Department civil servant in receipt of the letter was 'still of the opinion that ... he [Carvelli] could be trusted to be of good behaviour if permitted to return to Australia', he was doubtful that his recommendation would be effective. 'In view of his previous conviction and the opportunity that would be afforded the press ... it is presumed that the Minister will not be disposed to authorise his readmission,' Mr Peters wrote. A few months later Carvelli received a curt letter from an assistant secretary to the minister of the Home Department, informing him that his request to re-enter Australia had been denied. Veronique and her husband were trapped in Fascist Italy.[81]

Veronique could only bear the exile so long. After the failed attempt to gain her husband legal readmission, she left him in Italy and re-entered Australia at the end of 1926. She rejoined her family in Melbourne, where she began to plead once more on behalf of her deported husband with the help of her sister and brother-in-law. Playing on the growing suspicion of Mussolini's politics, she told Mr Peters that 'she cannot live in Italy', and that her family was willing to put up 'any reasonable bond' as a surety for Carvelli's good behaviour, if they permitted his re-entry.

It almost worked. Mr Peters, for his part, was totally convinced that this man, with a wife who came from 'an apparently good family', could be trusted in his assertion that he wanted nothing more than to 'live down the past and earn an honest living here'. The minister, however, remained suspicious. 'Although it is 19 years since Carvelli was last convicted the nature of the offences with which he was charged was such that it would be very difficult to overlook their effect on the public mind,' he wrote. He could not recommend readmission.

They would have to make it happen in the old way. In 1927 Veronique travelled back to Europe, where she met her husband at the Hotel de Marseilles in Monaco. A short while later she bought two steamship tickets on the SS *Borda*, travelling third-class to Sydney. She reported her name honestly to the ship's registrar as Veronique Carvelli. Her travel companion told the man with the form that he was Giuseppe Feraro; and then, judging Giuseppe to sound too Italian, corrected this to José. The annoyed registrar scratched it out and corrected the name. The SS *Borda* left the dock in Italy and continued on to Sydney. And with that, Carvelli was able to sneak back into Australia.

Their triumph was mixed with tragedy. In 1929 Veronique's father died at his beloved 'Trafford', although at least this time she could be at the deathbed. The Carvellis seemed to pass the next couple of years quietly, possibly in New Zealand, possibly in Australia: traces of Veronique in ships' manifests suggest regular trips back and forth across the Tasman Sea. The couple travelled back to Europe a year later, where they remained for some time. Then, in 1931, a more profound catastrophe befell them. In July, at the age of only fifty-two, the man who had been Veronique's husband, business partner and pimp in various measures for over two decades died.

Antonio Carvelli's obfuscations of who he was, where he was and what he was doing continued right up to the moment of his death. There is no trace of a death announcement in the Australian or New Zealand papers, despite the fact that he surely had friends and relations there. He died in Nervi, a small resort town just outside Genoa, but I have no idea what he was doing there. His cause of death is listed simply as 'unrecorded', and his profession was described as 'industrialist': an unlikely self-reinvention, even for him.[82]

In the absence of death announcements, letters and testimonies of grief, we cannot know how forty-eight-year-old Veronique Carvelli felt when she lost her husband. We can be certain that she mourned, because whatever the complicated and perhaps harmful nature of their relationship, it had lasted for almost twenty-five years. For two decades they were lovers; partners – quite literally – in crime; they visited her parents, were close with her sisters and their families; they travelled the world. They wore each other's precious gifts with pride. They danced together, slept together, posed for photographs and wrote letters when they were apart. They loved each other.

It seems Veronique returned to Wellington to live, after the loss of her husband – the city that she had always most liked to call home. But the death of Carvelli left Veronique adrift in more ways than one. She remained Italian, even after the man who had made her so had died. Thankfully, the daughters of the suffrage campaigners who had secured the early twentieth-century vote had now taken up the cause of citizenship reform, and by the mid-1930s they launched a concerted campaign in Australia and New Zealand, linked to others around the world, for women who had lost their nationality upon marriage to be able to renaturalise.[83]

Veronique must have learned about their success because, in late April 1938, she wrote to the New Zealand Department of Internal Affairs, asking them to naturalise her as a British subject. In an elegant but untidy hand, punctuated with unnecessary capitalisation, she explained her situation:

I am Australian born of English parents. I married an Italian Gentleman in N Zealand 25 years ago (not naturalised). I have resided here ever Since with the exception of trips abroad. My husband died 5 Years Ago. There are no children.

Then, underlined, she asked:

<u>Am I Still considered an Alien</u>? I have Never felt an alien. I am informed women married to foreigners can retain their own nationality now. I trust you will be able to Give me this good news. And instruct me how to go about Same.

Thank You in anticipating,

Believe me.

Yours truly

Veronique Carvelli

The Department of Internal Affairs evidently replied asking for more information in early May, because Veronique's next short letter stated that she did not have her birth certificate, but was able to procure it if necessary. Another letter elaborated on her marriage. 'My husband, Antonio Adolpho Carvelli, died in Italy in 1931.' In this letter she claimed that she married her husband in 1909 but had seen little of him since; that he had lived most of his life in Italy and she had lived her life in New Zealand. Of course this was categorically untrue, but it is difficult not to admire her brazen approach to manipulating state officialdom.

She was not a good enough liar to avoid the scrutiny from officials of the Department of Internal Affairs who, whether because they suspected something or because it was standard procedure, requested a report from the police, as to her past life in the country. It did not take long for the police in Auckland and Wellington to uncover Veronique's past. The police provided the Department with evidence of an arrest for brothel-keeping and intimated that she had once procured other women. They noted that she had used aliases in various cities. They reported that she had been convicted for 'keeping a house of ill-fame' in Auckland back in 1917; and one police officer, perhaps a little more canny than the rest, suggested that she may have 'brought other females into this form of livelihood'.[84]

And yet the police officers who wrote with this information in the two cities maintained that she was respectable, and declined to condemn her. 'Since [her arrest in 1917] she had been living a respectful life and her character is now above reproach,' wrote Detective Heenan of Auckland. Another, Sergeant Doel of Mount Eden station, said he remembered her well back in Auckland, where he knew her as Marie Williams. 'I have spoken to her on Queen Street on occasion,' he told the Department of Internal Affairs. 'I remember one occasion when speaking to her she told me that she had given up her old life of immorality and that she had ample means for the rest of her life.' She had recently sold a house in Melbourne for £1,450, another report noted. Constable Peterson wrote that she was 'held in high esteem' in her current neighbourhood.

The Department of Internal Affairs did not take long to adjudicate on Veronique's request. Her next letter thanked them warmly for her naturalisation certificate, and for the return of her documents, including the death certificate of her husband:

Please accept my Grateful thanks for all the trouble You have taken on my behalf,

Believe Me,

Yours respectfully,

Veronique Carvelli[85]

She continued to live in New Zealand until the early 1940s, when she returned to Melbourne and registered at 23 Riversdale Road: she had, it seems, gone back to her childhood home of Hawthorn, living just beside Fairview Park and the banks of the Yarra. Like many Australian women who had spent most of their lives abroad, or travelling, it appears she had come 'home to die'.[86]

It was around this time that Veronique began suffering from the disease that would eventually kill her: acromegaly, an excessive production of growth hormone from the pituitary gland. The signs were there even in the picture from her younger days – she was very tall, as though she had an enormous growth spurt in adolescence. Her hands were large. At thirty-five, in her prison photograph, it seemed as though her facial features had begun to enlarge. By the age of sixty-five in 1948, when she was first diagnosed, the symptoms were probably mild, but over the next decade she grew more and more fatigued, with painful joints and an inability to sleep. Veronique, always so elegant and stylish, was probably horrified by her excess hair growth, profuse sweating and body odour.

The 1940s were marked by the death of almost all her siblings – the *Argus* ran the obituary of Ethel Pitcher, who died in 1947. Keppel, her only brother, fell down the stairs and died in a lodging house in 1949. In every death notice she was named as Madame or Mrs Carvelli, even as the years that she had spent with her husband grew more distant.

She left little behind: no papers, no letters, no recollections, no regrets. We can assume she gave little thought to one mousy-haired girl from New Zealand whom she had once known. The only material that survives from the last twenty years of Veronique's life is a brief will. It suggests that she died in financial comfort, but with few human connections. Her only living sister, Beatrice, was named as executor, but she left her entire estate to the Australian RSPCA. The parrot was probably not the last animal that had kept loneliness at bay.

By 1964 Veronique Sarah White Carvelli was living at 880 Glenferrie Road, Kew, Melbourne, which was then the Lancewood Private Hospital. She found herself in a very different world from the one in which she had spent her working life. The Beatles were coming to Australia, to play music one couldn't tango to; and in new coffee shops and meeting halls around the country, women in short skirts and trousers demanded equal pay to men, having learned that, of the vote and the money, money was at least as important. We shall never know what Veronique thought of it all. Her acromegaly was by this point well advanced. Her heart was enlarging. She died when this organ failed on 15 February 1964 – two days after her late husband Antonio's birthday; he would have been eighty-five. She was eighty years old, but she would probably have claimed to be seventy-five. She outlived every other person in this story, in the end. Beatrice, her sister, certified her death and Veronique was cremated three days later. According to the records, her remains were scattered, but they do not say by whom, or where. Veronique White Carvelli's final resting place remains unknown, which may be exactly as she intended.

CHAPTER SEVEN

THE SAILOR'S WIFE

On the day that Lydia Harvey first appeared in the witness box at a London police court to testify against her trafficker, back in Oamaru life continued as normal. Her three oldest sisters helped their mother care for the one-year-old twins, rode their bicycles across the railway line and down to the beach, window-shopped and flirted with the local boys. Her mother taught piano lessons in her front room, a fire lit against the mid-winter chill. It could not have been further from the drama unfolding in Lydia's life, 12,000 miles away at the height of the northern summer.

Emily Louisa Badeley may have had her worries and suspicions when she heard so little from her eldest child, after she received her letter back in January 1910. She had met a couple at the photography studio, Lydia's letter explained, and they had hired her as their nursemaid and were taking her to London. Months passed in a state of distracted worry; but there were, after all, more pressing concerns, not to mention the hope that Lydia would soon send a little money back to the growing family.

Then, on 22 July 1910, as Lydia was settling into Eilidh MacDougall's rescue home after her harrowing testimony, Emily Badeley opened the *Oamaru Mail*. Nothing at first appeared amiss. There were the results of the Wellington horse-races, adverts for underskirts and condensed milk and tea. There was the usual from Parliament, the shipping news, the weather. Then, on page four, a headline caught her eye: 'White slave traffic in New Zealand', the small article was called, and reported briefly – via electric telegraph – on a trial that had taken place in London only the day before. Two men had been remanded in custody 'on several charges of white slavery'. One victim was from New Zealand and was using the assumed name Doris Williams. She had been working at a photographer's studio in Wellington before she was lured away.[1]

It was a brief report, only a handful of lines, but Emily Badeley could clearly read between them. It was the mention of the photographer's studio that made her stop whatever it was she was doing, leave the twin babies with Clara or a neighbour or her sister-in-law and rush to Oamaru Police Station, the newspaper clutched in her hand. Lydia's mother told the desk sergeant that she was very concerned about her daughter, Lydia Rhoda Harvey, who had written to her from Wellington many months ago to tell her she was leaving with a respectable couple, to work as a nursemaid in London. They were rich, Lydia said; the man O'Conner was a wool buyer. The paper stated that this girl – this 'white slave' who had been taken to Buenos Aires and London – was seventeen and had worked at a photographer's studio outside Wellington. How many girls could that possibly be? Emily had not heard from her daughter in months. Could they make enquiries at the photographer's studio? Her daughter had written that she had met these supposed O'Conners there.

The answer that came a week later from the Wellington police confirmed Emily's worst fears. Sergeant Stagpool knocked on the door of Chelmer Street and informed her that he had learned that Doris Williams was in fact Lydia Rhoda Harvey, and she had indeed just testified against her traffickers at a police court in London.

What would Emily Badeley have felt when she heard this news? Anger at her daughter's foolishness? Despair at her own naïvety and negligence? Desperation that no one else should find out who Doris Williams really was? Gut-churning worry and sadness surely mixed with all these other emotions as she stood, powerless and poor, in front of Sergeant Stagpool. She had no money, she explained, with which to bring her daughter home.[2]

The Vigilance Record, the organ of William Coote's National Vigilance Association, was clear about the role it expected parents to play in the crusade for moral right-eousness. That same year, for instance, it reprinted a speech from the Mothers' Union, castigating careless mothers and imbuing good mothers with profound responsibility. 'A mother should be the friend of her children now more than ever,' the speech intoned:

> She should try to win that confidence by an ever-ready sympathy and interest in their pleasures, in their recreations, in their interests and in their work. But above all, I would plead that every mother should make it her duty to know her child's friends and companions ... whose influence is brought to bear on that child, for that is the principal factor in the forming of character.

What kind of mother, then, was Emily Badeley, who had been so ignorant of her daughter's companions that she had no idea she had been trafficked until she read about it in her local newspaper? How was any working-class mother supposed to know these things, when their daughters were so often forced to work at great distances? 'The evil of our age,' the article continued, 'seems to me to be want of balance, impatience of control of any kind, and an unwholesome craving for excitement – and with that we mothers have to face the fact that we can no longer control our children the way we ourselves were controlled.'[3] But what hope did Emily Badeley, the poor single mother of seven, have of controlling her daughter, when middle-class women fretted over controlling theirs?

Sergeant Stagpool promised to relay Emily Badeley's wish for her daughter's return – and her limited means to enable it – to the authorities in Wellington. But he did not tell her what the Wellington police had actually learned about her daughter, or their real reasons for enquiring about her life in the capital city. The truth was that it was not the anxious mother's queries that had prompted the investigation into Lydia Harvey, and Emily Badeley was not the only person who read the story of 'white slavery in New Zealand' with particular concern. The Department of Justice, and the prime minister Sir Joseph Ward himself, were well aware of the ramifications, should the voting public believe that traffickers were allowed to operate with impunity in the young nation's capital, and that an innocent, young white New Zealand girl had been ruined on the watch of the Wellington police.

Luckily, a Supreme Court judge was in the mood to do the government favours and issued a suppression order on

Guy Scholefield's full report. Rumours about who this 'Doris Williams' really was had already begun to circulate, before Joseph Ward's office contacted Inspector Ellis at the Wellington police. Could he look into the past of this supposed 'white slave' and supply the government with any relevant information?[4]

Detective Lewis, well versed in the Wellington underworld, was charged with completing this delicate task. His first stop was the photography studio in Lower Hutt, where Mr Harlow told him that Lydia Harvey had been a good worker, although she'd only been with him for three weeks. She had left without giving notice, and all he knew was that she had been staying at Mrs Logan's boarding house in Ingestre Street. It was an address Detective Lewis knew well. When he arrived, Mrs Logan told him that Lydia Harvey had shared a bedroom with Doris Gray, a girl who the detective claimed was 'a bookmaker's prostitute and convicted thief'. Mrs Logan described further damning behaviour: the girls had been known to sneak out of their window after the rest of the household had gone to bed for the night. Then, a few weeks later, Lydia Harvey had left the boarding house and gone to live with someone she called 'Mrs Rae', telling Mrs Logan that she was 'going to England with some French people'. This was not how a trafficking victim was meant to behave. The supposed 'white slave' Lydia Harvey, concluded Detective Lewis, 'had been leading an immoral life for some months before leaving here'.[5]

The report was forwarded on to the Department of Justice and the prime minister's office, giving Sir Joseph Ward what he needed to wash his hands of the whole 'white slavery' question. On 29 August he stood up before the New

Zealand Parliament and made a statement 'in regard to the case in which a New Zealand girl named Doris Williams was concerned'. He commended the police in Wellington, who had investigated and forwarded to Scotland Yard everything they had learned about the suspects, in order to assist the prosecution. 'The inspector of Police then continued his investigation,' Ward told Parliament, 'with the result that it is now proved that the young woman, whose identity has been fully established, was living an immoral life in this city for some time before her departure for Monte Video.'

Ward continued, somewhat defensively, 'It is only right that I should make this statement, because the assumption was that some respectable girl or girls had been decoyed away. The last part of the statement put a different complexion on the matter.' He sat down to hearty shouts of 'Hear, hear!' from his honourable members.[6] Conveniently, this was the same day that the judge lifted the suppression order, and newspapers were now free to report the full particulars of the case: in light of, naturally, the prime minister's clarifying statement.

'The White Slave Traffic', ran the headline in the *New Zealand Herald* and the *Auckland Star*, and a dozen other newspapers, including the *Oamaru Mail*, on 30 August 1910. 'An Abominable Traffic', declared the *Bay of Plenty Times*; 'An Inhuman Traffic', said the *Ashburton Guardian*; while the *Wanganui Chronicle* dubbed it 'A Diabolical Trade'. The *Evening Post*, which had been sitting on Guy Scholefield's original story, finally got to put it in print.

The story ran twice in just about every newspaper in the country, but it was the *New Zealand Truth* that came closest to revealing the terrible secret of Lydia's real name to the whole of New Zealand. 'Who is Doris Williams?' the unscrupulous new tabloid asked. Guy Scholefield himself was *Truth's* first target. His 'latest and even ludicrous sensation' claimed that there was a 'white slave' traffic in New Zealand, but 'so sensational and sad a story of a pure, young, and innocent New Zealand girl going astray must naturally call for further and fuller particulars'. *Truth*, which clearly had an informant on the Wellington police force, was 'able to supply further information'. Though it was unable to discover Doris Williams's true identity, the newspaper could assure its 40,000 readers that she was indeed a 'soiled dove' and that 'there has been nothing in the shape of trafficking as suggested by the daily press'.[7] Taking this 'soiled dove' to Buenos Aires, concluded *Truth*, was just 'carrying coals to Newcastle'.[8]

Unsurprisingly, communications between London and Wellington were strained. In September 1910, shortly after Carvelli and Berard had pleaded guilty at the Old Bailey, assistant police commissioner Frederick Bullock and DI Ernest Anderson had begun to make enquiries about sending Lydia Harvey back to New Zealand, telling its high commissioner in London that if nothing could be done for her, she would be forced to go back on the streets.[9] The New Zealand high commissioner, Sir William Hall-Jones, who had in fact recently been interim prime minister, sent a cablegram to the Department of Justice. Translated from telegraphic code, it read like a strange poem:

Cellis and Berard convicted chief
Witness eighteen
Years of age

Said to be
Daughter of Mrs Harvey Chalmers Street
Oamaru who
Not acquainted with
Position been bad case Scotland Yard
Asking whether
You can do
Anything for her
Said to be
now reformed kindly advise.

The undersecretary at New Zealand's Department of Justice was perfectly acquainted with the government's stance on the matter, writing:

I do not think that the government is called upon to repay the cost of bringing this young woman back to New Zealand. She was not of good character, and I have no doubt she left the Dominion with a full knowledge of what she was going to do. I suggest that the High Commission be informed by cable that the Government cannot do anything for her.[10]

The cable to London was swift and brief: 'Mother desires daughter home but [she] cannot financially assist regret Government also unable pay passage money.'[11]

When the cable arrived at Scotland Yard, Frederick Bullock's fist must have hit his desk. As the assistant commissioner for legal matters and the central authority on the 'white slave' traffic, he was surely incensed at the New Zealand government's position. He had worked closely with anti-trafficking campaigners for years to ensure that the 1904 International Agreement for the Suppression of the 'White Slave Traffic' was written and ratified. Unclenching his fist and taking up his pen, Bullock replied to the undersecretary by letter, asking whether New Zealand was still interested in being party to the 1904 agreement, which obliged it to repatriate 'the destitute victims of the criminal traffic' who were New Zealand nationals.[12] This was a stickier issue than it might at first seem, because New Zealand had not, in fact, signed the agreement itself, but was assumed to come under the agreement by virtue of it being a British Dominion, a status it had been granted in 1907. Ward's insistence that New Zealand was not responsible for repatriating Lydia Harvey was not only a statement about her character, or even about the national character, but also about national sovereignty.[13]

As these diplomatic battles raged in the electrical pulses that fired through undersea cables, and in the letters that travelled back and forth by steamship, seventeen-year-old Lydia Harvey sat and waited to find out if she was officially a 'white slave' or a 'soiled dove' in the eyes of her government. She spent almost five months in the Metropolitan Police Home for Women and Girls, until Bullock managed to raise enough money from the Police Voluntary Fund to send the girl home and booked her a third-class berth. The cost of the passage over which Britain and New Zealand bickered was £28.[14]

At long last the day of Lydia's departure arrived, and DI Anderson collected her from the Police Home at 198 Lambeth Road on the morning of 13 October 1910. It would have been the first time Anderson had seen Lydia since the trial in early September, and almost five months since he had first spoken to her that evening in Piccadilly Circus. It is difficult to say what words, if any, would have passed between them. After saying farewell (tearily or happily, or both) to the Police Home matron and to Miss MacDougall, Lydia joined Anderson in a taxi that took them all the way through South London, across a bridge and through the docklands until they reached the Royal Albert Docks. If she had thought London large before, it must have seemed truly immense by the time they arrived.

They joined the crowds of embarking passengers on Shaw and Savill's 'magnificent' Royal Mail Steamer *Tainui*, which made monthly voyages from London to New Zealand and ports in between. A few months previously it had carried Veronique Carvelli back to Wellington. 'Cheap fares,' the company proclaimed, were available.[15] Anderson accompanied Lydia on board, meeting the ship's matron, Miss Gordon, and seeing her safely into her care. He probably explained in hushed tones what had happened to the girl, and why she was in particular need of attention and surveillance. As ship's matron, Miss Gordon was in charge of keeping men out of the single women's cabins, and keeping young women – especially those like Lydia Harvey – in line. For performing this duty, Miss Gordon earned herself a free passage, as well as a small amount of money. She and Anderson brought Lydia to the ship's captain, who assured them that he would put her under his direct care.

Meanwhile, William Coote had arranged for Mireille Lapara, Marguerite Bescançon and Victoria Bricot to be repatriated to France. Mercifully, France was closer than New Zealand, and the girls were easier and cheaper to repatriate, so this was

24: The RMS *Tainui*, a Royal Mail Steamer built in 1908 for Shaw, Savill and Albion. Lydia Harvey boarded this ship in London in October of 1910 to begin her long journey home in the third-class cabins.

undertaken in September, immediately following the trial. Coote instructed a National Vigilance Association worker to collect the first two girls at the Sisters of the Good Shepherd Convent in London and take them by boat-train to Dover and on to Dieppe.

This journey, according to the NVA worker, was fraught almost from the start. Nineteen-year-old Marguerite and seventeen-year-old Mireille, who were meant to have been cowed and shamed by their experience of being trafficked, were anything but. From the moment they left the convent 'they endeavoured to attract the notice of every man who came near us. On the boat, both when embarking and disembarking, their remarks called forth various replies from the men around us.' They had, as William Stead once put it, 'lost their moral sense'.

The pair settled down as they drew nearer to Paris and their brief respite from the confines of respectability drew to a close. Mireille was handed over to a Salvation Army captain in that city, who had agreed to take her on as a domestic servant: this was considered charity at the time. The girl, noted the NVA worker, was 'rather unwilling' to go with the Salvation Army woman, 'but nevertheless did so without trouble'. It is the last glimpse we get of the youngest victim of the traffickers, walking off to another job cleaning and cooking; either resigned to her fate or deciding that biding her time would make for a more effective and durable escape.

Then it was Marguerite's turn to be 'reformed', which was to take place at the French branch of the NVA in the avenue du Général Michel Bizot. Gone was the bubbly young woman who had flirted with men on the steamship. 'The poor child cried very much when we arrived there, and clung to me at the last, begging me not to leave her alone,' the NVA worker wrote in her report to William Coote. 'I talked to her seriously and kindly, and she promised to be good and obedient, and to do her utmost to remain in the home.'[16] There are no other definitive traces of Marguerite in the historical record: good and obedient, or otherwise.

Victoria Bricot, the oldest of the three French girls that Carvelli and di Nicotera had recruited, was another case entirely. Unlike the two younger girls, twenty-one-year-old Bricot appeared composed and compliant when she was collected at the Church Army home in Stourcliffe Street by a different NVA worker a few days later. 'Her behaviour was excellent until we reached Dieppe, when she became suddenly very sullen and independent,' the NVA worker wrote. Nonetheless, the pair successfully made the journey from Dieppe to Paris, where they had breakfast before getting the tram to avenue du Général Michel Bizot. Victoria refused to sit inside the tram and instead stood grasping the rail on the tram's outdoor platform, no doubt sullenly enjoying the frustration of her temporary mistress, and the noise and bustle of the Paris streets as they clanged by.

When they arrived they were told that the NVA home was quite full, and were made to wait while the matron tried to arrange a place. At last, in her beneficence, she called Bricot into her office and offered her a bed, but instead of gratitude she was greeted with 'insolence'.

'No, I shall not remain here,' Victoria informed the matron and the horrified NVA worker who sat beside her. 'I would rather return from where I came.'

'Why will you not remain?' the matron asked.

'This is a Patronage, and I do not intend to stay in such a place,' Victoria Bricot replied, meaning that she understood she had been going to some kind of boarding house, only to discover they had taken her to a reform home.

The matron asked what she knew of similar places and, free from the exigencies of the police interview room and the court, the young woman was frank. 'I have already been arrested three times, and have spent three years in a House of Correction at Rouen, so you may be sure I shall not willingly go into such a place again. No, I will go to my parents.'

When asked if her parents would be willing to receive her, after what she had done, her reply was 'Why not?'

She consented to be chaperoned as far as the tram stop,

but a few yards beyond the reform home's doors, Victoria Bricot stopped and turned to the woman beside her.

'Madam, *je suis libre, n'est-ce pas?*'

'Certainly,' the woman replied.

'Then I will go to my aunt, who is a laundress, for I cannot face my parents in this plight. I will take a cab and go alone, please.'

'But you will give me your aunt's address?' the woman asked.

'Why should I do so?' Victoria asked.

'Because I have brought you all the way from London, and should like to know where you intend to go now,' the woman replied.

'Well then, the address is 39 rue Rodier.' It was suspiciously similar to the rue Rodier address of the hotel where she had stayed with Carvelli, back when he had induced her to come with him to London in April. With that, Victoria Bricot hailed a passing cab, gave the address to the driver and left the NVA worker standing in the street.

Once she got over her initial shock, the worker sent a cable to William Coote at the NVA offices back in London, telling him what had happened, despite her best efforts to convince Victoria to choose a different path. Coote replied that she ought to give Bricot's name to the local police. This she did, and was pleased at the Chef de Division Mr Harouin's kind response. 'He promised that a watch should be kept on her movements in future, in the interest of other young girls.'[17]

Trafficking, it seems, was defined by very fine lines. As Victoria Bricot discovered when her name was handed over to the Paris police 'in the interest of other young girls', the difference between being a victim of trafficking and a criminal threat was razor-thin. Equally minute was the space between the benevolent idea of 'repatriation', written into the 1904 agreement, in the name of supporting and protecting victims should they wish to return 'to their family and friends', and forced removal in the form of deportation – which is what often happened in practice.

William Coote oversaw hundreds of 'repatriations' during his tenure with the NVA. Very few of these were done to assist trafficking victims who wanted to go home. The vast majority were thinly veiled deportations of women who had been prosecuted for soliciting on the streets of London and who professed no desire to leave. This makes the difficulties in repatriating Lydia Harvey particularly egregious: for all the talk of repatriation and anti-trafficking, two wealthy governments could not seem to get together to help this confirmed victim of 'the white slave trade' – who had actually expressed a desire to return home – pay for a third-class steamship ticket. As the line between 'repatriation' and 'deportation' continued to thin, the press, moral reformers and policy makers continued to operate under a false and impossible dichotomy of victimhood and villainy; of innocence and ruin. And young women like Lydia Harvey continued to live their life in the spaces in between.

The RMS *Tainui*'s horn sent out one loud blast and, after the heavy ropes were flung on deck, the ship began to pull away from the Royal Albert Docks. Lydia watched as the red-and-brown stone buildings of the docklands, the masts of the ships and the smoke and chimneys of London all grew smaller and she could barely see them at all. Soon the ship turned course, with Margate on her starboard side, and then the white cliffs of Dover came into view, glimmering and vast in the autumn sun. Having landed in Southampton when she had come with the Cellises from Buenos Aires, it was the first time Lydia had seen the cliffs. Whether she knew it or not, it would also be the last. She went below, and things settled into ordinary life on board a ship. She and the other single women would eat a small tea in the third-class dining room, before making their way down to the cabin where they slept: dozens of girls who were bound for Kalgoorlie, Sydney and Wellington, alone but for the stern-faced matron who had them in her temporary charge. The sound of the water and the steady hum of the ship's engine must have seemed strange to Lydia after all those months with the racket of Lambeth Road outside her window.

There is no record of what Lydia thought of being kept under the matron's watchful eye, nor of her feelings about leaving London. As much as she perhaps dreaded returning to New Zealand after her experiences, cloaked in nothing but the thin pseudonym of Doris Williams, she cannot have been sad to see the other side of the wet, cold city and its endless pavements. When they boarded the ship she was asked her occupation. 'Domestic,' she replied.[18] She was in good company. Seventy-five other single young women had joined the RMS *Tainui* on this voyage as 'domestics', many boarding the ship together, having answered New Zealand's call for British and Irish servants to work in 'good homes' for 'good wages'.[19] Perhaps one of them was bound for Mrs Batson's house in Karori. She had lost her maid-of-all-work, after all, in January of that year.

Lydia knew that her mother wanted her home, but could

not afford to pay for her passage. After all she'd done to prevent it, her mother had found out what had happened to her. It was this very threat – that the police would tell her parents – that had helped to keep Lydia quiet when she was with Mr Cellis, when she lay in the hospital bed, when she first encountered DI Anderson. And all those shillings and pounds she had earned, and yet she was penniless. 'Aldo will see you settled,' Marie had told her before she had left London. It had been a lie.

In early November 1910 the RMS *Tainui*, carrying Lydia Harvey, the ship's matron Miss Gordon and the dozens of farmers, miners, grocers and domestics who travelled with them, arrived at the Queen's Wharf in Wellington. On the dockside the ship's matron handed Lydia over into the care of a woman from the YWCA, to whom Miss MacDougall had written. They had secured her a live-in job as a ward maid in the city's hospital. Lydia hardly had time to readjust to the strangeness of being back in a familiar city as a much-changed person, before she was expected to begin in this new post. Her travel back to Oamaru – which the UK government, the New Zealand government and the NVA had refused to cover the cost of – would have to wait until she had saved enough for the fare.

She donned the crisp white apron and hat that she had seen the ward maids wear in the Paddington hospital, when she was the patient. She scrubbed the wooden floors and polished them, washed the dishes, served the bland meals and made the beds – which would have involved stripping soiled sheets, a filthy, smelly and unpleasant task. She lit coal fires and sometimes she would help with patients.[20] It was hard work. Because the hospital had a large staff, Lydia was probably not as lonely as she had been in Karori, though she had to work on Saturday and Sundays too. Nonetheless she used the precious little time she had between work and sleep to write those grateful letters to Miss MacDougall.

Such letters were apparently common, but, when they do survive, they read ambivalently. On the one hand, they can be interpreted as a moving account of a person saved from the brink of damnation; on the other, they can be seen as the rehearsed words of another young working woman who has learned to toe the line. There was, after all, a clear message inherent in the stories about trafficking, in which women who travelled for work and adventure wound up kidnapped and enslaved: stay in your place. Mobility – both physical and social mobility – was dangerous.[21] Dreaming of things beyond one's station was risky. Perhaps Lydia had learned her lesson.

But was life as a ward maid what this young woman who won the beauty contest, who moved out of domestic service into shop work, who jumped at the chance for a South American adventure, aspired to? Had Lydia been scared back into her place by her experience? Her pseudonym protected her from being publicly shamed, but it may also have put a great deal of power into the hands of the organisations that helped to ensure this anonymity, enabling them to shunt her into a low-status occupation that was experiencing a severe labour shortage.[22] Indeed, as Lydia made her way up to Wellington to work for Mrs Batson back in 1909, the *New Zealand Truth* defined the attempt to solve the servant crisis as a kind of trafficking, accusing middle-class women affiliated with the YWCA of demanding that the government use its funds to import 'household slaves'. 'The obvious remedy is a reasonable wage and reasonable hours,' the newspaper intoned.[23]

Lydia Harvey did not seem to want to wait for either her wages or her hours to change (and in any case, as a domestic worker she would still be waiting today, if she had). She worked until she had saved enough money to return to her mother's house, and by early 1911 had quit her new job and was back in Oamaru. Her mother and sisters probably greeted her lovingly, but the truth of what she had experienced hung heavily between them.

It must have been difficult for Lydia to settle back into an ordinary life. While there is no hint that the local press in her home town had discovered that Oamaru's very own Lydia Harvey was the 'white slave' 'Doris Williams', this knowledge – which the local police definitely had – may well have made its way unofficially around the area. In fact some of Lydia's recent past had followed her home: Mrs Batson had returned to Oamaru around the same time as Lydia, opening a tobacconist to make ends meet after the death of her banker husband. A fundraising concert was held at the opera house for the widow and her four young children.[24] We can only assume that Lydia studiously avoided contacting her former employer, who must have had her suspicions about the connections between the 'white slave' from the newspapers, who had worked at a photographer's studio, and the wayward girl who had left her service to go and work for Mr Harlow the year before.

Even if Lydia Harvey escaped being the talk of the town, the news that her mother was expecting another baby out of wedlock surely got round. In July 1911 Emily gave birth to Amalina Alexandra, her eighth daughter. Chelmer Street was now even more crowded than it was before, and there would be no concert at the opera house to help the Badeleys. Whatever the circumstances that greeted her in Oamaru, Lydia did not stay there long. Around September 1911 she went to nearby Dunedin and a short while later sent her mother a letter, telling her that she had taken a job with a vaudeville company called 'Brennan's', leaving shortly for Australia.

Lydia Harvey signed her contract with Brennan's at the height of vaudeville's golden age. Originally an export from America, vaudeville was a descendant of the older American minstrel show, the salacious burlesque styles that could be found in brothels and bars around the world and the raucous working-class music hall of Victorian Britain. More respectable and modern than its ancestors, vaudeville was also known as 'variety theatre' or simply 'varieties', and took the world by storm in the early twentieth century with its mix of comedy sketches, dancing, singing, acrobatics, animal acts, pantomime and more. It was variety theatre that had filled the seats of London's West End, through which Lydia had walked miserably back in the spring of 1910, and it was no less popular in Australia.

James Brennan was one of Australia's most well-known vaudeville entrepreneurs who, in the early twentieth century, founded one of the country's main circuits: Brennan's Amphitheatre in Melbourne and the Gaiety in Sydney, as well as a touring company that travelled to Hobart, Adelaide, Brisbane and elsewhere.[25] Alongside the more famous Harry Clay and the Tivoli circuit, Brennan helped to make vaudeville the most popular form of mass entertainment, before cheap cinemas dramatically poached the theatre's clientele in the years after the First World War.[26]

James Brennan stands as a typical example of the way that this middle-class, respectable entertainment industry continued to rub shoulders with the underworld of gambling, sex and crime. Brennan began life as a bookmaker, moving in the same circles as Carvelli and di Nicotera, who also arranged bets on horses while operating brothels in New Zealand. Bookmakers were notorious go-betweens for the licit and illicit entertainment industry, and frequently kept bad company. Only a few years into his vaudeville venture, Brennan sold his company to Fuller's and returned to the bookmaking scene.[27]

Vaudeville companies kept few records, and fewer still about the chorus girls, dancers and stagehands who supported the headline acts. Vaudeville had a seemingly insatiable demand for star power to sell tickets, but it was also hungry for the anonymous performers who underwrote the circuit. It is unsurprising that Lydia Harvey had been recruited in Dunedin – Brennan's must have been permanently on the lookout for pretty young women who could sing or dance. Raised by a music teacher and pianist, we can presume that Lydia could boast at least one of these talents.

Working on the circuit, she would have supported darling child stars, joined dance acts, watched from the wings as acrobats and wire-walkers made the audience gasp. She shared the stage with sketch artists and comedians, illusionists and musicians. The troupe toured Australia's major cities: Melbourne, Sydney, Brisbane, Adelaide and even Hobart, Tasmania, where Brennan's Vaudeville played Her Majesty's Theatre, to delighted reviews.[28]

To anti-trafficking campaigners, Lydia had simply changed one form of moral danger for another: life in the theatre exposed young women to the temptations of drink and nightlife, and often encouraged them to flirt with – and even sell sex to – theatre and cabaret patrons. But it wasn't so much the drink or the late hours, or even the flirting, that posed the real danger to young women like Lydia. It was the contracts they were forced to sign. Up until at least the 1930s, when the industry was finally regulated in some countries, performers' contracts usually required the signee to work on commission, to pay for their own board, to work long hours and unpaid overtime, and to be at the mercy of their directors and producers as to when and where they worked. The company was also under no obligation to provide them with return passage home, should they be fired, or should the troupe fold. Young women like Lydia Harvey were seen as expendable, easily recruited workers: for every dancing girl onstage there were another two waiting in the wings.

It is unlikely that Lydia cared much about what men like Mr Brennan or like Mr Coote thought of her. In her eyes, she had managed to cast off a life of drudgery and respectability and exchange it for one of travel, excitement and the stage. For several years she seems to have travelled around the towns and cities of Australia, performing in pantomimes like *Puss in Boots* and musicals like *HMS Pinafore*. The venues may not have been as grand and famous as the Alhambra in London, but it must have felt good to be on the other side of the stage lights, and not up in an overcrowded balcony gazing down. Between 1911 and 1915 Lydia performed at first for an audience in evening wear, and later for an audience studded with military uniforms. *Puss in Boots* made young men laugh before they poured onto steamships and set off for the Western Front.

At least, that is what she told her mother. The police in New Zealand, on the other hand, had other ideas about what had happened to Lydia Harvey. Their suspicions arose when, back in March 1911, they received a report from DI Anderson, who returned to the case just before Carvelli and di Nicotera were released from prison. It was his job to arrange their deportation to Italy. It was also his job to be cynical: with no police escort and no coordination from the Italian authorities, there was little chance the men would actually reach their destination. And so Anderson wrote to the Australian and New Zealand police, warning them that according to 'information received' (most likely from the plain-clothes, undercover work of Mead and Burmby and their informants), the 'two despicable ruffians' were most likely headed for Paris and then on their way back to the Antipodes.

The information gleaned by the Metropolitan Police proved accurate. Carvelli and di Nicotera did indeed travel to Paris, where they found Victoria Bricot waiting for them at the rue Rodier. They had promised to set her up with her own house and business in New Zealand, and it seems she intended to hold them to their word. Carvelli arranged for her steamship tickets, which she booked in the name of Violette Baron, the name she would use for the rest of her career. She arrived in Sydney in September 1911, off the SS *Scharnhorst*, the same ship as Carvelli (now going by the name of Courrier).[29] And then, a few months later, her name appeared on a police list of 'one-woman brothels in Auckland'. She had taken a place on Hobson Street, working alongside Veronique Carvelli, running a brothel disguised as a sweet shop.

The police knew that Carvelli and di Nicotera, and quite possibly a larger network of pimps and traffickers, were behind this system of 'one-woman brothels', which they were powerless to stop, despite regular excoriation of police inaction in the press. The network seemed to extend across the Tasman Sea: Carvelli and his associates had been spotted in Sydney, Melbourne and even Brisbane, as well as in Auckland and Wellington. Seeing that one of the former 'white slaves' in London had seen fit to rejoin the gang, and given what they knew of Lydia Harvey's long-standing immoral behaviour before she left Wellington, it was only natural to assume that she had reconnected with her traffickers as well. In an effort to gain more information about Carvelli's newest scheme, Senior Sergeant Stagpool was sent once more to Emily Badeley's house on Chelmer Street.

He explained to Lydia's mother that Aldo Cellis, aka Antonio Carvelli – the man against whom her daughter had testified in September 1910 – had been released from prison and was spotted disembarking in Sydney. There was some suggestion that Lydia was still associated with him. Did she know the whereabouts of her daughter? Emily Badeley replied with concern. She explained to the officer that her daughter had said Carvelli had threatened her before he went to prison, that he told her that he would 'do for her' if he ever saw her again.

Stagpool was unimpressed by Lydia's mother's concern, writing in his report that it was 'quite possible' Lydia Harvey knew where Carvelli was and, far from fearing harm from him, was probably keen to work for him again.[30] The recipient of his report in Wellington took the threat more seriously, underlining it twice and asking for it to be investigated more thoroughly.

Further enquiries came up with nothing that supported either Lydia's story or the police's suspicions. Brennan's vaudeville company did not have any Lydia Harvey on its list of employees, but, the owner explained, he did not know all his performers personally. What is more, it is very likely that, given her experience in London, Lydia would have signed up with a new pseudonym. When it became clear that finding 'The White Slave Lydia Harvey' (as the New Zealand police had come to refer to her) was not going to get them any closer to Antonio Carvelli, the police abandoned their search.[31]

Had she, like Victoria Bricot, returned to selling sex, and to working with Carvelli and his associates? The latter seems very unlikely indeed, considering how strongly she spoke against them in her witness statement, and the fact that Carvelli had openly threatened her with violence if he ever got his hands on her. 'I wish I had never met them,' she had told Miss MacDougall. The former, however, is not beyond the realms of possibility. Many women who had been trafficked or exploited in prostitution returned, once they escaped their exploiters, to sex work on their own or on someone else's terms. In some cases, traffickers were persistent, seeking out their former victims and re-trafficking them. In more cases, women had been in the sex industry prior to being trafficked and continued to sell sex afterwards, striving to do so on better terms. When you didn't have to hand over all your earnings to a pimp or trafficker, selling sex was the single best way to make a lot of money, paying many times more than any other form of skilled or unskilled employment for women, usually for far fewer hours of work.

Rumours continued to fly over the next four years. As far as her family was concerned, Lydia Harvey was working the vaudeville circuit in Australia. The police in New Zealand, on the other hand, continued to monitor the network of pimps, traffickers and prostitutes and to suspect that she was among them. Indeed, she was even named in an anonymous letter sent to the police by 'A Victim', which alleged that Lydia Harvey was in Melbourne, working this time for Alessandro di Nicotera. Such letters were surprisingly common, part of a culture of denouncement, jealousy and turf war that was typical of networks of people who had business interests in the sex industry, but also romantic entanglements. The police put little stock in them, and neither should we. Indeed, the letter that named Lydia Harvey, sent in late July 1915, suggests that the writer had the wrong woman and had mistaken Lydia for Victoria Bricot, who was indeed working for, and in a romantic relationship with, Di Nicotera. A picture taken around the same time shows her and Alessandro in domestic repose, with a cat and a dog by their side; and confiscated letters bear witness to their tumultuous love and business affairs.[32]

Whether she returned to the sex industry or not, one thing is for certain: free from the scrutiny of the police, the courts, the prime minister and the newspapers, Lydia Harvey continued to live her life. And sometime in 1915 that life was about to change dramatically, when she met a young sailor by the name of Herbert Ockenden. He had been born in 1885 into a middle-class, servant-keeping family in Brighton, England. His father was an accountant, but Herbert found the prospect of a life in finance unappealing and had got his Masters and Mates Certificate of Competency at nineteen. From there, it was a decade on the open seas, working his way up the ranks of the merchant marine on ocean liners and mail

25: Alessandro di Nicotera and his lover (possibly wife) Victoria Bricot (going by Violet Barron). The photograph, alongside a series of letters, was seized as evidence when Victoria's brothel was raided by police in 1915.

steamers that travelled back and forth across the Tasman Sea and along the coast of Australia. He was a third mate aboard the SS *Bombala* of the Australian Steamships Line when he met Lydia. Such meetings, so quotidian in world history and so monumental for individual people, are rarely recorded, so we are left to imagine the circumstances. Perhaps he saw her perform in a local theatre in Sydney or Melbourne while on shore leave; or perhaps they met through a mutual acquaintance. Perhaps they met while she was selling sex in a local hotel or brothel. Perhaps it was a chance meeting on the street, in the heady atmosphere just after war had been declared in 1914, when life all of a sudden seemed to shift into a new and faster gear.

They were married in Sydney on 27 July 1915 at St James's Church at the top of Hyde Park, on a cool and rainy day. It was around the same time the police received the anonymous letter suggesting that Lydia was working for di Nicotera in Melbourne, casting still more doubt on this account. Two friends stood as witnesses, but whether the rest of the church was empty or full, we will never know. The couple said their vows and the reverend filled in the parish register. Ockenden was recorded as a mercantile marine officer; Lydia as 'household duties'. Herbert told the reverend that his father was an accountant; Lydia told him that her father was Harry Kenneth Harvey, a New Zealand Supreme Court judge.[33]

It is difficult to adjudicate on what this official document can tell us about Lydia, her relationship with her new husband and that with her late father. Her misnaming of her father's profession may well have been an honest mistake, demonstrating how little she really knew about the man. 'Kenneth', after all, sounds like 'Cannon', and she may have always heard it incorrectly on her mother's lips (or perhaps the reverend misheard it on hers). And how was she to know the difference between a father who was a solicitor and one who was a Supreme Court judge? Neither version of him had stuck around. It would certainly have been easier not to know more; to be unaware of the wealth and social standing that were so nearly hers, had she been Harry George Cannon Harvey's legitimate daughter.

Or perhaps the truth – that she was a bastard child among eight bastard children – was so harmful that Lydia felt she needed to hide it behind a larger falsehood. Her new husband's family was well-to-do, and her husband was making something of himself, moving quickly up the ranks of the Australian Steamship Line. He might have command of his own ship one day. Lydia, by now well used to playing many roles, may have begun to form a new version of herself: the daughter of one of the highest-ranking New Zealand public officials; the respectable future captain's wife.

If the couple's future was promising, their present was respectable but modest, and being the wife of a sailor meant one didn't stay anywhere very long. This may well have suited Lydia, accustomed at this point to a life on the move. From Sydney they moved to Melbourne, where they rented a flat in Fitzroy, in a stately building with high ceilings and huge windows, a stone's throw from the Fitzroy Gardens and just round the corner from the bustle of Victoria Parade. It was also just round the corner from Veronique White's last address before she had left home in 1908. Indeed, at this point in 1915, the Carvellis were making regular trips to Melbourne to see the Whites at Jolimont Terrace, though there is no evidence that their lives collided with Lydia's ever again.[34] Later that year the Ockendens had moved to New-castle, New South Wales, where they established a home, and Herbert took work as first mate on the SS *Saros*. Lydia settled down to life as a housewife.

Did she ever tell him? Did she tell her sailor that she had

steamed across the Pacific Ocean, through the incredible Magellan Strait? Did she describe the dock in Buenos Aires and its squares filled with electric lights; did she say that she had crossed the Atlantic, gazing upon the beaches of Tenerife and then arriving in England? Did she tell him about the streets of Soho and the crowds, about the white cliffs of Dover; about how she steamed down the European coast, through Gibraltar, the Suez Canal, past Colombo, Brisbane and then home? Did she tell him that she had sold sex, that she had been abused and exploited by a man she knew as Aldo Cellis and his Australian wife; that she had attended a trial at the Old Bailey; that she had caught venereal disease? Or did she stay silent, allowing Herbert to assume that her vaudeville years were the raciest part of her personal history?

Perhaps the newly married Ockendens maintained parallel silences about their experiences with prostitution. Herbert, after all, had been a merchant mariner since his teenage years, living and working in ports: it is impossible for him not to have encountered the commercial sex trade regularly, and highly unlikely that he had never participated in it. He may have been a regular buyer of sex.

In fact in this way their pasts were well matched. The only group of people in this era who came close to generating the same kind of social concern as trafficked women were merchant seamen. It was widely acknowledged that mariner culture was drink-soaked and often miserable, particularly for those men who worked in the stoke holes and engine room.[35] The moral welfare of seamen – from the firemen, to the mates like Herbert Ockenden – preoccupied early internationalists and moral reformers, and they saw it as inextricably tied to the question of regulated prostitution, public health and moral fitness. By the interwar years, merchant mariners were the subject of several investigations and committees at the International Labour Organization and the League of Nations.[36] They, like the women in the global sex industry, were caught up in a nexus of labour, mobility, commerce, health and sex. Their labour facilitated the labour of others: the extraction of resources, the manufacture of goods and the movement of products. This army of permanently mobile men represented some of the most frequent and most numerous customers in the brothels and vice-districts around the world.

Herbert certainly had some skeletons in his closet. In 1908 the *Auckland Observer* reported that Mr Herbert Ockenden, of Brighton, England, was engaged to Miss Violet S. Hunt, whose father was captain of the SS *Hinemoa* out of Onehunga harbour.[37] No marriage followed, and we can presume that Herbert made sure he never worked out of Onehunga harbour again. Perhaps he never knew about Aldo Cellis, and Lydia never knew about Miss Violet S. Hunt, the captain's jilted daughter. It wouldn't have been the first or last marriage to have held parallel secrets.

Some truths may have emerged when Lydia did not conceive a child. This was often a slow process for the wives of sailors, but perhaps after four years the Ockendens decided it was time to see the doctor. Had this trip been undertaken, the doctor would have examined Lydia with a cold metal speculum that surely took her back to those horrible days at the Harrow Road hospital. Then, as was in keeping with medical practice in 1916, he may have pulled her husband aside for a frank conversation, telling Herbert that his wife had been infected with venereal disease in the past, which may have affected her ability to have children. As was also in keeping with medical practice, this information would not have been passed on to Lydia. Despite the advances in women's rights, her body remained in many ways the legal property of her husband.[38] Indeed, Herbert Ockenden had more legal control over Lydia than Aldo Cellis ever did. We can only hope that he was kind.

There is no trace of her married life, either way. Lydia guarded her secrets well. But whatever labels people may have given her back in 1910, Lydia Harvey was – as so many victims of sexual abuse and exploitation choose to be called today – a survivor. Her life did not end in a brothel in Buenos Aires, or in the seedy streets of London; not even in a rescue home. She continued to live. She worked in theatre. She travelled. She married well.

She probably didn't see much of this fine husband, however, over the next three years. He was the chief officer aboard the SS *Saros* and was more often at sea than not, particularly during the busy war years. While he was away, Lydia made a home for them in Waratah, a suburb of Newcastle, Australia, far from the port and the bars and cafés that her seventeen-year-old self would have sneaked out to get to, less than a decade before. Perhaps she made friends with other officers' wives, and with the wives of the coal-mine managers, doctors and lawyers whose society she now belonged to.

Letters from home probably eased the loneliness. Her mother wrote to tell her that she had finally married, after all those years alone: a local man named Thomas Jones. Her sisters told Lydia all the news and gossip from home: the new trees that now lined Thames Street, the shows at the opera house, the boys who had left for the Somme, and the equally cataclysmic incident in which a horrible girl called Amy Bond accused Clara of stealing a bicycle and she had to appear at the magistrates' court. It was even in the papers.[39] Then, sometime during the war, the happy news came that her little sister Lynda had decided to join Lydia in Newcastle, where she had found a post as a children's nurse at a local hotel.[40]

Her sister's company was surely a blessing, with her husband so often at sea. During the war Herbert worked as a merchant mariner on the ships that carried people and supplies across the Tasman Sea and up and down the coastal waters of Australia. And although it was far away, war seemed to change the very blood in people's veins. People searched the paper every morning for names of young men they knew; Guy Scholefield spent the late hours of the night in London telegraphing the names of New Zealand's dead sons back to the offices of Wellington's *Evening Post*. The ship upon which Lydia had sailed home became a troop carrier. Crowds gathered on the Wellington docks as the RMS *Tainui* made berth in 1919.

Many other ships like her were held in quarantine in the harbours of Australia and New Zealand when war ended in 1918, in an effort to prevent troops from bringing the new 'Spanish flu' to the Antipodes. New Zealand managed the threat to its own and surrounding countries badly, and the Maori and Samoan populations were hit especially hard. Australia, by contrast, avoided the worst of the 1918 pandemic that was ravaging Europe and India.

But the 1918 outbreak was not to be the worst one in Australia, and the returning troops – no longer under quarantine in 1919 – helped to spread the most virulent and deadly wave of the H1N1 virus. It rode on the currents of unprecedented human movement around the globe; it thrived on the great traffic in young bodies that was the First World War and its devastating aftermath. In Newcastle, Waratah hospital was taken over by the government as an influenza epidemic hospital.[41] This particular strain of flu – like the war itself – was remarkable for having its highest mortality rate among young adults. Unlike most flus, it did not kill mostly the very young and very old, but rather people in their twenties and thirties. Most died from bacterial pneumonia: the secondary infection that followed on the heels of the virus in an era two decades away from the discovery of antibiotics. Schools were closed, businesses shuttered and bodies were stacked in temporary morgues. The death rate in New South Wales peaked in June 1919, and the median age of death was twenty-six. On 24 June 1919, shortly after her twenty-sixth birthday, Lydia Harvey Ockenden became one of its victims.

She did not lie in the makeshift bed in the overcrowded Waratah hospital for long. She had not been ill for a week before pneumonia saw her draw her last breath.[42] Perhaps it happened to be one of the rare times that her seafaring husband was at home with her. Her sister Lynda was close by at least, but because she was another of the hundreds of patients who crowded into the influenza hospital that June, it is unlikely she had the strength to sit by her sister's bedside. She may have received the horrible news of her sister's death while lying in her own hospital bed. Lydia's illness and death were too quick for her mother or her sisters to make it from Oamaru to Newcastle – no steamship could ever be that fast. Her husband, had he been at sea, would have rushed back, but may only have arrived in time to grieve for her, not to say goodbye.

Herbert, surely bereft, placed Lydia's death announcement in the *Newcastle Sun* just a few weeks short of what should have been their fourth anniversary. Among a shockingly long list of names of other young people was Lydia Rhoda, 'beloved wife of Herbert Ockenden, 26 years'. 'New Zealand papers,' requested the short notice, 'please copy.' He buried her, he mourned her, and it was surely with a heavy heart that he returned as the first mate on the SS *Saros*. The following June, Herbert Ockenden, still mourning his love and reeling from the imagined future that he no longer had, took out a memorial announcement to mark the first anniversary of Lydia's death. He posted it to the *Newcastle Sun* from some port along his travels. Her sister Lynda, who had survived the epidemic, took out another memorial notice below it.[43]

Then, on 23 June 1920, Herbert Ockenden was carried off his ship in ill health. He was admitted to the Mater Misericordia Hospital in Brisbane. The next day, the anniversary of his wife's death, he dictated his last will and testament in the presence of friends and fellow officers, leaving everything to his father in Brighton, England. In the wee hours of 28 June, he died.[44] All the ships in the Australian Steamer Line lowered their flags to half-mast in his honour and he was buried two days later in Brisbane. Back in Newcastle, the plot beside Lydia Harvey's grave, which he probably bought when he buried her, remained an empty stand of dried grass.

When I first set out to find Lydia Harvey, I wanted to find a story that challenged the sensational tales of 'white slavery' and – in defiance of those misogynistic moralists who would condemn to misery, disease and death a girl who had sold sex – I had hoped for a happy ending. Of course a grave was always where I was going to find this girl who had disappeared more than a hundred years ago, and Lydia Harvey's death was just a small moment in a century that saw hundreds of millions of unjust and untimely deaths: the most violent and deadly century by far in all of human history. And yet it is difficult not to mourn especially for her and the long life she ought to have lived. All I can do is lay her to rest.

AFTERWORD

I am on a train slowly snaking its way up the Australian central coast, through dense forests of gum, bloodwood and apple, travelling between Sydney and Newcastle. More than ten years ago I sat in the National Archives in London, looking out over different treetops, wondering what had happened to the young woman Lydia Harvey after Inspector Anderson had sent her home. At the time she was one of many women whom I had glimpsed in the case files of the Metropolitan Police, about whom I knew little other than that which their brief appearance in the archive, in a moment of duress, told me. Lydia was just another girl who had disappeared. First, from her home and workplace, and into the global commercial sex market. Second, from the historical record. I did not expect to learn anything about her past or her future.

Yet I felt compelled to try to find this girl who had been disappeared both by her traffickers and by the anti-trafficking movement, which had reduced her complicated experiences to a short, sensational anecdote. And so, in the time since first discovering Lydia in an archive file, I have followed her around the world. I have pieced together her life, and the lives of those whom she encountered. I have glimpsed her on an opera-house stage in Oamaru; in the kitchen of a suburban home in Wellington; in a brothel in Buenos Aires; beneath the lights of the Criterion Theatre in Piccadilly Circus; in a vaudeville show in Melbourne. Around a hundred years ago Lydia herself may have ridden this train from Sydney to her husband's new posting in Newcastle.

I have glimpsed Lydia Harvey through many other people's eyes, and their stories shape this history as well. Had it not been for Detective Inspector Ernest Anderson's keen eye that morning in the Marlborough Street police court, when he noticed the men who were strangely interested in the case of Marguerite Leroy, I would never have learned of Lydia Harvey's existence, or of her traffickers'. DI Anderson is the person who kept them under observation, who wrote hundreds of pages of reports, who liaised with Scotland Yard, rescue and reform organisations and the Home Office; as well as police and consular officials in Italy, Australia and New Zealand. If it wasn't for him, Lydia Harvey might have remained in London, stranded and coerced into selling sex, for many years. Antonio Carvelli and Alessandro di Nicotera, who really were, as Anderson put it, 'the most despicable ruffians', might have gone completely unpunished.

DI Anderson, alongside PC William Mead and Sergeant Walter Burmby and Sergeant George Nicholls, all received commendations for their work on the Carvelli case. For two of them, this was the beginning of illustrious careers with the Met. Sergeant Burmby went on to work primarily with what would become the Clubs and Vice Unit.[1] He became widely known as the best anti-vice officer in the Met by the time he reached the rank of inspector in the 1920s. He oversaw the largest criminal investigation into drug trafficking in London in that era, and was celebrated in the press for bringing down a gang that had been responsible for providing thousands of pounds' worth of cocaine to the bright young things of Soho. He retired in 1936 and died in Sussex in 1960.[2]

George Nicholls's star rose higher still. A few years after the Carvelli case was closed, when the First World War began, he was – not least because of his ability to speak French – seconded to the Special Branch in Europe to become a counter-intelligence officer for the Allies. Upon his celebrated return, he became a famous inspector at the CID, sent by Scotland Yard around the country to work difficult and infamous cases.[3] At the end of his career he had reached 'the big five', becoming superintendent inspector of the Metropolitan Police. He was named one of the most influential police officers of his generation at the 100th anniversary of the Met in 1928, and was known for his meticulousness and professionalism until he retired in 1934.[4]

William Mead's epilogue is far less impressive, although it does provide some important counterpoints to the well-travelled narrative of the honourable cop. Like Burmby, Mead continued to work vice-cases after the Carvelli trial had closed. But by the First World War rumours had begun to surface about the men who had been selected for this duty. They spent their days bouncing around the clubs and bars of Soho, chumming with gangsters and pimps and, increasingly, with the men and women who had begun to supply cocaine to the growing wartime market. There were hints that they took protection money; that they extorted women for money or sex, in exchange for not being arrested and harassed. They drank and used cocaine on the job, and took cuts from bookies.

None of this was written down, not in 1915. The behaviour of PC Mead and the other plain-clothes vice constables left only the scantest of paper trails. In a single letter, hastily written by Trevor Bingham, chief constable of the CID, to Edward Henry, the commissioner of the Metropolitan Police, he noted that 'the highly unsatisfactory conduct of PC Mead' was part of a larger problem of plain-clothes vice officers. 'They are almost exclusively employed in cases of living on immoral earnings, and their work involves constant associations with prostitutes and the like.' Bingham never used the word 'corruption'. 'There is a danger of losing their efficiency over time,' he judiciously put it. As for William Mead specifically, 'Superintendent Sutherland feels he has been too long in C Division. He is said to have done very good work for the White Slave Branch but his conduct on this present occasion was most improper.' The official record-keepers of the London Metropolitan Police, like forces the world over, made sure historians would never be able to know just how many policemen like William Mead operated, and how many women like Lydia Harvey suffered at their hands.

Whatever Mead did, and whomever he did it to, it would be the last time he would do so in Soho. By the end of 1915 William Mead could no longer wear his day-suit and over-coat to work, and instead found himself back in the uniform of the bobby. With his chin-strap helmet, his shiny-buttoned coat and his polished boots, he finished out his career as a desk clerk, never reaching any higher rank than constable, in leafy and quiet Hampstead.[5]

Ernest Anderson stayed with the case the longest. He oversaw the repatriations of all four victims, and he wrote to the authorities in France, New Zealand and Australia when the men were released from prison, warning them that they might be coming their way. He penned the final report, closing the case on 4 March 1911. Two years later his career in the police was suddenly ended when he suffered a hernia and a painful and debilitating testicular torsion. He moved back to Oxfordshire, to the town of Eynsham, to live with his elderly mother. He remained in the area, unmarried, for the rest of his life, until he died in 1956.[6]

Unlike many of his fellow detectives who spent their retirement years in the 1920s and 1930s penning memoirs about their time at the Yard, Ernest Anderson never published a single word about his work with the Metropolitan Police. As an early police historian put it, 'the tongues of those who have taken part in dramatic episodes, more stirring than any in fiction, are locked'.[7] We will never know whether in those long years that he collected his police pension he ever spared a thought for the young women he had found on the streets back in 1910, or for the men he had fought so hard to bring to justice, who, just six short months later, escaped back into the global underworld.

It was a world in which Antonio Adolpho Carvelli (aka Aldo Cellis, aka Anton Courrier, aka Anthony Coty) thrived. Despite his many legal and financial setbacks, Carvelli remained a wealthy international criminal, a convincing trickster, larger than life. He was one of a number of men in the early twentieth-century world who made their money in semi-licit, interconnected global economies that were defined by high profit, frequent exploitation and businesses of thrill and pleasure: commercial sex, the traffic in arms and drugs, gambling and bookmaking, the silk and oriental-goods trade, and the entertainment and liquor industry. Such men lived in a world of possibility, consumption, misogyny and hyper-masculinity. They had a hunger for money and status, often at any cost, and a talent for self-reinvention. Back in 1910 they were in the vanguard of the internationalisation and organisation of crime that would later help to shape the twentieth- and twenty-first-century worlds.

Many of these men also had their own stories of exploitation and deprivation. Pimps and traffickers usually came from poor families and difficult, dangerous, badly paid and unstable jobs. Many had experiences of abuse, trauma, abandonment and disability. Carvelli, on the other hand, could not explain himself with such a story. He was very well educated, worked in the entertainment industry and could have sustained himself modestly and stably with a job in the arts or in teaching. He pimped and trafficked women because he wanted to be rich, and because he enjoyed it. He was also good at it: it is not difficult to sense the charisma he wielded even at a hundred years' distance. I have left his violence, his reprehensible acts and his vivid, charming humanity deliberately unreconciled. The historical record presents us with a series of seemingly contradictory images: a young military officer, a student of music, an opera singer, a thief, a pimp, a trafficker, a rapist, a dancing master, a businessman and artiste regretting the folly of his youth; a deportee, a self-proclaimed war hero, a desperate victim of sensationalised reporting, a loving husband trapped in Fascist Italy. Antonio Carvelli was a complex, charming and contemptible human being. He was, in the end, neither grotesque and monstrous nor romantic and picaresque – only a human like the rest of us, and a fascinating one at that; though assuredly not one of the best.

But he would never be anything but a monster – a fiend in the shape of a man – to those who marketed tales of 'white slavery' to a global audience. By the early twentieth century the trope of 'white slavery' was pervasive and powerful. Lydia Harvey's story, in which a poor, young and naïve white girl was trafficked to Buenos Aires by a continental pimp disguised as a gentleman and a debauched, unredeemable prostitute, was like something ripped straight from the salacious headlines. And yet, despite this, Lydia still was not allowed to claim victimhood. She was, to Guy Scholefield – the accidental 'white slavery' reporter – a 'warning to girls' because of the poor decisions she had made. To the prime minister of New Zealand, she was a woman to be denounced as 'already immoral' before she left the country. To the tabloid newspapers, trafficking her to Buenos Aires was 'carrying coals to Newcastle'. Most of all, Lydia was someone to be forgotten. In the 1920s New Zealand proudly reported to the League of Nations that it had never had any cases of 'white slavery' in its country.[8]

By the end of his career, Scholefield had established himself as one of his nation's great early historians and record-keepers. In addition to his work as parliamentary librarian and comptroller of the Dominion Archive, he oversaw the archiving of many of New Zealand's early newspapers, which remain today a crucial historical source for the country's past, and were the place where I first glimpsed the early life of Lydia Harvey. He founded and was the author of the earliest editions of *Dictionary of New Zealand Biography*, filled with great men (and a handful of women) and their great deeds. It is not surprising, of course, that Scholefield did not even consider a young woman like Lydia Harvey worthy of a footnote in his country's history. She had played her role and then blended once more into the background, joining the thousands of young women whose lives went unremarked in the early twentieth-century world. In a long and illustrious career in journalism, scholarship and record-keeping, Guy Scholefield never breathed a word about Lydia Harvey ever again.

The stories that Scholefield and hundreds of other journalists told about girls like Lydia Harvey fuelled widespread concern about trafficking, and helped to fund and legitimise the early anti-trafficking movement. Like the stories that underwrote it, this movement was filled with contradictions and ironies. Men and women in the National Vigilance Association and the International Bureau for the Suppression of the 'White Slave Traffic', who involved themselves in Lydia Harvey's case and hundreds of others, did so in the name of saving and protecting innocent girls, yet they also seethed with contempt for any girl who dared to strut her stuff, to perform, to dream of fame and riches. Many campaigners in the early anti-trafficking movement wanted to save women from sexual exploitation even if – or perhaps because – this meant incarcerating them, deporting them and exploiting other aspects of their labour.

This approach was not without its ardent critics, and many early feminists railed against the mistreatment of young women in the name of anti-vice crusades. They were especially opposed to measures that claimed to combat trafficking by controlling and surveilling women's migration, and to measures that used incarceration as a means of 'moral reform'. But these feminist voices were increasingly drowned out by more conservative, coercive and carceral ideas, not least because they were so palatable to the statesmen and police officers whom the anti-trafficking movement counted as allies. Anti-trafficking was a useful tool in the legal and cultural campaign to control migration, and some of the earliest anti-trafficking laws functioned as ways to control and prevent the immigration of people whom white Western nations had deemed 'undesirable'. It was also a way to criminalise a symptom of global inequality and exploited labour, without addressing the root causes that made people so ready to accept the promises of traffickers.

The League of Nations, founded in the aftermath of the First World War, was tasked with continuing the international fight against 'the traffic in women and children'. A dedicated section of the League spent the next two decades meeting, writing and signing international agreements, and investigating the nature of the international sex trade. The findings from these investigations, which sit in boxes on shelves at the United Nations Archive, are filled with women and men explaining how working poverty had driven them into the sex trade; how migration restrictions and the cost of travel had seen them turn to illegal brokers and agents to help them move, often resulting in high levels of debt; how endemic police corruption facilitated exploitation; and how work in the sex trade could be better paid, safer and more reliable than any other job that was available to them. Trafficking, far from being a distinct crime that operated apart from the early twentieth-century global economy, was completely entangled with it, and was a direct product of its fundamental inequalities.

Law and policy in the decades that followed largely

ignored these findings. To acknowledge them would be to acknowledge women's unpaid and underpaid work as mothers, wives, domestic servants and sweated labourers. It would be to see traffickers as pimps, not as animals or the ultimate evil, but as amoral opportunists who made good in a world economy in which the exploitation of mobile people was increasingly common. It would be to admit that the immigration restrictions that had been in part fuelled by a fear of traffickers and foreign prostitutes were in fact contributing to higher rates of trafficking. It would be to recognise that solutions that turned to the criminal law to fix these problems put inordinate power in the hands of police forces and immigration bureaux, which could not properly administer them. This era, in other words, gave us the highly imperfect legal frameworks that we continue to use today, which link trafficking to immigration law and use detention and deportation to control both perpetrators and victims.

These laws were passed in the name of disappearing girls, but they overwhelmingly targeted other kinds of women – women like Veronique Sarah White. These were women who chose to sell sex for money; women who valued lives of leisure and adventure and wealth. They travelled freely to better markets, they mined the miners, they fleeced the ranchers, they tempted young innocent men in London's West End. They cared little for the morality of anti-trafficking campaigners and crusading journalists, especially if being moral meant being compliant, working long hours in domestic service for mere shillings, and aspiring to nothing more than a good character reference from their mistress, marriage and child-bearing. These women overwhelmingly saw themselves as workers who provided for themselves and their families in a world where their choices were limited and the alternatives were equally, if not more, harmful.

Veronique White (later Carvelli) was a woman who, despite coming from a well-off, stable family, began to sell sex in her early twenties. We can't know why, but we can know that she made a fortune, which perhaps speaks for itself. Her story is one of family, work, adventure, travel, luxury and social mobility. It is also a story of crime and abuse; of her exploitation of at least one other young woman; and, perhaps, of her own exploitation at the hands of her husband or of unnamed and unknown others. Whatever the truth, it is a history that will for ever remain hidden. Veronique Carvelli sought no redemption or reform in her long life and has proved particularly resistant to my efforts to rescue her from the condescension of posterity.

Women like Veronique were also highly resistant to efforts to rescue them in their own time, but that did not stop women like Eilidh MacDougall from trying. Miss MacDougall was one of a legion of early social workers who built careers and volunteered at rescue homes, shelters, ports, railway stations and in the streets, in the name of protecting girls and young women from sexual exploitation. Some travelled abroad as rescue workers; others, like Miss MacDougall, stayed closer to home. She may not have known it, as she sat, writing letters to beg for money, in her crowded office in the front room of a crumbling terrace house in Lambeth Road in July 1910, but Miss Eilidh MacDougall was quietly making history. She was the first woman ever employed to take statements for the police in the UK. She was an outspoken advocate for victims of sexual assault, long before this became an official part of the criminal-justice system. She ran the first safe-house for trafficking victims. Throughout her career in early social work she encountered and cared for a small army of lost, wayward and abused girls and young women.

Many of her contemporaries believed that international trafficking and cross-border prostitution were the chief source of women's sexual exploitation, but others – and no one more than Eilidh MacDougall – knew that most cases of sexual abuse and violence happened within the borders of neighbourhoods. Lydia Harvey was sent to a special home that was established because of the panic over sex trafficking, but the majority of this home's residents were victims of intimate abuse, not trafficking. Their stories, which unfolded in quiet homes, churches and schools, did not map comfortably onto 'white slavery' narratives, in which nasty foreigners kidnapped innocent women and took them to brothels abroad. And so these stories did not get told.

Even when young women's stories matched the narrative expectations, few really cared about what happened afterwards. Eilidh MacDougall was one of a very small number of people who engaged in what she called 'aftercare': providing shelter for victims, arranging for work or a ticket home, maintaining a support network for them in the years to come. The meagre funding for the home that she ran was cut to nothing in the 1930s, the home was closed and her lifetime of work was largely forgotten. Yet she stands as testament to the important work that was being done within problematic frameworks of rescue work and anti-trafficking – work that could be a crucial lifeline to victims of sexual crime. Unlike the writers and consumers of sensational stories of 'white slavery', MacDougall was deeply concerned about what happened to women afterwards, when they stopped being headline fodder and continued to be complex and individual human beings.

The Metropolitan Police Home for Women and Girls, opened in 1910 and closed in 1933, was the first and last official Police Home for victims of trafficking. Indeed, Lilian Wyles's 'new plan' to house victims in various homes and shelters run by charities and religious groups set the foundation for the present-day relationship between the government and anti-trafficking and safe-house NGOs. Today it is still religious and other philanthropic institutions that shelter victims of trafficking, and they compete with each other for state funding and private donations. After testifying, victims are usually deported, if they are not also put on trial for a related offence such as brothel-keeping. Barristers can fight to get trafficking victims recognised as needing asylum in rare cases, navigating some of the same legal inconsistencies that MacDougall did a hundred years before. The story that began at 198 Lambeth Road continues to unfold across the UK in the twenty-first century in complicated ways. Today governments have placed themselves at the centre of crime control around trafficking, while moving to the furthest edge of victim support, asylum and rehabilitation.

The story of the home founded to house 'white slaves', and the work of its founder, turned out to be as much about the abuse suffered by girls in their own homes, and in domestic work, as it was about the exploitation and assault they endured while crossing oceans and national borders. Mac-Dougall bore witness for years, as girls and children spoke their quiet accusations in hospital beds and police stations, and she had experienced the silence that followed: the lack of punishment, the erasure of experience, the absence of reporting. Unlike the public, who remained more interested in stories of kidnap and trafficking, Eilidh MacDougall knew that the most dangerous place for a girl was not a railway station or a port, or a steamship or even Buenos Aires. It was the intimate and institutional spaces of her daily life – and, very often, her own home.

We continue to live today within many of the legal and ideological parameters set by the early twentieth-century anti-trafficking movement, where the idea of anti-trafficking as anti-immigration, and of rescue as incarceration and punishment, predominates. Dichotomies of 'victim' and 'criminal' continue to simplify and efface human and structural complexity.[9] Non-governmental anti-trafficking organisations (much like the NVA more than a hundred years before) receive immense amounts of funding from private and government sources and are given extraordinary political power, in exchange for helping states identify and deport trafficking victims and perpetrators.[10] As I write, around the world there are hundreds of thousands of women in prison for prostitution-related offences, and hundreds of thousands more have been deported. Violent raids on brothels, police harassment and immigration detention are regular features of the state's approach to anti-trafficking. The idea that the ideal victim of trafficking is white and Western remains alive and well, and migrant women and women of colour are at the sharp end of this more than 100-year-old prejudice.[11] Brothel raids, arrests, incarceration and, of course, deportations, all fall disproportionately hard on them.

Just as they were in the early twentieth century,

twenty-first-century newspaper columns are filled with stories of young women who disappear from their home countries and are found in brothels, farmers' fields and nail bars. We traffic in these stories and call them 'awareness campaigns'.[12] We use them to raise money for humanitarian organisations and political parties. We use them to put up borders, to build more detention centres, to hire highly paid officials to monitor 'modern slavery'. These stories fill out the plots of hit series, get bums on cinema seats and are splashed across newspaper front pages. Here, girls who dreamed of better things appear abused, exploited, simplified, attenuated and cut off from their real lives and complex contexts. We ask few questions about why they could not find safe and legal work that could sustain them and their families. We live in a global economy where cheap food, services and clothing are more important than girls who disappear. We refuse to acknowledge that, for many, sex work provides the only well-paid, meaningful work available to them; and for some, perhaps not unlike Veronique White, it provides enjoyment, wealth and social mobility. Ultimately we are uninterested in trafficking victims as human beings who make complicated choices within systems of global inequality that we are doing little to mitigate. We care little where they came from and why they left home; and still less about what happens to them afterwards.[13] As Carol Vance puts it, these stories 'entertain and absolve' us.[14] Then the women disappear again just as quickly from our consciousness, lost amid what Rachel C. Riedner calls the 'melodramatic yet brutal rhetoric of human interest stories'.[15]

Then, when the case reaches the criminal-justice system, this traffic in stories comes crashing down, when juries see the real women on the witness stands, the real people who trafficked them, and neither quite fits their expectations. The rules for what a victim and what a criminal looks like blur as the testimony unfolds; the tidy categories of 'trafficking victim' and 'illegal immigrant' break down.[16] The case fails. The perpetrator walks free. And, most grotesquely of all, the complainant – the woman who failed to live up to popular culture's idea of victimhood – is charged with crimes herself, thrown into a detention centre and processed for deportation.[17]

Even when a case does make it through systems designed, not unlike the early rescue movement, to separate the 'real' victims from the 'seasoned prostitutes', there is little support to be found. Shelters and support systems like MacDougall's continue to be extremely rare today, and are equally underfunded. Some continue to operate as thinly veiled prisons and labour camps. Most anti-trafficking money in the humanitarian sector goes into salaries, meetings and campaigns; while most government expenditure on trafficking goes towards the costs of incarceration and deportation.[18] Lydia Harvey's story, and the story of Ernest Anderson, Guy Scholefield, Eilidh MacDougall, Antonio Carvelli and Veronique White, show us how little has changed and how much needs to.

Back at Newcastle Interchange, I take the local train to Sandgate Cemetery, travelling along the same track as the funeral train leaving Newcastle that the 'friends of Herbert Ockenden' were invited to take, to attend the funeral of his beloved wife, at 2.40 p.m. on 25 June 1919.[19] The train passes the building that housed the hospital where Lydia died. Its partially hidden Victorian facade overlooks the suburb of

Waratah, her last place of residence. It would have been a lovely view from the upper windows, out over the city and the sea.

I arrive in Sandgate and cross a road bridge, where dozens of orb spiders have made their webs. I make my way along a grassy verge: Sandgate is now made for cars, not pedestrians. The cemetery's online grave locator, with latitude and longitude coordinates, helps me navigate amid the long lines of faded headstones. I march around in the dry grass, swatting at salt-marsh mosquitoes and squinting at my phone's location and direction beacon in the brightness of midday. The unseasonably hot autumn sun beats down, and the humidity sends trickles of sweat down my back. I long for the cool breezes of New Zealand's South Island.

Amid a forest of white granite and marble, I find her. Among all the other plainer tombstones, Lydia's stands out because it is in the shape of a heart: the romantic choice of a heartbroken man, married for just four years. It reads:

> To my loving wife, Lydia Rhoda Ockenden.
> Died 24 June 1919, age 26 years.

The stone has weathered significantly. The lead lettering now stands out from the surface, and much of it has fallen off. I pick up the 'R' of Rhoda, the '6' of 26, and push them back into the perforated holes they fell out of. I can't find the 'L' of Lydia anywhere on the dusty ground. The little carved posy of daisies on the bottom remains mostly intact; but the engravings on the foot of the stone are illegible. The plot beside it lies empty, waiting for a husband who wound up buried 500 miles away.

26: The grave of Lydia Rhoda (Harvey) Ockenden, Sandgate
Cemetery, Newcastle, New South Wales, Australia.

In a small shipping-news column in the *Newcastle Sun*, I discover that Lydia's mother and her six other younger sisters travelled to Newcastle from Oamaru in July 1920, and I can only assume it was, in part, to visit Lynda and to see Lydia's grave.[20] Visiting graves was of the utmost importance in this period, though the distance from the Badeleys' home ensured that such a trip could never be – as it was for many – an annual event. I picture the then Mrs Emily Louisa Jones holding the arm of her new husband Thomas for support, stepping off the train onto the little brick platform in the heart of Sandgate Cemetery, back when that small branch line still operated. Three young women, one teenage girl, twin eleven-year-olds and a nine-year-old step off the train behind them, and the family forms a small procession behind Lynda and winds its way through the lines of headstones until they reach the one in the shape of a heart. Maybe some of the scraps of coloured fabric that lie caught in the pebbles and dust around the grave are the remnants of the tokens left over the years by Lynda, who married a local clerk and stayed in Newcastle for the rest of her life. As the decades passed, real flowers and satin gave way to plastic petals and polyester ribbons, until 1959, the year that Lynda died and there was no one else left to visit Lydia Harvey's grave.

I unwrap the dozen red roses that I bought around the corner and place them on the ground beside the heart-shaped granite. Their blossoms are a flash of deep colour against the wind- and sun-bleached stone. I stand quietly, completely alone in the cemetery, at the end of a story. The fact that I am here at the graveside of this young woman, whom I had once assumed to have disappeared from the historical record, feels profoundly important.

Yet words fail to come, despite the lengths I have gone to for this pilgrimage. I think about Lydia's own words instead. When Lydia Harvey made her brief mark on the historical record, she told us that she wanted safe and valued work that paid a living wage. That she dreamed of a life made meaningful by travel and adventure, by pleasure and comfort. She said that she wanted respect and justice.

What would I say to Lydia Harvey if I could? I would tell her that one day, perhaps, we will live in a world where this is never too much for anyone to ask.

ACKNOWLEDGEMENTS

This story began, for me, in the National Archives in London, when I untied the string around a thick bundle of paper that the police had filed away when the Carvelli case was finally closed in 1911. But it certainly did not end there. Alongside consulting hundreds of other files from the UK's National Archives, I worked in the London Metropolitan Archive and the Women's Library at the London School of Economics in London, an invaluable repository of material on early feminist and social campaigns. I also travelled to the League of Nations Archive at the UN in Geneva, where the materials related to the Advisory Committee on the Traffic in Women and Children, established after the First World War, are held in neatly labelled boxes and files.[1] From Geneva it was on to Turin and its Archivio di Stato, where I found a slim but crucial file about Antonio Carvelli. In Paris I searched, to no avail, for more information on the other girls who were trafficked to London alongside Lydia. In New Zealand and Australia I worked in the Victoria Public Record Office, the Australian National Archives in Melbourne, Archives New Zealand in Dunedin and Wellington, as well as many local archives and libraries in both countries.

I am indebted to funding from the British Academy and

the Arts and Humanities Research Council, which made these journeys possible. I would like to explicitly acknowledge the AHRC's family travel policy, which enabled me to conduct my research in New Zealand and Australia without being forced to be away from my then one-year-old for an extended period of time. This kind of funding is game-changing for people who do not want to choose between the work of an academic and the work of a carer. I am lucky to have got it; and only hope more funders will move towards making such costs eligible.

I am also indebted to the archivists who have overseen the massive digitisation projects upon which this project relies, and who also continue to work with the paper records of the past. They answered the random email queries I sent them and joined my international scavenger hunt with enthusiasm, searching for names on registers, calling up files 'just in case' and contacting colleagues at other institutions.[2] Their expertise and enthusiasm have solved more than one mystery along the way.

Local historians, and local-history books, have also been invaluable in helping me imagine the material and social conditions of life on a small scale. I would like to especially recognise the work by Lenore Layman and Criena Fitzgerald on Leonora and the Gwalia mine, which, alongside a very helpful local-history web site, enabled me to paint a rich picture of life in this corner of the goldfields, even though I was unable to go there myself. Liz Yewers, from the Hawthorn Local History Society, corresponded with me regularly, and her daughter Penney carted books from Melbourne to London. Michael Shelford, a historian and expert in the local histories of Fitzroy, helped me understand this changing neighbourhood. James Dalton, with the Australian Historical Railway Society in New South Wales, assisted with descriptions of the journey to Sandgate Cemetery in 1919.

In reconstructing the experiences of the marginal, largely forgotten people whose lives intersected for a moment in 1910, I am deeply indebted to hundreds of other historians. Sometimes a single sentence in this book is the product of a dozen other historians' work. Not only has their excellent written work been invaluable, but many have been generous enough to speak to me and answer my questions about their area of expertise. I would like especially to thank Bill Burke and his family, who contacted me after the book was first published to share their memories of Lynda, Lydia's younger sister who was near her when she died. Lynda went on to become a beloved wife, mother, grandmother, and great-grandmother to many, who still remember her gentle warmth and humour to this day.

This book would have been far poorer without the particular insights of Charlotte MacDonald, Barbara Brookes and Anabel Cooper, whose work has not only been instrumental in helping me reconstruct the life and world of Lydia Harvey, but who have also taken the time to read and comment extensively on the manuscript. I want to thank Mark Seymour, for being such a kind host at the University of Otago and enthusiastic supporter of the book, and for his sharp insights on Italian masculinity and microhistory. Violetta Gilabert organised a wonderful seminar on the project in Dunedin and inspired the book's title. Alana Piper, an expert in women and crime in Australia, and Raelene Frances, whose work on prostitution in modern Australia was of seminal importance to the book, have been invaluable. Louise Jackson's comments on Eilidh MacDougall's chapter enriched it immensely, and Anna Sergei and Steven Bennets warmly entertained my random questions about Italian organised crime in the turn-of-the-century Antipodes. Generous help was also given by Chris Hilliard and Felicity Barnes. Lucy Smyth provided crucial material for my work on Eilidh MacDougall, and Catherine Gillies of Ergadia Heritage and the Dunollie Museum in Oban, Scotland, provided other precious details about her life. Thanks are also owed to Sadiah Qureshi for her generous advice on publishing outside academia.

This book was workshopped in many forums and emerged better and richer after each one, and I am especially grateful to the Creative Histories network for helping to shape the project. Other readers were crucial in shaping the book as well, including Harriet Phillips, Alison Stockham, Matt Houlbrook, Lucy Bland, Lucy Delap and Deborah Thom. I also want to highlight the work of Saidiya Hartman and Marissa Fuentes. While I draw no equivalences between the experience of Lydia Harvey – as a white girl within a coerced labour system – and the experiences of black enslaved women, I must acknowledge my debt to, and admiration of, those scholars who have shown me new ways to reimagine survival and aspiration, however hopeless, as a crucial form of resistance.

I would never have considered writing this book were it not for the pioneering work of Judith Walkowitz, Ruth Rosen, Donna Guy and others, who convinced their own and later generations of readers that prostitution, far from being a marginal social phenomenon, was at the heart of the most fundamental debates about gender, health, public order and labour in the past and in the present. This book has been written amid a wonderful collaboration with Philippa Hetherington, my co-investigator on the AHRC Trafficking Past project, as well as with Rose Holmes and Tom Clark, the research associate and developer behind the Trafficking Past web site. It is from the work of Magaly Rodriguez, Gunther Peck, Paul Knepper, Jessica Pliley, Elisa Camiscioli, Mir Yarfitz, Eileen Boris, Julia Martinez, Caroline Sequin, Rachael Attwood, Tara Suri, Sandy Chang and others in the Trafficking Past Network that I have learned about the intricacies of the international debates and national political developments, the campaigners and their campaigns; the flows of licit and illicit migration into and out of Europe, North and South America, Asia, India and Africa; and the thousands of women who did their best to navigate a dangerous, mobile world of exploitation and opportunity.

Equally important has been the vibrant social research into trafficking in the present day. I would especially like to recognise the work of the founding editors of the Open Democracy series 'Beyond Trafficking and Modern Slavery' (Genevieve LeBaron, Joel Quirk, Neil Howard, Samuel Okyere, Cameron Thibos, Prabha Kotiswaran and Julia O'Connell Davidson) and all the excellent contributors; as well as the work of the editorial board of the journal *Anti-Trafficking Review*. I hope that my own critical approach to the subject can help social scientists and activists, who are campaigning for rights, justice and safety for migrant women in the sex industry, as much as their work has helped me.

I want to thank all of my colleagues at Birkbeck for making the college such a fruitful place to do research, but especially Brodie Waddell for being such an excellent reader, and for many a conversation about microhistory and history-from-below across time and space; Louise Hide and the incredibly thought-provoking 'sensitive sources' workshops that she organised; and Joseph Viscomi, who not only spoke to me at length about modern microhistory and Italian migration, but went on a treasure hunt for me at the Archivio Centrale in Rome. I want to thank my Birkbeck students as well, whose diverse insights have made my book better, and who have made my job teaching them so incredibly rewarding. As I finished the manuscript, I thought often of Chris Youé, who died while I was writing it. As my undergraduate mentor at Memorial University of Newfoundland, he was the first person who made me think I was a historian, and I wish he could have read this book.

To my mentors in writing and publishing: to Hallie Rubenhold, for shouting loudly about the history of sex work with me in London restaurants, for putting forgotten women on the map of popular history writing and for giving me the evocative phrase 'history in the round'; to my editor at Profile, Louisa Dunnigan, who understood the project instantly and has been instrumental in shaping it since; to my agent, Rachel Calder, whose attentive reading and astute early suggestions helped take this project from an idea into a book.

I also want to thank my friends who are not among those already named, and my family. To my partner Will Alcock, who has listened to me talk about Lydia Harvey and Antonio Carvelli for half a decade and who carted our children around Australia and New Zealand while I bounced from archive to archive. To my children Owen and Finn, who always mercilessly drag me back into the present. To my sister, for being so cool; and to my extensive, wonderful, warm and supportive family. To the circle of people in Cambridge alongside whom I am lucky to parent; to my other friends spread around the world; and to my precious gang of ancient friends in Newfoundland, who are all there with smart conversation, commiseration, wine and laughter whenever I need it. To my parents, for decades of unwavering support. To everyone who helped me find the girl I thought had disappeared; to everyone who believed this was an important thing to do: thank you.

NOTES

Prologue

1   On domestic service, see Charlotte Macdonald, 'Strangers at the Hearth: The Eclipse of Domestic Service in New Zealand Homes *c.*1830s–1940s', in *At Home in New Zealand*, ed. Barbara Brookes (Wellington, 2000); Lucy Delap, *Knowing Their Place: Domestic Service in Twentieth-Century Britain* (Oxford, 2011); Carolyn Steedman, *Labours Lost: Domestic Service and the Making of Modern England* (Cambridge, 2009).

2   Charles Byron Crysler, *White Slavery: Our Daughters* (London, 1911), p. 23.

3   Frank 'Nutty' Sharpe, *Sharpe of the Flying Squad* (London, 1938), p. 79.

4   J. P. Wilson, *The White Slave Traffic* (London, 1912).

5   Clifford G. Roe, *The Girl Who Disappeared* (Michigan, 1914), p. 24.

6   Saidiya Hartman, 'Venus in Two Acts', *Small Axe*, no. 26 (vol. 12, no. 2), June 2008, pp. 1–14.

Chapter 1: The Disappearing Girl

1   *Otago Daily Chronicle*, 25 May 1909.

2   On the opera house, see oamaruoperahouse.co.nz/visiting-our-venue/history/ (accessed 26 November 2018).

3   For an example of these films, see www.theguardian.com/film/video/2012/dec/03/le-faune-1908-pathe-video (accessed 26 November 2018). For more on beauty contests, see N. Smith,

'The modern girl: Dale Austen, Miss New Zealand in Hollywood', in R. Bell (ed.), *New Zealand Between the Wars* (Auckland, 2017), pp. 256–79. See also *Sites of Gender: Women, Men and Modernity in Southern Dunedin, 1890–1939*, ed. Barbara Brookes, Annabel Cooper and Robin Law (Auckland, 2003); Kerryn Pollock, 'Beauty contests – Beauty contests, 19th century to the 1950s', *Te Ara – The Encyclopedia of New Zealand*, www.TeAra.govt.nz/en/beauty-contests/page-1 (accessed 26 November 2018).

4 Marriage Certificate, Edward Badeley and Esther Hyams, 9 June 1881, Hobart, Tasmania, Australian Marriage Register, 277; Tasmania, Australia, Police Gazettes, 1884–1933 for Edward Badeley 1886, page 204; 1841 England Census Essex Chelmsford District 1, 11, Ancestry.co.uk (accessed 10 October 2018).

5 J. A. Tuck, 'The Devil's Half-Acre, 1900–1910', BA (Hons) dissertation, University of Otago, 1983.

6 *North Otago Times*, 17 October 1894.

7 'Minnie Dean's last statement', Wellington, Archives New Zealand, J1 1895/643, page 25; Lynley Hood, *Minnie Dean: Her Life and Crimes* (Sydney, 1995).

8 Peter Shaw, cited by Gavin McLean, *Oamaru: History and Heritage* (Dunedin, 2002), p. 7.

9 Ibid., p. 16.

10 Ibid., p. 26.

11 St Luke's Anglican Church baptism register, 20 April 1884–15 October 1902, entry 684, Oamaru, Waitaki District Archive, 63888.

12 *Oamaru Mail*, 29 January 1897.

13 Avon Lodge, Riccarton Road, File Reference CCL Photo Collection 22, Img01500, Christchurch City Council Libraries, christchurchcitylibraries.com/heritage/photos/collection22/01500.asp (accessed 19 June 2020).

14 Clare Wood, '"Bastardy Made Easy"?' Unmarried Mothers and Illegitimate Children on Charitable Aid – Dunedin 1890–1910' (Otago, 1990).

15 Hislop and Creagh, Solicitors, to Edward Towsey, 13 January 1904, Oamaru, Waitaki District Archive, Hislop, Creagh, and Main Day books, 29 April 1901–17 June 1905 [1345].

16 Oamaru Criminal Record Book, 1904–6, Archives New Zealand, Dunedin, DABP D548 20742 Box 25.

17 Clara Kathleen, 1895/8432, Lynda Harvey? *c*.1900, no registration, Gertrude Mildred Hawthorn, 1903/6229, Doris Winnifred, 1906/12357, New Zealand Registry of Birth, Marriage and Death, www.bdmhistoricalrecords.dia.govt.nz/Home/ (accessed 30 June 2020).

18 *Oamaru Mail*, 29 January 1897.

19 Mary Isabella Lee, *The Not So Poor: An Autobiography*, ed. Annabel Cooper (Auckland, 1992). *Oamaru Mail*, 10 June 1907. Emily Badeley was called as a witness in the drunken-neighbour case.

20 McLean, *Oamaru: History and Heritage*, pp. 165, 181, 224, 226.

21 Michael Brown, '"A Piano in Every Other House?" The Piano in New Zealand Trade Statistics, 1877–1931', *New Zealand Journal of History*, vol. 51, no. 2, 2017, pp. 26–53 (pp. 29, 60).

22 Index of the Oamaru Middle School and Oamaru Middle School pupils, 1906–7, Waitaki District Archive, Oamaru, 6046P.

23 Anne Phyllis, 1909/22634; Evaline Rose, 1909/22611, New Zealand Registry of Birth, Marriage, Death, www.bdmhistoricalrecords.dia.govt.nz/Home/ (accessed 30 June 2020).

24 Rosemary Goodyear, 'Black Boots and Pinafores: Childhood in Otago, 1900–1920' (Otago, 1992), pp. 143–57.

25 Harry George Cannon Harvey death notice, *Star*, 8 March 1909.

26 Harry George Cannon Harvey probate record, 1909, Probate Records, 1843–1998, Christchurch Court, Wellington, New Zealand National Archive, P6595/09-P6631/09.

27 These advertisements could be found in the *Otago Daily Times* and the *Oamaru Mail*.

28 *North Otago Times*, 17 April and 6 August 1909.

29 Charlotte Macdonald, 'Why Was There No Answer to the "Servant Problem"? Paid Domestic Work and the Making of a White New Zealand, 1840s–1950s', *New Zealand Journal of History*, vol. 51, no. 1, April 2017, pp. 7–35; and Macdonald, 'Strangers at the Hearth' in *At Home in New Zealand*, ed. Brookes.

30 Witness statement of Mrs Batson, 7/1/10, Archives New Zealand, Wellington, AAAJ W3289 6813 Box 9, CR 13/26.

31 Brookes, Cooper and Law, *Sites of Gender*; Wendy M. Gordon, *Mill Girls and Strangers: Single women's independent migration in England, Scotland, and the United States, 1850–1881* (Albany, NY, 2002); Katherine Mullin, *Working Girls: Fiction, Sexuality and Modernity* (Oxford, 2016).

32 Witness statement of Mrs Batson, 7/1/10, Archives New Zealand, Wellington, AAAJ W3289 6813 Box 9, CR 13/26. I take this description of the journey from Wellington to Karori from Katherine Mansfield's short story 'Prelude', in which two young girls travel by cart from central Wellington to their new home.

33 See Macdonald, 'Strangers at the Hearth' in *At Home in New Zealand*, ed. Brookes. Katherine Mansfield, 'Prelude', *New Zealand Stories*, ed. Vincent O'Sullivan (Auckland, 1999), p. 44.

34 This description of the work Lydia would have been doing comes from various historical and oral-history sources. See Lucy Delap, *Knowing Their Place*; Pamela Horn, *Life Below Stairs in the Twentieth Century* (Stroud, 2003). For sociological perspectives on this kind of work, see Linda McDowell, *Working Bodies: Interactive Service Employment and Workplace Identities* (Chichester, 2009); and Eileen Boris and Rhacel Salazar Parreñas (eds), *Intimate Labors: Cultures, technologies, and the politics of care* (Stanford, CA, 2010).

35 This description is drawn from the character of Alice, the

servant in Mansfield's short story 'Prelude', *New Zealand Stories*, p. 63.

36 Ibid., p. 62.

37 *Travellers' Aid Society Annual Report for 1910* (Bristol, 1911), p. 13.

38 Jane Addams, *A New Conscience and an Ancient Evil* (New York, 1912), p. 170.

39 Mansfield, 'Prelude', *New Zealand Stories*, p. 63.

40 Witness statement of Mrs Batson, 7/1/10, Archives New Zealand, Wellington, AAAJ W3289 6813 Box 9, CR 13/26. Ingestre Street is today's Vivian Street. Williams Minchin, *Wellington – The Dark Side: Murder, Mayhem and Nefarious Activity in the Capital of Crime* (Auckland, 2005), p. 35.

41 Report of Detective W. E. Lewis re interview with Mr Harlow, 2 August 1910, Archives New Zealand, Wellington, AAAJ W3289 6813 Box 9, CR 13/26.

42 *New Zealand Truth*, 3 September 1910, p. 3.

43 See various reports in *New Zealand Truth*, 1909–11.

44 Report of Detective W. E. Lewis, 2 August 1910, Wellington, Archives New Zealand, AAAJ W3289 6813 Box 9, CR 13/26.

45 Lydia mentions her sweetheart in her witness statement on 9 July 1910, London, The National Archives (TNA), MEPO 3/197; his name is mentioned in Report of Con. H. P. Anderson, Lower Hutt, 12 January 1910, Archives New Zealand, Wellington, AAAJ W3289 6813 Box 9, CR 13/26.

46 On sexuality and sexual experience among early twentieth-century young women, see Hera Cook, *The Long Sexual Revolution: English Women, Sex, and Contraception, 1800–1975* (Oxford, 2004).

47 Ellice Hopkins, as cited by Havelock Ellis, *Studies in the Psychology of Sex*, vol. IV: *Sex in Relation to Society* (Philadelphia, 1920), p. 289.

48 Eaton S. Lothrop, Jr., 'The Brownie camera', *History of Photography*, vol. 2, no. 1, 1978, pp. 1–10.

49 Witness statement of Lydia Rhoda Harvey, 9 July 1910, London, TNA, MEPO 3/197.

50 Wellington, Archives New Zealand, AAAJ W3289 6813 Box 9, CR 13/26.

51 Witness statement of Lydia Rhoda Harvey, 9 July 1910, London, TNA, MEPO 3/197.

52 C Division Police Report, 20 October 1910, Wellington, Archives New Zealand, 1915/1032.

53 Witness statement of Lydia Rhoda Harvey, 9 July 1910, London, TNA, MEPO 3/197.

54 For domestic service, emigration schemes and employment agencies, see Katie Pickles, 'Empire Settlement and Single British Women as New Zealand Domestic Servants during the 1920s', *New Zealand Journal of History*, vol. 35, no. 1, 2001, pp. 22–44; Macdonald, 'Why Was There No Answer to the "Servant Problem"?', pp. 7–35; Lisa Chilton, *Agents of Empire: British Female Migration to Canada and Australia, 1860–1930* (Toronto, 2007); Jan Gothard, *Blue China: Single Female Migration to Colonial Australia* (Melbourne, 2001); Eileen Boris, *Making the Woman Worker: Precarious Labor and the Fight for Global Standards, 1919–2019* (Oxford, 2019).

55 International Labour Office, 'The Moral Protection of Young Women Workers', in *Prevention of Prostitution: A Study of the Measures Adopted or Under Consideration Particularly with Regard to Minors*, ed. League of Nations Advisory Committee on Social Questions (Geneva, 1943), p. 70.

56 'Domestic workers call for 68-hour week', nzhistory.govt.nz/page/domestic-workers-call-68-hour-working-week (Ministry for Culture and Heritage), updated 13 March 2018. See also Boris, *Making the Woman Worker*.

57 See Chilton, *Agents of Empire*; Gothard, *Blue China*.

58 Nora Glickman, *The Jewish White Slave Traffic and the Untold Story of Raquel Liberman* (London and New York, 2000), p. 45.

59 'The Ruahine's Cargo', *New Zealand Herald*, 9 January 1910.

60 Avril de St Croix letter, London, LSE, The Women's Library, 3/ AMS/B11/12 box 75.

61 Torsten Feys, Lewis R. Fischer, Stephane Hoste and Stephan Vanfraechem (eds), *Maritime Transport and Migration: The Connections between Maritime and Migration Networks* (Liverpool, 2017).

62 Dirk Hoerder, *Cultures in Contact: World Migrations in the Second Millenium* (Durham, NC, 2002); Leo Lucassen, 'Migration and World History: Reaching a New Frontier', *International Review of Social History*, vol. 52, 2007, pp. 89–96.

63 Frances Steel, *Oceania Under Steam: Sea Transport and the Cultures of Colonialism, c.1870–1914* (Manchester and New York, 2011), p. 50.

64 Witness statement of Lydia Rhoda Harvey, 9 July 1910, London, TNA, MEPO 3/197.

65 James R. Scobie, *Buenos Aires: Plaza to Suburb, 1870–1910* (New York, 1974), p. 21.

66 Ibid., p. 13.

67 Daniel K. Lewis, *The History of Argentina* (Westport, CN, and London, 2001), chapter 4. Samuel L. Bailey, *Immigrants in the Land of Promise: Italians in Buenos Aires and New York City, 1870–1914* (Ithaca, NY, 1999). V. Mirelman, *Jewish Buenos Aires, 1890–1930: In search of an identity* (Detroit, 1990). William Glade, 'Latin America and the International Economy, 1870–1914', in *The Cambridge History of Latin America*, ed. Leslie Bethell (Cambridge, 1986), vol. 4, pp. 1–56. Nicolás Sánchez-Albornoz, 'The Population of Latin America, 1850–1930', in *The Cambridge History of Latin America*.

68 Donna J. Guy, *Sex & Danger in Buenos Aires: Prostitution, Family, and Nation in Argentina* (London, 1991), pp. 59–64.

69 Albert Londres, *The Road to Buenos Aires* (Cornwall, 1928), pp. 40–41.

70 For a discussion of these methodological issues, see Shani D'Cruze, *Crimes of Outrage: Sex, Violence and Victorian Working Women* (DeKalb, IL, 1998).

71 Londres, *The Road to Buenos Aires*, p. 162.

72 Special Body of Experts Files, Kinsie Notebooks, CE: Code book and Argentina, League of Nations, United Nations Archive, Geneva, S171.

73 Londres, *The Road to Buenos Aires*, pp. 196–204.

74 Scobie, *Buenos Aires*, p. 26.

75 Ibid., p. 143.

76 Ibid., p. 181.

77 Adriana Bergero, *Intersecting Tango: Cultural Geographies of Buenos Aires, 1900–1930* (Pittsburgh, 2008), p. 150.

78 Witness statement of Lydia Rhoda Harvey, 9 July 1910, London, TNA, MEPO 3/197.

79 Report of the Special Body of Experts on the Traffic in Women and Children, Part 2, League of Nations, C. 52. M. 52 1927 (IV) Geneva, 17 February 1927: Table b, 'Nationality of newly registered prostitutes in Buenos Aires, 1910', p. 19.

80 Witness statement of Lydia Rhoda Harvey, 9 July 1910, London, TNA, MEPO 3/197.

81 *Travellers' Aid Society Annual Report*, 1910, p. 71.

82 London Lock Hospital and Asylum, vol. 1: Correspondence and Papers, London, London Metropolitan Archives, A/FWA/C/D/078/001.

83 Judith R. Walkowitz, *Prostitution and Victorian Society: Women, Class and the State* (Cambridge, 1980).

84 On venereal disease, lock hospitals and the Contagious Diseases Acts see, for instance, ibid.; Pamela Cox, 'Compulsion, Voluntarism, and Venereal Disease: Governing Sexual Health in England after the Contagious Diseases Acts', *Journal of British Studies*, vol. 46, 2007, pp. 91–115.

85 Witness statement of Lydia Rhoda Harvey, 9 July 1910, London, TNA, MEPO 3/197.

86 Anne Hanley, '"The Great Foe to the Reproduction of the Race": Diagnosing and Treating Infertility Caused by Venereal Diseases, 1880–1914', in *The Palgrave Handbook of Infertility in History Approaches, Contexts and Perspectives*, ed. Gayle Davis

and Tracey Loughran (London, 2017), pp. 335–58; Simon Szreter, *Hidden Affliction: Sexually Transmitted Infections and Infertility in History* (Rochester, 2019).

87 Witness statement of Lydia Rhoda Harvey, 9 July 1910, London, TNA, MEPO 3/197.

88 Julia Laite, *Common Prostitutes and Ordinary Citizens: Commercial Sex in London, 1885–1960* (Basingstoke, 2011).

89 Witness statement of Lydia Rhoda Harvey, 9 July 1910, London, TNA, MEPO 3/197.

90 *The Times*, 11 July 1910, p. 13.

Chapter 2: The Detective

1 Robert Fabian, *London after Dark: An Intimate Record of Night Life in London, and a Selection of Crime Stories from the Case Book of Ex-Superintendent Robert Fabian* (London, 1954), p. 16.

2 Report of DI Ernest Anderson, 10 April 1910, London, TNA, MEPO 3/197.

3 This description is drawn from the cells that remain part of the bar area in what is now the Courthouse Hotel, Great Marlborough Street, London, which I visited in April 2019.

4 Report of Anderson, 10 April 1910, London, TNA, MEPO 3/197. For more on the physical space of the court and police station, see Neil R. A. Bell, *Capturing Jack the Ripper: In the Boots of a Bobby in Victorian London* (Stroud, 2014).

5 Great Marlborough Street Police Court Register, April 1910, London, London Metropolitan Archives (LMA), PS/MS/A.

6 *The Sketch*, Wednesday 30 March 1910, p. 8; *Islington Gazette*, Wednesday 30 March 1910, p. 5.

7 Great Marlborough Street Police Court Register, April 1910, London, LMA, PS/MS/A.

8 Report of Anderson, 10 April 1910, London, TNA, MEPO 3/197.

9 For more on the practice of Coote's National Vigilance Association, lady visitors and expulsion orders, see London, TNA, HO 45/15041.

10 Letter from 'Antoinette' to '*Chère Maman*', translated in a report from 9 April 1910, London, TNA, MEPO 3/197.

11 'Weather', *The London Times,* 6 April 1910, p. 19.

12 'I get more handshakes from crooks and ex-crooks than any other class of people,' wrote Detective Frank 'Nutty' Sharpe in his memoir. They were, in his words 'pretty decent fellows'. Sharpe, *Sharpe of the Flying Squad*, pp. 9–10.

13 Fabian, *London after Dark*, p. 54.

14 Paul Knepper, *The Invention of International Crime: A Global Issue in the Making, 1881–1914* (Basingstoke, 2010).

15 *Illustrated Police News*, Saturday 13 June 1903, p. 1.

16 Jennifer Davis, 'A Poor Man's System of Justice: The London Police Courts in the Second Half of the Nineteenth Century', *The Historical Journal*, vol. 27, no. 2, 1984, pp. 309–35.

17 Report of Police Constable William Mead, 6 April 1910, London, TNA, MEPO 3/197.

18 Robert Fabian, *Fabian of the Yard: An Intimate Record*, 2nd edn (London, 1950), p. 16.

19 Census Returns of England and Wales, 1901, TNA, 1901, Class: RG13; Piece: 183; Folio: 28; Page: 10, Ancestry.com (accessed 10 April 2019); Marriage Register of England and Wales, 5 February 1905, St Andrew's Church, Islington, no. 196, p. 98., Ancestry.com (accessed 10 April 2019).

20 George Dilnot, *Scotland Yard: Its History and Organisation 1829–1929* (London, 1929), p. 154.

21 Walter Burmby in 1881, 1891, 1901 and 1911 Census Return; Census of England & Wales, Ancestry.com (accessed 12 April 2018).

22 Fabian, *Fabian of the Yard*, p. 17.

23 Census Returns of England and Wales, 1871, TNA, Class: RG10; Piece: 1450; Folio: 34; Page: 13; GSU roll: 828789, Ancestry.com (accessed 20 October 2018).

24 Sharpe, *Sharpe of the Flying Squad*, p. 162.

25 Lilian Wyles, *A Woman at Scotland Yard: Reflections on the*

Struggles and Achievements of Thirty Years in the Metropolitan Police (London, 1952), p. 129.

26 Census Returns of England and Wales, 1911, TNA, Class: RG14; Piece: 425, Ancestry.com (accessed 13 February 2018).

27 David Petrucelli, *A Scourge of Humanity: International Crime, Law, and Policing in Interwar Europe* (New Haven, CT, 2015).

28 Dilnot, *Scotland Yard*, p. 14.

29 Early twentieth-century ocean liners, despite their dramatic increase in tonnage, travelled at a speed of up to 27 knots, while ships in the 1870s travelled at 15 knots.

30 Dilnot, *Scotland Yard*, p. 15.

31 Fabian, *London after Dark*, pp. 11, 22.

32 Fabian, *Fabian of the Yard*, p. 155.

33 Fabian, *London after Dark*, p. 10.

34 Sharpe, *Sharpe of the Flying Squad*, p. 69.

35 Fabian, *London after Dark*, pp. 52–3.

36 Edward Henry memorandum, 21 April 1915, MEPO 3/228.

37 George Dilnot, *The Real Detective* (London, 1933), p. 83.

38 Fabian, *Fabian of the Yard*, p. 158.

39 Bell, *Capturing Jack the Ripper*, p. 58.

40 Haia Shpayer-Makov, 'Relinking Work and Leisure in Late Victorian and Edwardian England: The Emergence of a Police Subculture', *International Journal of Social History*, vol. 47, 2002, pp. 213–41.

41 For more on the working lives of police constables and detectives, see Haia Shpayer-Makov, *The Making of a Policeman: A Social History of a Labour Force Metropolitan London, 1829–1914* (Aldershot, 2002); Haia Shpayer-Makov, *The Ascent of the Detective: Police Sleuths in Victorian and Edwardian England* (Oxford, 2011); *Police Detectives in History, 1750–1950*, ed. Clive Emsley; Haia Shpayer-Makov, *Police Detectives in History, 1750–1950* (Aldershot, 2006).

42 Report of Anderson, 14 June 1910, London, TNA, MEPO 3/197.

43 Dilnot, *Scotland Yard*, pp. 116, 119, 123.

44 1883–1951 Dilnot George, *Scotland Yard: The Methods and Organisation of the Metropolitan Police* (Project Gutenberg, 2010), p. 33.

45 Fabian, *London after Dark*, p. 98.

46 Witness statement of Ernest Anderson, 25 June 1910, London, TNA, MEPO 3/197.

47 Census Returns of England and Wales, 1901, TNA, Class: RG13; Piece: 187; Folio: 61; Page: 19, Ancestry.com (accessed on 18 February 2018); Examination certificate for George Robert Nicholls, The Met heritage centre London, Report of particulars, pension number 34324, 20 Feb 1934, MEPO 21/69.

48 On the Alhambra Theatre, see Arthur Lloyd: The Music Hall and Theatre History Site (dedicated to Arthur Lloyd, 1839–1904): www.arthurlloyd.co.uk/Alhambra.htm#alhambra (accessed 2 May 2019); and British History Online, www.british-history.ac.uk/survey-london/vols33–4/plate-35 (accessed 2 May 2019). For more on music halls, see Peter Bailey, *Music Hall: The Business of Pleasure* (Milton Keynes, 1986).

49 Fabian, *London after Dark*, p. 25.

50 *London Daily News*, Friday 17 June 1910.

51 *Illustrated Police News*, Saturday 9 July 1910.

52 'Alex' to Marguerite Dennis, undated, Wellington, Archives New Zealand, AAAJ W3289 6813 Box 9, CR 13/26.

53 Mireille Lapara witness statement, 23 June 1910, London, TNA, MEPO 3/197.

54 Marguerite Bescançon witness statement, 23 June 1910, London, TNA, MEPO 3/197.

55 Victoria Bricot witness statement, 24 June 1910, London, TNA, MEPO 3/197.

56 Judicial statistics, England and Wales, 1909. Part I, 'Criminal statistics. Statistics relating to criminal proceedings, police, coroners, prisons, reformatory and industrial schools, and criminal lunatics, for the year 1909', Cd. 5473, 5501, 1911.

57 Report of Anderson, 22 July 1910, London, TNA, MEPO 3/197.

58 Witness statements of Mary Alice Wood and Robert Edwin Eddison, 30 June 1910, London, TNA, MEPO 3/197.

59 Witness statement of Luigi Carvelli, 5 July 1910, London, TNA, MEPO 3/197.

60 Report of Detective E. Lewis, Wellington Police Department, 7 and 11 July 1910, London, TNA, MEPO 3/197.

61 Agent General, Western Australia to the Commissioner of Police, 17 August 1910, London, TNA, MEPO 3/197.

62 Inspector R. Connell to the Commissioner of Police, 17 August 1910, London, TNA, MEPO 3/197.

63 Questore of Turin to Ernest Anderson, c/o the Italian Consul, London, 16 July 1910, London, TNA, MEPO 3/197.

64 *Smith's Weekly*, 7 March 1925.

65 Judith G. Coffin, *The Politics of Women's Work: The Paris Garment Trades, 1750–1915* (Princeton, NJ, and Chichester, 1996).

66 David Von Drehle, *Triangle: The Fire That Changed America* (New York, 2004).

67 Coffin, *The Politics of Women's Work*, pp. 175–200.

68 *The Times*, 11 July 1910, p. 17.

69 Witness statement of Inspector Anderson, 25 June 1910, London, TNA, MEPO 3/197.

Chapter 3: The Newsman

1 Felicity Barnes, *New Zealand's London: A Colony and Its Metropolis* (Auckland, 2012).

2 Guy Scholefield, Autobiography, Alexander Turnbull Unpublished Manuscript Collection, Wellington, MS-Papers-0212–67, p. 62.

3 Ibid., pp. 53–6.

4 Ibid., pp. 59–61.

5 Ibid., p. 66.

6 *Illustrated London News*, 28 February 1885, p. 1; 25 April 1885; 21 November 1885; 12 December 1885.

7 Laurel Brake, 'Journalism and Modernism: Continued', in

Transatlantic Print Culture, 1880–1940: Emerging Media, Emerging Modernisms, ed. Ann Ardis and Patrick Collier (Basingstoke, 2008), pp. 149–66; Laurel Brake and Mark W. Turner, 'Rebranding the News of the World: 1891 and After', in *The News of the World and The British Press, 1843–2011: Journalism for the Rich, Journalism for the Poor* (Basingstoke, 2015), pp. 27–42; Mark Hampton, *Visions of the Press in Britain, 1850–1950* (Chicago, 2004); Mark Hampton, 'Representing the Public Sphere: The New Journalism and Its Historians', in *Transatlantic Print Culture, 1880–1940*, pp. 15–29.

8   William T. Stead, 'Government by Journalism', *The Contemporary Review*, vol. 49, 1886, pp. 653–74. See also Julia Laite, 'Justifiable Sensationalism', *Media History*, vol. 20, no. 2, 2014, pp. 126–45.

9   Roger Lockhurst, Laurel Brake, James Mussel and Ed King (eds), *W. T. Stead: Newspaper Revolutionary* (London, 2012).

10 Stead, 'Government by Journalism', pp. 653–74.

11 For more on the 'Maiden Tribute', see Deborah Gorham, 'The "Maiden Tribute of Modern Babylon" Re-Examined: Child Prostitution and the Idea of Childhood in Late-Victorian England', *Victorian Studies*, vol. 21, no. 3, 1978, pp. 353–80; Judith R. Walkowitz, *City of Dreadful Delight: Narratives of Sexual Danger in Late-Victorian London* (London, 1992).

12 *New York Times*, 7 September 1885, p. 11.

13 'The Maiden Tribute of Modern Babylon', *Pall Mall Gazette*, Part III, 8 July 1885.

14 *West Coast Times*, 9 September 1885.

15 Guy Hardy Scholefield, *Epic Year, 1893* (Dunedin, 1946), pp. 2–4.

16 Scholefield, Autobiography, p. 86.

17 Ibid., p. 92.

18 Ibid., p. 99.

19 For more on the National Vigilance Association, see Rachael Attwood, 'Stopping the Traffic: The National Vigilance Association and the International Fight against the "White

Slave" Trade (1899–*c*.1909)', *Women's History Review*, vol. 24, no. 3, 2015, pp. 325–50; Paula Bartley, *Prostitution: Prevention and Reform in England, 1860–1914* (London, 2000); Lucy Bland, *Banishing the Beast: English Feminism and Sexual Morality, 1885–1914* (London, 1995).

20 W. A. Coote, *A Romance of Philanthropy* (London, 1916), pp. 109–10.

21 Stephanie A. Limoncelli, *The Politics of Trafficking: The First International Movement to Combat the Traffic in Women, 1875–1960* (California, 2007).

22 Frances Porter, 'Scholefield, Guy Hardy', first published in the *Dictionary of New Zealand Biography*, 1998; *Te Ara – The Encyclopedia of New Zealand*, teara.govt.nz/en/ biographies/4s12/scholefield-guy-hardy (accessed 17 June 2020); Christopher Hilliard, *The Bookmen's Dominions: Cultural Life in New Zealand, 1920–1950* (Auckland, 2006).

23 Yska Redmer, *Truth: The Rise and Fall of the People's Paper* (Nelson, NZ, 2010).

24 George Kibbe Turner, 'The Daughters of the Poor: A Plain Story of the Development of New York City as a Leading Centre of the White Slave Trade of the World, under Tammany Hall', *McClure's Magazine*, vol. 34, November 1909, pp. 45–61.

25 Ben Brewster, '"Traffic in Souls": An Experiment in Feature-Length Narrative Construction", *Cinema Journal*, vol. 31, no. 1, 1991, pp. 37–56; Eric Olund, 'Traffic in Souls: The "new woman," Whiteness and Mobile Self-possession', *Cultural Geographies*, vol. 16, no. 4, 2009, pp. 485–504; Shelley Stamp Lindsey, '"Oil upon the Flames of Vice": The Battle over White Slave Films in New York City', *Film History*, vol. 9, no. 4, 1997, pp. 351–64.

26 Anon., *The White Slave Traffic*, revised edn (London, 1916), p. 48.

27 Anonymous, *The Dangers of False Prudery: A Book for Parents* (London, 1912), p. 52.

28 Ibid., p. 53.

29 Ibid., p. 12.

30 Anon., *The White Slave Traffic*, p. 18.

31 T. A. Bingham, *The Girl That Disappears* (New York, 1911), pp. 37, 10.

32 For an analysis of these, see Brian Donovan, *White Slave Crusades: Race, Gender, and Anti-Vice Activism 1887–1917* (Urbana, IL, and Chicago, 2006), pp. 17–37.

33 Unattributed, *The Dangers of False Prudery: A Book for Parents* (London, 1912).

34 Anon., *The White Slave Traffic*, p. 15.

35 Gunther Peck, 'Feminizing White Slavery in the United States: Marcus Braun and the Transnational Traffic in White Bodies, 1890–1910', in *Workers Across the Americas: The Transnational Turn in Labor History*, ed. Leon Fink (Oxford, 2011), pp. 222–41.

36 Ernest Bell, *Fighting the Traffic in Young Girls; Or, War on the White Slave Trade* (Chicago, 1910), p. 90.

37 Julia Laite, 'Traffickers and Pimps in the Era of White Slavery', *Past & Present*, vol. 237, no. 1, 2017, pp. 237–69.

38 'Some Arguments Against the Compulsory Repatriation of Prostitutes', *The Shield*, November 1927.

39 Raelene Frances, 'Sex Workers or Citizens? Prostitution and the Shaping of "Settler" Society in Australia', *International Review of Social History*, vol. 44.S7, 1999, pp. 101–22; Jessica Pliley, *Policing Sexuality: The Mann Act and the Making of the FBI* (Cambridge, MA, 2014).

40 Scholefield, Autobiography, p. 24.

41 Census Returns of England and Wales, 1911, TNA, RG14, 1911, Ancestry.com (accessed 10 February 2019).

42 Scholefield, Autobiography, p. 160.

43 *Evening Post*, 30 August 1910, p. 6.

44 Ibid., p. 153.

45 *Evening Post*, 30 August 1910, p. 6.

46 High commissioner to Prime Minister's Office, 21 September

1910, Wellington, Archives New Zealand, AAAJ W3289 6813
Box 9, CR 13/26.

47 Report of Anderson, 30 July 1910, London, TNA, MEPO 3/197.

48 *Oamaru Mail*, 31 August 1910.

49 *New Zealand Truth*, 3 September 1910, p. 3.

50 Scholefield, Autobiography, p. 124.

Chapter 4: The Rescuer

1 Metropolitan Police Home for Women Annual Report, 1910.

2 Alexander William MacDougall, 14 April 1837. Jamaica, Select
Births and Baptisms, 1752–1920 Ancestry.com.

3 See the *Legacies of British Slave Ownership* web site, www.ucl.
ac.uk/lbs/ (accessed 29 June 2020).

4 Marriage banns of William Alexander MacDougall and
Cassandra Bird, Gloucestershire Archives; Gloucester, England;
Gloucestershire Anglican Parish Registers; Reference Numbers:
GDR/V1/478a; Church of England Marriages and Banns,
1754–1938 Ancestry.com (accessed 12 July 2018); Baptism of
Lorna Eilidh Louisa MacDougall, 18 October 1872, Scotland,
Select Births and Baptisms, 1564–1950 Ancestry.com (accessed
12 July 2018).

5 1901 England Census, Class: RG13; Piece: 540; Folio: 84; Page:
13; Ancestry.com (accessed 12 July 2018). Kew, Surrey, England:
The National Archives, 1901.

6 Charles Booth's London: Poverty Maps and Police Notebooks,
London School of Economics, booth.lse.ac.uk/ (accessed 12 July
2018).

7 Greenwich and Deptford Workhouse Girls' Aid Committee:
annual reports for 1894/5, 1895/6, London, London
Metropolitan Archives, ACC/2201/B/22/002/009–011.

8 Lavinia Talbot et al., fundraising letter, to the editors of the
Morning Post, Outdoor Rescue Work in Lambeth Casebook
(November 1907), London, LMA, ACC2201/H3/3/1.

9 Southwark Diocesan Association, Outdoor Rescue Work in
Lambeth Casebook, p. 26, London, LMA, ACC2201/H3/3/1.

10 Ibid., p. 44.

11 Ibid., p. 5.

12 Ibid.

13 Ibid., p. 24.

14 On histories of sexual abuse and assault, see Lucy Delap, '"Disgusting Details Which Are Best Forgotten": Disclosures of Child Sexual Abuse in Twentieth-Century Britain', *Journal of British Studies*, January 2018, vol. 57, 2018, pp. 79–107; Louise Jackson, *Child Sexual Abuse in Victorian England* (London, 2000).

15 *Oamaru Mail*, 10 April 1899.

16 Witness statement of Lydia Rhoda Harvey, 9 July 1910, London, TNA, MEPO 3/197.

17 Miss MacDougall, Lady Assistant to the Metropolitan Police, Minutes of Evidence, Select Committee on Assaults on Young Persons, Friday 5 December 1924, London, TNA, HO 45/25434.

18 For more on women's statements and self-narration, see Elisa Camisicioli, 'Coercion and Choice: The "Traffic in Women" between France and Argentina in the Early Twentieth Century', *French Historical Studies*, vol. 42, no. 3, 2019, pp. 483–507.

19 Southwark Diocesan Association, Outdoor Rescue Work in Lambeth Casebook, p. 26, London, LMA, ACC2201/H3/3/1.

20 Letter from Miss MacDougall to Lavinia Talbot re obit. for Miss Hogg, London, LMA, ACC 2201/B22/1/7.

21 MacDougall, as cited in M. Penelope Hall and Ismene V. Howes, *The Church in Social Work: A study of moral welfare work undertaken by the Church of England* (Abingdon, 1965), p. 39.

22 April Haynes, paper given to the Berkshire Conference of Women Historians, June 2017; see also April Haynes, *Tender Traffic: Intimate Labors in the Early American Republic* (forthcoming).

23 Constance Tite, 'Is Rescue Work a Failure?', *The Shield*, vol. 3, October 1916.

24 International Bureau for the Suppression of the White Slave Traffic in Argentina (correspondence with Rosalie Lighton Robinson), London, The Women's Library, 4IBS/6/001 FL112.

25 Minutes of Evidence, Select Committee on Assaults on Young Persons, Friday 5 December 1924, London, TNA, HO 45/25434.

26 Police Home for Women Annual Report (London, 1911).

27 Ibid., p. 48.

28 Minutes of Evidence, Select Committee on Assaults on Young Persons, Friday 5 December 1924, London, TNA, HO 45/25434. For more on reporting sexual violence in the newspapers, see Daniel Grey, '"Monstrous and Indefensible"? Newspaper Accounts of Sexual Assaults on Children in Nineteenth-Century England and Wales', in *Women's Criminality: Patterns and Variations in Europe, 1600–1914*, ed. Manon van der Heijen, Marion Pluskota and Sanne Muurling (Cambridge, 2020).

29 Report of Detective Inspector Anderson, 22 July 1910, London, TNA, MEPO 3/197.

30 Francis Finnegan, *Do Penance or Perish: A Study of Magdelene Asylums in Ireland* (Kilkenny, 2001).

31 Police Home for Women Annual Report (London, 1912).

32 Erika Rappaport, *Shopping for Pleasure: Women in the Making of London's West End* (Princeton, NJ, and Oxford, 2000), p. 125.

33 Minutes of Evidence, Select Committee on Assaults on Young Persons, Friday 5 December 1924, London, TNA, HO 45/25434.

34 Executive committee notes from the Outdoor Rescue Work committee, Lambeth, 1905–11, London, LMA, ACC 2201 H3/4/1.

35 Eilidh MacDougall, 'The Administration of the Law', paper read at a private conference of rescue workers arranged by the NUWW, Lincoln, 12 October 1910.

36 *Daily Telegraph and Courier*, Tuesday 13 September 1910.

37 *The Common Cause*, vol. 2, no. 83, 10 November 1910.

38 Minutes of Evidence, Select Committee on Assaults on Young Persons, Friday 5 December 1924, London, TNA, HO 45/25434.

39 Jackson, *Child Sexual Abuse*, p. 3.

40 1910 Police Home for Women Annual Report (London, 1911).

41 Ibid.

42 1916 Police Home for Women Annual Report (London, 1917).

43 Police commissioner Edward Henry to the Home Office, 17 June 1914, London, TNA, MEPO 3/5561.

44 Kim Stevenson, 'These Are Crimes Which Are Inadvisable to Drag into the Light of Day: Disinterring the Crime of Incest in Early Twentieth Century England', *Crime, Histoire et Societes/ Crime, History and Societies*, 2016, pp. 15, 27.

45 Victoria Bates, *Sexual Forensics in Victorian and Edwardian England: Age, Crime and Consent in the Courts* (Basingstoke, 2016); Kim Stevenson, 'Unequivocal Victims: The Historical Mystification of the Female Complainant in Rape Cases', *Feminist Legal Studies*, vol. 8, 2000, pp. 346–66; Kim Stevenson, '"Crimes of Moral Outrage": Victorian Encryptions of Sexual Violence", in *Criminal Conversations: Victorian Crimes, Social Panic, and Moral Outrage*, ed. Judith Rowbotham and Kim Stevenson (Ohio, 2005).

46 Jackson, *Child Sexual Abuse*, p. 16.

47 Eilidh MacDougall to Police Commission Edward Henry, 1917, London, LMA, ACC2201/B22/4/20.

48 1932 Police Home for Women Annual Report (London, 1933).

49 Louise Jackson, *Women Police: Gender, Welfare and Surveillance in the Twentieth Century* (Manchester, 2006).

50 Dorothy Peto, *The Memoirs of Miss Dorothy Olivia Georgiana Peto, OBE* (London, 1993), p. 4.

51 Wyles, *A Woman at Scotland Yard*, p. 104.

52 Ibid., p. 121.

53 Rosalie Lighton Robinson to F. R. Sempkins, 26 November 1930, London, The Women's Library, 4IBS/6/001 FL112.

54 Treasurer of Buenos Aires NVA to F. R. Sempkins, Lighton

Robinson to Sempkins 1931 (n.d.), London, The Women's Library, 4IBS/6/001 FL112.

55 1919 Police Home for Women Annual Report in London, TNA, ACC/22/01/B22/6.

56 Police commissioner Edward Henry, 17 June 1914, to the Home Office, London, TNA, MEPO 3/5561.

57 Regina G. Kunzel, *Fallen Women, Problem Girls, Unmarried Mothers and the Professionalization of Social Work, 1890–1945* (New Haven, CT, and London, 1993); Carolyn Taylor, 'Humanitarian Narrative: Bodies and Detail in Late-Victorian Social Work', *British Journal of Social Work*, vol. 34, no. 4, 2008, pp. 680–96.

58 Letter from MC to police commissioner, 10 November 1932, London, TNA, MEPO 3/5561.

59 Lillian Wyles to the Commissioner of Police, 18 June 1934, London, TNA, MEPO 2/5561.

60 Memorandum from Dorothy Peto, 9 January 1934, London, TNA, MEPO 2/5561.

61 Peto, *Memoirs*, p. 4.

62 Wyles, *A Woman at Scotland Yard*, p. 104.

63 Minutes of Evidence, Select Committee on Assaults on Young Persons, Friday 5 December 1924, London, TNA, HO 45/25434.

64 Letter from Winnifred MacDougall to Miss Robinson of the Southwark Diocesan Association, London, LMA ACC2201/B22/1/3.

65 Letter from Winnifred MacDougall to Miss Robinson of the Southwark Diocesan Association, London, LMA ACC2201/B22/1/3.

66 Miss Robinson to Winnifred Hadfield, 24 March 1954, LMA, ACC2201/B22/1/1.

Chapter 5: The Dancing Master

1 Archivio centrale dello Stato Roma, Casellario Politico Centrale, di Nicotera, Alessandro, b.1729.

2   Stephen Hobhouse and Fenner Brockway, *English Prisons Today* (London, 1922), p. 356.

3   'Alex' to Marguerite Dennis, undated, Wellington, Archives New Zealand, AAAJ W3289 6813 Box 9, CR 13/26.

4   Birth certificate of Antonio Adolfo Carvelli, 13 February 1879; Nascita, citing Torino, Torino, Italy, entry 432, Tribunale di Torino [Torino Court, Torino]; FHL microfilm 2,334,846. Marriage certificate of Luigi Carvelli and Maria Courrier, Certificato di Matrimonio, 8 August 1878, Verona, Italy.

5   Edmondo De Amicis, *La città*, in *Torino* (Turin, 1880), pp. 40–41.

6   I draw this description from De Amicis's novel *Cuore, or Heart: A Schoolboy's Journal*, which is set in the fictional Baretti school in San Salvario, Turin, in 1886. Edmondo de Amicis, *Heart: A School-Boy's Journal*, trans. Isabel J. Hapgood (Amsterdam, 2003), p. 3.

7   In other places it says these were published in 1894: but fifteen is still a fine age to be reading adventure novels. 'Emilio Salgari', *Encyclopaedia of Italian Literary Studies*, ed. Gaetana Marrone and Paolo Puppa (London, 2006), pp. 1654–5. Later Salgari would write for younger readers, but the first novels were for an adult audience.

8   Albert Londres, *Le Chemin de Buenos-Aires* (Paris, 1927), p. 45.

9   Ben L. Reitman, *The Second Oldest Profession* (London, 1936), p. 36.

10 Mark Seymour, *Debating Divorce in Italy: Marriage and the Making of Modern Italians, 1860–1974* (Basingstoke, 2006).

11 Furti, Informazione Varie, Cara-Cav; Questore di Torino, 1898–1906, Turin, Archivio di Stato di Torino, box 175. With many thanks to the archivist Silvia Corino at the Archivio di Stato for help with the translation and orthography.

12 Silvana Patriarca, *Italian Vices: Nation and Character from the Risorgimento to the Republic* (Cambridge, 2010), chapter 1. On other aspects of Italian sexuality and morality, see Valeria

P. Babini, Chiara Beccalossi and Lucy Riall, *Italian Sexualities Uncovered, 1789–1914* (London, 2015).

13 On the military, volunteerism and masculinity, see Lucy Riall, 'Men at War: Masculinity and Military Ideals in the Risorgimento', in Silvana Patriarca and Lucy Riall (eds), *The Risorgimento Revisited: Nationalism and Culture in Nineteenth Century Italy* (Basingstoke and New York, 2012), pp. 152–70.

14 Frank Mort, *Dangerous Sexualities: Medico-Moral Politics in England since 1830*, 2nd edn (London, 2000).

15 Mary Gibson, *Prostitution and the State in Italy, 1860–1915* (New Brunswick and London, 1986). After some attempts to scale back or abolish regulation, it was reinstated by Mussolini in 1923.

16 For other examples of state regulation, see Alain Corbin, *Women for Hire: Prostitution and Sexuality in France after 1850* (London, 1990).

17 Police Notebook, *c.*1898, Charles Booth Survey Documents, London, LSE Archives, B358, 371 138–140; Summary Report of District Superintendents, 24 June 1909, London, TNA, MEPO 2/1287. For more references to ex-servicemen as pimps, see Report of B division, 28 August 1933, MEPO 3/769.

18 Mary S. Gibson, 'The Criminalization of Youth in Late Nineteenth- and Early Twentieth-Century Italy', in *Crime, Punishment and Reform in Europe*, ed. Louis A. Knafla (Westport, CT, and London, 2003), pp. 121–44 (p. 125).

19 Gina Lombroso-Ferrero, *Criminal Man: According to the Classification of Cesare Lombroso* (London, 1911).

20 'Mandato di Arresto', Questore di Torino, in London, TNA, MEPO 3/197.

21 Samuel L. Bailey, *Immigrants in the Land of Plenty: Italians in Buenos Aires and New York City, 1870–1914* (Ithaca, NY, 1999); Donna R. Gabaccia, *Italy's Many Diasporas* (London, 2000); Donna Gabaccia, Franca Iacovetta and Fraser Ottanelli, 'Laboring across National Borders: Class, Gender, and

Militancy in the Proletarian Mass Migrations', *International Labor and Working-Class History*, no. 66, 2010.

22 Gunther Peck, *Reinventing Free Labor: Padrones and Immigrant Workers in the North American West, 1880–1930* (Cambridge, 2000).

23 Gabaccia, *Italy's Many Diasporas*.

24 Mark Choate, *Emigrant Nation: The Making of Italy Abroad* (Cambridge, MA, 2008).

25 James Jupp, *From White Australia to Woomera: The Story of Australian Immigration*, 2nd edn (Cambridge, 2007), p. 9; Frances, 'Sex Workers or Citizens?' 127–41

26 Carlotta Sorba, 'The Origins of the Entertainment Industry: the Operetta in Late Nineteenth-Century Italy', *Journal of Modern Italian Studies*, vol. 11, no. 3, 2006, pp. 282–302.

27 Alison Gyger, *Opera in the Antipodes: Opera in Australia, 1881–1939* (Sydney, 1990), pp. 107–17.

28 Cecil Bishop, *From Information Received* (London, 1932), p. 49.

29 *Evening News*, 2 May 1901, p. 6.

30 Carvelli, Australian criminal record, London, TNA, MEPO 3/197.

31 Londres, *The Road to Buenos Aires*, p. 45.

32 Robert Pascoe and Patrick Bertola, 'Italian Miners and the Second-Generation "Britishers" at Kalgoorlie, Australia', *Social History*, vol. 10, no. 1, 1985, pp. 9–35.

33 *The West Australian*, 19 November 1904, p. 8; *The Daily News*, 11 November 1904, p. 10; *The West Australian*, 5 November 1904, p. 10.

34 *The Daily News*, Tuesday 8 August 1905, p. 1.

35 On Italian masculinity in this era, see Charlotte Ross, 'Critical Approaches to Gender and Sexuality in Italian Culture and Society', *Journal of Modern Italian Studies*, vol. 65, no. 2, 2010, pp. 164–77; Mark Seymour, 'Contesting Masculinity in Post-Unification Italy: The Murder of Captain Giovanni Fadda', *Gender & History*, vol. 25, no. 2, August 2013, pp. 252–69; Steven C. Hughes, *Politics of the Sword: Dueling, Honor and*

Masculinity in Modern Italy (Columbus, 2007); Suzanne Stewart-Steinberg, *The Pinocchio Effect: On Making Italians, 1860–1920* (Chicago, 2008).

36 I discovered this after asking an archivist at the University of Turin to search the student records. No one by the name of Antonio Carvelli had ever taken a degree there.

37 'A Brief History of Gwalia and the Sons of Gwalia Mine', www. leonora.wa.gov.au/a-brief-history-of-gwalia-and-the-sons-of-gwalia-mine.aspx (accessed16 July 2018).

38 Lenore Layman and Criena Fitzgerald (eds), *110° in the Waterbag: A History of Life, Work and Leisure in Leonora, Gwalia and the Northern Goldfields* (Perth, 2011).

39 For a brief mention of the market for bought sex among Italian male émigrés, see Gabaccia, *Italy's Many Diasporas*, p. 86.

40 *Truth* (Sydney), 14 June 1925.

41 Reitman, *The Second Oldest Profession*, p. 36.

42 Layman and Fitzgerald, *110° in the Waterbag*, p. 14.

43 *Kalgoorlie Miner (WA)*, Friday 4 December 1908, p. 2.

44 For later tensions between Anglo miners and Italians, see Pascoe and Bertola, 'Italian Miners'.

45 *Kalgoorlie Miner* (WA), Tuesday 27 October 1908, p. 4.

46 Including *The Mercury* (Hobart), Saturday 31 October 1908, p. 3; *The Argus* (Melbourne), 28 October 1908, p. 8; and the *Chronicle* (Adelaide), Saturday 31 October 1908, p. 38, which did not clock that Cellis was actually Carvelli, the 'hotel barber' from seven years prior.

47 *Kalgoorlie Western Argus* (WA), Tuesday 10 November 1908, p. 9.

48 'Arcadia Private Hotel' advertisement, The Pamphlet Collection of Sir Robert Stout, vol. 78, p. 141, Victoria University of Wellington Library, Wellington; nzetc.victoria.ac.nz/tm/scholarly/Stout78-fig-Stout78P009150a.html.

49 National Archives in Washington, DC, Records of the Immigration and Naturalization Service, 1897–1957, Record Group 85, Passenger and Crew Lists of Vessels Arriving at

New York, NY, 1897–1957, microform publication T715, roll 254, p. 274, line 17; p. 278, line 4; Belgium, Antwerp Police Immigration Index, 1840–1930, 5, www.ancestry.com (accessed 18 July 2017).

50 Report of the Prefettura di Milano, 8 December 1906, Archivio centrale dello Stato Roma, Casellario Politico Centrale, di Nicotera, Alessandro, b.1729.

51 *New Zealand Truth* clipping, White Slave Traffic – Procuring Girls for Prostitution – issuing forged 10 pound notes, Wellington, Archives New Zealand. [AAAJ 6813 W3289/9 CR 13/26] (R22342274).

52 Report of Detective W. E. Lewis, Wellington, 7 July 1910, London, TNA, MEPO 3/197.

53 Bronwyn Dalley, 'Lolly Shops "of the Red-Light Kind" and "Soldiers of the King"', *New Zealand History*, vol. 30, no. 1, 1996, pp. 3–24 (pp. 6–7).

54 *Trafficking in Women 1924–1926: The Paul Kinsie Reports for the League of Nations, Vol. I*, ed. Jean-Michel Chaumont, Magaly Rodríguez García and Paul Servais (Geveva, 2017), p. 33.

55 'Our History', Club Garibaldi web site, www.clubgaribaldi.org.nz/history/ (accessed 14 December 2018).

56 New Zealand Marriage Certificate, Veronique Sarah White and Antonio Aldo Carvelli, 27 January 1910, Registrar of Births, Deaths and Marriages New Zealand, Registration number 1910000969.

57 Loose image, Archives New Zealand, Wellington, AAAJ W3289 6813 Box 9, CR 13/26.

58 Scobie, *Buenos Aires*, p. 17.

59 Ibid., pp. 25, 35.

60 Bergero, *Intersecting Tango*, p. 25.

61 *Report of the Special Body of Experts on the Traffic in Women and Children* (Geneva, 1927).

62 Chaumont, Rodríguez García and Servais, *Trafficking in Women*, p. 33.

63 Ibid., p. 37.

64 Judith R. Walkowitz, *Nights Out: Life in Cosmopolitan London* (Princeton and Oxford, 2012), pp. 17–42.

65 Report of C Division, 18 May 1910, London, TNA, MEPO 3/197.

66 Max Kassel's story is retold by Frank 'Nutty' Sharpe in his police autobiography, *Sharpe of the Flying Squad*, pp. 88–106. See also London, TNA, MEPO 3/795.

67 Chaumont, Rodríguez García and Servais, *Trafficking in Women*, p. 151.

68 1911 Census of England and Wales, 40 Wells Street, schedule 229.

69 Witness statement of Lydia Rhoda Harvey, 9 July 1910, London, TNA, MEPO 3/197.

70 On sore feet and walking to solicit in London, see Marthe Watts, *The Men in My Life* (London, 1960), p. 42.

71 Londres, *The Road to Buenos Aires*.

72 Witness statement of Lydia Rhoda Harvey, 9 July 1910, London, TNA, MEPO 3/197.

73 'South Coast Municipal Orchestras, I, Brighton', *The Musical Times,* vol. 50, no. 796, 1 June 1909, pp. 379–81.

74 Brighton Municipal Orchestra programme, week of 8 February 1908, The Keep, Brighton, Brighton Pamphlet Box 21c 1b.

75 For Italian restaurants in Soho, see Walkowitz, *Nights Out: Life in Cosmopolitan London*, pp. 92–143.

76 Aldo Cellis and Alexander Berard Criminal Trial, Old Bailey Online, ref. t19100906–76.

77 London & River Plate Bank to Scotland Yard, 25 January 1911, London, TNA, MEPO 3/197.

78 *The Sunday Times* (Perth), 17 September 1911, p. 1.

79 Ibid.

80 Police report, 15 October 1915, Wellington, Archives New Zealand, AAAJ W3289 6813 Box 9, CR 13/26.

81 Gillian Abel et al., *Taking the Crime out of Sex Work: New Zealand Sex Workers' Fight for Decriminalisation* (Bristol, 2010).

82 Karen Agutter, 'Belligerent Broken Hill', *History Australia*, vol.

8, no. 2, 2011, pp. 36–59; Brian (Brian Ernest) Kennedy, *Silver, Sin, and Sixpenny Ale: A Social History of Broken Hill, 1883–1921* (Carlton, Victoria, 1978).

83 *The Truth* (Melbourne), 7 March 1925, clipping from 'Cellis and Berard – White Slavery Suspects', Australian National Archives, 1926/20254, n.p.

84 Carvelli, *Albo dei Caduti Italiani della Grande Guerra*, www.cadutigrandeguerra.it/ (accessed 18 December 2018).

85 Paul Bleakley, 'Six o'Clock Closing and the Growth of Prostitution in Sydney, 1916–27', *Journal of the Royal Australian Historical Society*, vol. 100, no. 2, 2014, pp. 176–93.

86 'One-woman brothels in Hobson St Auckland, 1910–1915', Wellington, Archives New Zealand, P1300, 1915/1032.

87 Guy, *Sex & Danger in Buenos Aires*, p. 142.

88 Martínez Estrada writing in 1933, as cited in ibid., p. 154.

89 Report of DI Gleeson, 2 March 1925, Melbourne, National Archives of Australia, NAA: A1, 1926/20254.

90 91 AR, 19 November 1926, 'Cellis and Berard – White Slavery Suspects', Canberra, Australian National Archives, 1926/20254.

91 *Smith's Weekly News*, 7 March 1925, clipping from 'Cellis and Berard – White Slavery Suspects', Canberra, Australian National Archives, 1926/20254, n.p.

92 Barbara Brookes and Catherine Smith, 'Styling Gender: From Barber Shops and Ladies' Hairdressers to the Unisex Salon, 1920–1970', *New Zealand Journal of History*, vol. 51, no. 1, 2017, pp. 184–207.

93 *Smith's Weekly News*, 7 March 1925, and *The Truth* (Melbourne), 7 March 1925, clippings from 'Cellis and Berard – White Slavery Suspects', Canberra, Australian National Archives, 1926/20254, n.p.

94 *The Truth* (Queensland), 15 March 1925; *Smith's Weekly News*, 7 March 1925.

Chapter 6: The Woman Unknown

1 Sarah Jane Daley and Frederick Soutten White, *Australia,*

Marriage Index, 1788–1950, 1875, 395 [database online]. Provo, UT, USA: Ancestry.com Operations Inc., 2010.

2   Sarah Jane Daley, Class: H0107; Piece: 2407; Folio: 86; Page: 44; GSU roll: 87085, Ancestry.com. 1851 England Census [database online]. Provo, UT, USA: Ancestry.com Operations Inc., 2005; Sarah Daley, Inward Overseas Passenger Lists (British Ports). Microfiche VPRS 7666, copy of VRPS 947. Public Record Office Victoria, North Melbourne, Victoria.

3   Victoria Peel, Deborah Zion and Jane Yule, *A History of Hawthorn* (Melbourne, 1993), p. 52.

4   Ibid., p. 51.

5   Ibid., pp. 136, 212.

6   *The Australasian* (Melbourne, 1864–1946), Saturday 16 December 1893, p. 34.

7   Peel, Zion and Yule, *A History of Hawthorn*, p. 79.

8   Angela Woollacott, *To Try Her Fortune in London: Australian Women, Colonialism, and Modernity* (Oxford, 2001), p. 207.

9   With thanks to Peter and Mary Brady of 36 George Street, Fitzroy.

10 *Sands & McDougall's Directory*, 1905 (Melbourne, 1905), pp. 281–2, 288, 293; *The Outcasts of Melbourne: Essays in Social History*, ed. Graeme Davison, David Dunstan and Chris McConville (Melbourne, 1985); Chris McConville, 'The Location of Melbourne's Prostitutes, 1870–1920', *Historical Studies*, vol. 19, no. 74, 1980, pp. 86–97.

11 Frederick Soutten White et al., 36 George Street, Fitzroy, *Australia, Electoral Rolls, 1903–1980* Ancestry.com (accessed 15 January 2018).

12 Teresa Billington-Greig, 'The Truth about White Slavery', *The English Review*, June 1913, pp. 428–46. For 'white slavery' in an Australian context, see Raelene Frances, *Selling Sex: A Hidden History of Prostitution* (Sydney, 2007), pp. 178–97.

13 Billington-Greig, 'The Truth about White Slavery'.

14 Susan Margery, 'Sexual Labour: Australia 1880–1910', in *Debutante Nation: Feminism Contests the 1890s* (St Leonards,

NSW, 1993), p. 91; Russel Ward, *The Australian Legend* (Melbourne, 1958).

15 Louise Mack, *An Australian Girl in London*, 1902, as cited in Woollacott, *To Try Her Fortune in London*, p. 3.

16 Alys Eve Weinbaum et al., 'The Modern Girl as Heuristic Device: Collaboration, Connective Comparison, Multidirectional Citation', in *The Modern Girl Around the World*, ed. Alys Eve Weinbaum et al. (Durham and London, 2008), pp. 1–24 (p. 18).

17 For more on the reality and representation of child sexual abuse in Australia and elsewhere, see Andy Kaladelfos and Lisa Featherstone, 'Sexual Assault by Teachers: Historical, Legislative, Policy and Prosecutorial Responses', in *The Sexual Abuse of Children: Recognition and Redress*, ed. Yorick Smaal, Andy Kaladelfos and Mark Finnane (Clayton, Victoria, 2016), pp. 20–34; Shurlee Swain, 'Narratives of Innocence and Seduction: Historical Understandings of Child Sexual Abuse in Australia', in *The Sexual Abuse of Children*, ed. Smaal, Kaladelfos and Finnane, pp. 32–9.

18 *Wise Directory*, Western Australia, 1904, p. 684; *Wise Directory*, Western Australia, 1902, p. 578, *Wise Directory*, Western Australia, 1910, p. 578.

19 Gail Reekie, 'The Sexual Politics of Selling and Shopping', in *Debutante Nation: Feminism Contests the 1890s*, ed. Susan Magarey, Sue Rowely and Susan Sheridan (St Leonards, NSW, 1993), pp. 59–70 (p. 65).

20 McNess Royal Arcade, *Heritage Perth*, heritageperth.com.au/properties/mcness-royal-arcade/ (accessed 6 June 2019).

21 *New Zealand Police Gazette*, 29 September 1909; Anita Boyd, 'The Private and Public Life of Nellie Stewart's Bangle', *Journal of Popular Romance Studies*, vol. 4, no. 2, 2014.

22 Australian Heritage Commission, 'Linking a Nation: Australia's Transport and Communications 1788–1970', *Australia: Our national stories; A research series on significant themes in Australia's history*; web.archive.org/web/20080229151856/;

www.ahc.gov.au/publications/linking-nation/chapter-5.
html#western (accessed 6 June 2019).

23 Unattributed, *The Dangers of False Prudery*, p. 58.

24 Maude Royden, 'Downward Paths: An Inquiry into the Causes
Which Contribute to the Making of the Prostitute' (London,
1916); Laite, *Common Prostitutes and Ordinary Citizens*, chapter 2.

25 G. P. Merrick, *Work among the Fallen as Seen from the Prison
Cell* (London, 1890); Mary Chesterton, *Women of the
Underworld* (London, 1928); Mary Higgs, *Glimpses into the
Abyss* (London, 1906).

26 Shurlee Swain and Renate Howe, *Single Mothers and Their
Children: Disposal, Punishment and Survival in Australia*
(Cambridge, 1995). For an overview on the history of sexuality
in Australia, see Frank Bongiorno, *The Sex Lives of Australians:
A History* (Collingwood, Victoria, 2012).

27 Stead, 'The Maiden Tribute of Modern Babylon, Part II', *Pall
Mall Gazette*, 1885.

28 L. Featherstone, 'Rethinking Female Pleasure: Purity and desire
in early twentieth-century Australia', *Women's History Review*,
vol. 2, no. 5, 2012, pp. 715–31. Ellen Warne, 'Sex Education
Debates and the Modest Mother in Australia, 1890s to the
1930s', *Women's History Review*, vol. 8, no. 2, 1999, pp. 311–27.

29 Warne, 'Sex Education Debates', pp. 311–27 (p. 311).

30 *The Sun* (Kalgoorlie), 8 April 1900, p. 3.

31 *The Sun* (Kalgoorlie), 15 April 1900, p. 3.

32 Raelene Frances, 'Australian Prostitution in International
Context', *Australian Historical Studies*, vol. 27, no. 106, 1996,
pp. 127–42.

33 Julia Laite, 'Historical Perspectives on Industrial Development,
Mining and Prostitution', *Historical Journal*, vol. 52, 2009,
pp. 739–61.

34 Advertisement, *Leonora Postal Directory*, 1908, p. 218.

35 Layman and Fitzgerald, *110° in the Waterbag*.

36 *Leonora Postal Directory*, 1908, pp. 218–19.

37 May Vivienne, *Travels in Western Australia* (London, 1901), p. 285.

38 I draw these attitudes from those recorded in Rosalind Wilkinson, *Women of the Streets: A Sociological Study of the Common Prostitute*, ed. C. H. Rolphe (London, 1955).

39 *Kalgoorlie Miner*, 22 February 1909, p. 2.

40 *Kalgoorlie Miner*, 23 July 1909, p. 4.

41 *Leonora Postal Directory*, 1908, p. 219.

42 *Evening Star*, 25 March 1908, p. 3.

43 Frederick Southon [*sic*] White, 28 Jolimont Terrace, 1913, Australia, Electoral Rolls, 1903–80 Ancestry.com (accessed 14 January 2018).

44 Raelene Frances, *The Politics of Work: Gender and Labour in Victoria 1880–1939* (Cambridge, 1994), chapter 4.

45 *Kalgoorlie Miner*, 27 October 1908, p. 4.

46 *New Zealand Police Gazette*, 26 September 1909.

47 *Truth* (New Zealand), 3 September 1910, p. 3.

48 *New Zealand Police Gazette*, 26 September 1909.

49 Loose photograph in Wellington, Archives New Zealand, AAAJ W3289 6813 Box 9, CR 13/26.

50 Veronique Sarah White and Antonio Aldo Carvelli, New Zealand marriage certificate, 27 January 1910, 1910000969.

51 'Meteorological', *Wairarapa Daily Times*, 28 January 1910; *Melbourne Argus*, 2 April 1910, p. 13.

52 Steel, *Oceania Under Steam*, pp. 50–57.

53 Julia Laite, 'Between Scylla and Charybdis: Women's Labour Migration and Sex Trafficking in the Early Twentieth Century', *International Review of Social History*, vol. 62, no. 1, 2017, pp. 37–65.

54 Bergero, *Intersecting Tango*, pp. 22, 24, 36, 51, 71, 77.

55 Ibid.

56 Lydia Harvey Witness Statement, 13 July 1910; and Report of Inspector Anderson, 1 July 1910, London, TNA, MEPO 3/197.

57 Edward C. Ramsay, 'The Psittacosis Outbreak of 1929–1930', *Journal of Avian Medicine and Surgery*, vol. 17, no. 4, 2003,

pp. 235–7. The most popular bird for sale in Argentina in this period was the monk parakeet, which was native to the country, so I am making an educated guess here.

58 Lydia Harvey Witness Statement, 13 July 1910, London, TNA, MEPO 3/197.

59 Lydia Harvey Witness Statement, 13 July 1910, London, TNA, MEPO 3/197; for more on brothels in Buenos Aires, see Guy, *Sex & Danger in Buenos Aires.*

60 *The Times*, 11 July 1910, p. 17.

61 'One-woman brothels in Hobson St Auckland, 1910–1915', Wellington, Archives New Zealand, P1300, 10=915/1032; see also Dalley, 'Lolly Shops "of the Red-Light Kind"', pp. 3–24; *New Zealand Herald*, 2 March 1912, p. 3.

62 *New Zealand Herald*, 15 June 1912, p. 3.

63 *Auckland Star,* 18 January 1913, p. 3; Wellington Police to Inspector General of Police, Sydney, 15 October 1912, Wellington, Archives New Zealand, AAAJ W3289 6813 Box 9, CR 13/26.

64 'Scholefield, Guy Hardy', *Te Ara – The Encyclopaedia of New Zealand*, teara.govt.nz/en/biographies/4s12/scholefield-guy-hardy (accessed 5 June 2019).

65 Bronwyn Dalley, '"Come Back with Honour": Prostitution and the New Zealand Soldier, at Home and Abroad', John Crawford and Ian McGibbon (eds.), *New Zealand's Great War: New Zealand, the Allies, and the First World War* (Auckland, 2007), pp. 364–77.

66 Katherine Sanders, '"The Sensational Scandal Which Has Worried Wellington": The Kelburn Raid, Sex, and the Law in First World War New Zealand"', *New Zealand Journal of History*, vol. 48, no. 2, 2014, pp. 91–118.

67 As cited by Dalley, 'Lolly Shops "of the Red-Light Kind"', p. 19; Nicholas Boyack, *Behind the Lines: The Lives of New Zealand Soldiers in the First World War* (Wellington, 1989), pp. 131–46; Jock Phillips, *A Man's Country! The Image of the Pakeha Male*

(Auckland, 1987), pp. 187–92; Tolerton, p. 12, cited by Dalley, 'Lolly Shops "of the Red-Light Kind"', p. 13.

68 Superintendent Ellison, 1915, as cited by Dalley, 'Lolly Shops "of the Red-Light Kind"', p. 13.

69 Dalley, 'Lolly Shops "of the Red-Light Kind"', fn. 9, p. 5; *Evening Post*, 27 May 1916.

70 Dalley, 'Lolly Shops "of the Red-Light Kind"', p. 16.

71 Ibid., p. 22.

72 *New Zealand Herald*, 28 May 1917.

73 Dalley, 'Lolly Shops "of the Red-Light Kind"', p. 317.

74 Carvelli Veronique [Veronica]: Nationality – Italian: First registered at Sydney, Canberra, National Archives of Australia, MT269/1.

75 'Hobart' in *The Companion to Tasmanian History*, www.utas. edu.au/library/companion_to_tasmanian_history/H/Hobart. htm (accessed 29 June 2020).

76 *News* (Hobart), Monday 5 January 1925, p. 5; Wednesday 14 January 1925, p. 6.

77 *News* (Hobart), Tuesday 20 January 1925, p. 4.

78 Ibid.

79 Ibid.

80 Ibid.

81 Memorandum 19/11/26; Assistant Secretary F. J. Quinlan, Australian Home Department, to Antonio Carvelli c/o General Cornaro, 23 November 1926, 'Cellis and Berard – White Slavery Suspects', Canberra, Australian National Archives, 1926/20254.

82 'Antonio Carvelli', Certificato di Morte, Citta' di Genoa, 8 Nervi, Part I, series 83, Casellario Politico Centrale, Rome, Archivio Centrale dello Stato, Carvelli Antonio Adolfo, b.1122.

83 For more on this, see Harriet J. Mercer, 'Citizens of Empire and Nation: Australian Women's Quest for Independent Nationality Rights 1910s–1930s', *History Australia*, vol. 13, no. 2, 2016, pp. 213–27. Dorothy Page, 'A married woman, or a minor, lunatic or idiot: the struggle of British women against disability in nationality, 1914–1933', thesis submitted for the degree of

Doctor of Philosophy at the University of Otago, Dunedin, New Zealand, 1984.

84 Report of Constable J. Neeham, 27 June 1938, Archives New Zealand, Wellington, Naturalization – Application for – Carvelli, Veronique Sara Mrs, 1A12295; 115/210.

85 Veronique Carvelli to Department of Internal Affairs, 7 August 1938, Archives New Zealand, Wellington, Naturalization – Application for – Carvelli, Veronique Sara Mrs, 1A12295; 115/210.

86 Woollacott, *To Try Her Fortune in London*, p. 215.

Chapter 7: The Sailor's Wife

1 *Oamaru Mail*, 22 July 1910, p. 4.

2 Sergeant Stagpool to Wellington Police Department, 16 August 1910, Wellington, Archives New Zealand, AAAJ W3289 6813 Box 9, CR 13/26.

3 *The Vigilance Record*, April 1911, p. 27.

4 Report of Detective Lewis, 2 August 1910, Wellington, Archives New Zealand, AAAJ W3289 6813 Box 9, CR 13/26.

5 Ibid.

6 See, for instance, the *Marlborough Express*, 2 September 1910, p. 6; New Zealand Parliamentary debates, v.151, 1910, p. 134.

7 Redmer Yska, *Truth: The Rise and Fall of the People's Paper* (Nelson, NZ, 2010), p. 19.

8 *Truth* (New Zealand), 3 September 1910, p. 3.

9 William Hall-Jones, high commissioner, to New Zealand Department of Justice, 16 September 1910, Wellington, Archives New Zealand, AAAJ W3289 6813 Box 9, CR 13/26.

10 From the Undersecretary for the Department of Justice, Wellington, to William Hall-Jones, high commissioner, 21 September 1910, Wellington, Archives New Zealand, AAAJ W3289 6813 Box 9, CR 13/26.

11 Confidential cablegram, 15 September 1910, Wellington, Archives New Zealand, AAAJ W3289 6813 Box 9, CR 13/26.

12 F. S. Bullock to Undersecretary of State, NZ, 30 August 1910,

Wellington, Archives New Zealand, AAAJ W3289 6813 Box 9, CR 13/26.

13 International Agreement for the suppression of the 'White Slave Traffic', Paris, 18 May 1904, United Nations Treaty Collection, treaties.un.org/Pages/ViewDetails. aspx?src=TREATY&mtdsg_no=VII-8&chapter=7&clang=_en#3 (accessed 5 June 2019).

14 Report of Inspector Anderson, 24 September 1910, London, TNA, MEPO 3/197.

15 *The Times*, 30 September 1910, p. 1.

16 Undated National Vigilance Association Report, London, MEPO, 3/197.

17 Ibid.

18 Passenger list for RMS *Tainui*, 14 October 1910, Passenger Lists leaving UK 1890–1960, London, TNA, BT27; on FindMyPast. co.uk (accessed 5 June 2019).

19 'New Zealand wants Domestic Servants', Government Poster, *c.*1912, *Te Ara – The Encyclopaedia of New Zealand*, teara.govt. nz/en/ephemera/21778/new-zealand-wants-domestic-servants (accessed 5 June 2019); John E. Martin, *Holding the Balance: A History of New Zealand's Department of Labour, 1891–1995* (Christchurch, NZ, 1996), p. 109.

20 I take this description of a ward maid's work from oral histories used in Linda MacDowell, *Migrant Women's Voices: Talking About Life and Work in the UK Since 1945* (London, 2016).

21 Guy, *Sex & Danger*.

22 For more on the systematic way in which rescue organisations and other women's organisations shuttled 'rescued' women into domestic service, see Haynes, *Tender Traffic* (forthcoming).

23 *Truth* (New Zealand), 6 March 1909, p. 4. See also Macdonald, 'Why Was There No Answer to the "Servant Problem"?'

24 *Oamaru Mail*, 29 May 1911; 6 February 1912.

25 Richard Waterhouse, 'Minstrel Show and Vaudeville House: The Australian Popular Stage, 1838–1914', *Australian Historical Studies*, vol. 23, no. 93, 1989, pp. 366–85 (p. 380).

26 Ibid., p. 369.

27 Clay Djubal, 'Entrepreneurs', in 'Australian Variety Theatre Archive: Popular Culture Entertainment, 1850–1930', www. ozvta.com (accessed 3 March 2020).

28 *Daily Post*, 1 September 1911, p. 4.

29 'V. Bricot', 21 September 1911, New South Wales, Australia, Unassisted Immigrant Passenger Lists, 1826–1922 Ancestry.com (accessed 20 February 2020).

30 Report of Senior Sergeant Stagpool, Police Station, Oamaru, 20 October 1911, Wellington, Archives New Zealand, AAAJ W3289 6813 Box 9, CR 13/26.

31 Ibid.

32 Report of Mount Count police station, 20 August 1915, and 'Alec to Marguerite', 12 December 1912, Wellington, Archives New Zealand, AAAJ W3289 6813 Box 9, CR 13/26.

33 Herbert Ockenden and Lydia Rhoda Harvey, New South Wales Marriage Certificate, 27 July 1915, 8613/1915.

34 Inspector General of Police, Sydney, to the Commissioner of Police, Wellington, 14 October 1914, Wellington, Archives New Zealand, AAAJ W3289 6813 Box 9, CR 13/26.

35 For more on this, see Steel, *Oceania Under Steam*, pp. 85–90.

36 Boris, *Making the Woman Worker*, pp. 39, 42–7; Leon Fink, *Sweatshops at Sea: Merchant Seamen in the World's First Globalized Industry, from 1812 to the Present* (Chapel Hill, NC, 2011).

37 *Auckland Observer*, 27 June 1908.

38 See, for instance, Walkowitz, *Prostitution and Victorian Society*.

39 Emily Louisa Badeley and Thomas Jones Marriage Certificate, 1914, New Zealand, 6517; *Oamaru Mail*, 22 July 1914, p. 4.

40 *Newcastle Morning Herald and Miners' Advocate*, 12 July 1919, p. 9.

41 35th Annual Report of the Newcastle and Northumberland Benevolent Society for the year ending 31 December 1919, p. 5.

42 *Singleton Argus*, Thursday 26 June 1919, p. 2.

43 *The Newcastle Sun*, Thursday 24 June 1920, p. 5.

44 *Daily Mail* (Brisbane), 29 June 1920, p. 4; 'Australia, New
    South Wales, Deceased Estate Files, 1880–1923', database,
    FamilySearch; familysearch.org/ark:/61903/1:1:Q2TW-K13G
    (accessed 3 February 2017), Herbert Ockenden, 1921.

Afterword

1   Fabian, *Fabian of the Yard*, p. 22.

2   Census Returns of England and Wales, 1911. Class: RG14; Piece:
    1956, Ancestry.com (accessed 6 March 2018). General Register
    Office. England and Wales Civil Registration Indexes. London,
    England: General Register Office, United Kingdom; Volume:
    1d; Page: 437, Ancestry.com , (accessed 10 April 2018). General
    Register Office. England and Wales Civil Registration Indexes.
    London, England: General Register Office, Volume: 5h; Page:
    899, England & Wales, Civil Registration Death Index, 1916–
    2007, Ancestry.com (accessed on 10 April 2018).

3   Robin Quinn, *The Man Who Broke the Bank at Monte Carlo:
    Charles Deville Wells, Gambler and Fraudster Extraordinaire*
    (Cheltenham, 2016); Christopher Hilliard, *The Littlehampton
    Libels: A Miscarriage of Justice and a Mystery about Words in
    1920s England* (Oxford, 2017). See also Steve Adams, 'Murder at
    the Star: Investigating the unsolved murder of Thomas Thomas
    at Star Stores in the Carmarthenshire village of Garnant on
    February 12, 1921', personal blog (accessed 2 May 2019).

4   Wyles, *A Woman at Scotland Yard*, p. 195.

5   Correspondence re Mead, 21 April 1915, London, MEPO 2/228;
    William John Mead Pension Certificate, 11 September 1927,
    Metropolitan Police Pension Registers MEPO 21, London,
    England, Metropolitan Police Pension Registers, 1852–1932,
    Ancestry.com (accessed 10 April 2018).

6   Ernest Anderson Pension Certificate, 23 June 1913;
    Metropolitan Police Pension Registers MEPO 21, Ancestry.
    com. London, England, Metropolitan Police Pension Registers,
    1852–1932. England & Wales, Civil Registration Death Index,

1916–2007, Volume: 6b; Page: 892 Ancestry.com (accessed 12 October 2018).

7   George Dilnot, *Great Detectives and Their Methods* (London, 1927), p. 12.

8   Annual Report on the Traffic in Women and Children: Dossier Concerning New Zealand, 13 August 1924, Geneva, United Nations Archive, R665/12/22343/33415.

9   Rutvica Andrijasevic, 'Beautiful Dead Bodies: Gender, Migration and Representation in Anti-Trafficking Campaigns', *Feminist Studies*, vol. 86, no. 1, 2007, pp. 24–44.

10 See 'Following the Money: Spending on Anti-Trafficking', *Anti-Trafficking Review*, no. 3, 2014; and Igor Bosc, 'The Political Economy of Anti-Trafficking', *Beyond Trafficking and Modern Slavery (Open Democracy)*, 2018, www.opendemocracy.net/en/beyond-trafficking-and-slavery/political-economy-of-anti-trafficking/ (accessed 29 June 2020).

11 Siobhan Brooks, 'Innocent White Victims and Fallen Black Girls: Race, Sex Work, and the Limits of Anti-Sex Trafficking Laws', *Signs: Journal of Women in Culture & Society*, 2020, n.p. See also 'Special Issue – Trafficking Representations', *The Anti-Trafficking Review*, no. 7, 2016.

12 Dina Haynes, 'The Wastefulness of Human Trafficking Awareness Campaigns', *Beyond Trafficking and Modern Slavery (Open Democracy)*, 2019, www.opendemocracy.net/en/beyond-trafficking-and-slavery/wastefulness-of-human-trafficking-awareness-campaigns/; Kelli Lyon Johnson, 'Cutting Corners to Make a Compelling Story: Trafficking Awareness Campaigns as Fake News and Alternative Facts', *Beyond Trafficking and Modern Slavery (Open Democracy)*, 2019, www.opendemocracy.net/en/beyond-trafficking-and-slavery/cutting-corners-to-make-compelling-story-trafficking-awareness-camp/; Christine Sardina, 'Marketing Mass Hysteria: Anti-Trafficking Awareness Campaigns Go Rogue', *Beyond Trafficking and Modern Slavery (Open Democracy)*, 2019, www.opendemocracy.net/en/beyond-trafficking-and-slavery/

marketing-mass-hysteria-anti-trafficking-awareness-campaigns-go-rogue/; Joel Quirk and Elena Shih, 'Introduction: Do the Hidden Costs Outweigh the Practical Benefits of Human Trafficking Awareness Campaigns?', *Beyond Trafficking and Modern Slavery (Open Democracy)*, 2019, www.opendemocracy.net/en/beyond-trafficking-and-slavery/introduction-do-hidden-costs-outweigh-practical-benefits-of-huma/.

13 See 'Special Issue – Public Perceptions and Responses to Human Trafficking', *The Anti-Trafficking Review*, no. 13, 2019.

14 Carol S. Vance, 'Innocence and Experience: Melodramatic Narratives of Sex Trafficking and Their Consequences for Law and Policy', *History of the Present*, vol. 2, no. 2, 2012, pp. 200–218.

15 Rachel C. Riedner, *Writing Neoliberal Values: Rhetorical Connectivities and Globalized Capitalism* (Basingstoke, 2015).

16 *Representations of Transnational Human Trafficking Present-Day News Media, True Crime, and Fiction*, ed. Christiana Gregoriou (London, 2018).

17 Kate Roberts, 'Life after Trafficking in the UK: Uncertainty, Destitution and Neglect', *Beyond Trafficking and Modern Slavery (Open Democracy)*, 2019, www.opendemocracy.net/en/beyond-trafficking-and-slavery/life-after-trafficking-uk-uncertainty-destitution-and-neglect/.

18 Laura Maria Augustin, *Sex at the Margins: Migration, Labour Markets, and the Rescue Industry* (London, 2007); Anne Elizabeth Moore, 'Rich in Funds but Short on Facts: The High Cost of Human Trafficking Awareness Campaigns', *Beyond Trafficking and Modern Slavery (Open Democracy)*, 2019, www.opendemocracy.net/en/beyond-trafficking-and-slavery/rich-in-funds-but-short-on-facts-high-cost-of-human-trafficking-a/.

19 *Newcastle Morning Herald and Miners' Advocate*, 25 June 1919, p. 6.

20 Inward Bound Passengers, SS *Osterley*, 7 July 1920, Passenger Lists, New South Wales.

Acknowledgements

1 League of Nations Advisory Committee on the Traffic in Women 'Committee of Experts' files, UN Archive, Geneva.

2 These include Amy Coleman, Archives New Zealand Dunedin Regional Office; Chris Meech, Waitaki District Archives, Oamaru; Kari Wilson Allen, Hocken Collections Assistant, Hocken Library, Dunedin; an unknown archivist from the University of Turin archives; and Silvia Corno, Archivist at the Archivio di Stato in Turin.

LIST OF ILLUSTRATIONS

INDEX

Page references for illustrations are in *italic*